Easy Writer II

EASY WRITER II
BASIC SENTENCE COMBINING
AND COMPREHENSIVE SKILLS

DIANNA S. CAMPBELL

Mount Mary College

TERRY RYAN MEIER

Milwaukee Area Technical College

1817

HARPER & ROW, PUBLISHERS, New York

Cambridge, Philadelphia, San Francisco, Washington,
London, Mexico City, São Paulo, Singapore, Sydney

Sponsoring Editor: Phillip Leininger
Text Design: Robert Sugar
Text Design Adaptation: Caliber Design Planning, Inc.
Cover Design: Miriam Recio
Production Manager: Jeanie Berke
Production Assistant: Brenda DeMartini
Compositor: ComCom Division of Haddon Craftsmen, Inc.
Printer and Binder: The Murray Printing Company

**Easy Writer II: Basic Sentence Combining and
Comprehensive Skills**
Copyright © 1987 by Harper & Row, Publishers, Inc.

Library of Congress Cataloging-in-Publication Data

Campbell, Dianna S., 1949–
  Easy writer II.

  Includes index.
  1. English language—Rhetoric. 2. English language—
Grammar—1950–   . I. Meier, Terry Ryan, 1948–
II. Title.
PE1408.C2824 1987   808′.042   86-19571
ISBN 0-06-041158-9
    88 89 9 8 7 6 5 4 3

To the memory of Mrs. Marguerite Lauder (1894–1984)
and to all teachers
who expect their students to do great things.

Contents

To the Teacher

If you have been using *Easy Writer* for several semesters or quarters, you are familiar with the Easy Writer system for teaching basic writing skills on the college level, and you know that it works. You also know that when you're teaching highly motivated students, you can never have too much material. That's what *Easy Writer II* provides: the same effective system and completely new classroom-tested material.

We've kept our basic sentence-combining approach, which means that, once again, the emphasis is not merely on teaching students to avoid errors but on helping them create good sentences with a great deal of variety and style. The goals of *Easy Writer* and *Easy Writer II* are identical. You'll find all the same chapter and unit headings and, within them, the same variety of exercises designed to help students develop sound basic writing skills.

What's different is the content of the exercises. In *Easy Writer*, for instance, there's a Chapter 1 sentence structure exercise based on an episode in the life of Rosa Parks; in *Easy Writer II* the corresponding exercise is based on the childhood of the Marx brothers. Where the legend of Dracula supplies the content for a run-on exercise in *Easy Writer*, the roots of hypochondria supply it here. In *Easy Writer* students learn to use logical and consistent verb tenses by rewriting an essay about Jim Thorpe; in this alternate edition, they revise problems of verb tense in an essay on Vincent van Gogh.

As in *Easy Writer*, we've tried to create exercises that will nourish and encourage lively, curious minds. If your students are like ours, you'll continue to find that they appreciate exercises that teach them basic skills and entertain them or inform them about the world at the same time. Who can resist the humor of Winston Churchill or the charm and spunk of Ruth Gordon? How many readers wouldn't be curious about why Indian dance was once illegal in the United States? And what students, in the event that they're ever stranded at sea, wouldn't want to know how to discourage shark attacks? It's really very simple: we try to keep them thinking, keep them laughing, and keep them working on the basics.

Although we've preserved the basic design and sequence of *Easy Writer*, we have made a few changes in some explanations, mostly in the nature of clarifying and expanding our discussions of rules and strategies. We've also included more fill-in-the-blank items within the explanatory sections. Most of these short items contain their own answer keys on the same page so that students can be more certain about whether or not they really understand a particular point before they begin an exercise.

If you have not taught with *Easy Writer*, we want you to know that you certainly can choose *Easy Writer II* for your students; the book is completely self-contained, just as *Easy Writer* is. The second edition of *Easy Writer*, which has been widely used since its publication in 1984, will continue to be available and will itself be revised and updated at regular intervals. So teachers who want to use *Easy Writer* one year and *Easy Writer II* the next will have that option. In a given year one edition can be a principal teaching tool for a basic writing course or lab while the other edition provides supplemental exercises. The next year the roles of the two texts can be reversed.

Both *Easy Writer* and *Easy Writer II* come complete with their own Instructor's Manuals, each of which contains a complete answer key for the book and a set of tests. (Each chapter has two tests; there is also a final exam that covers all the material in the book, and *Easy Writer II* includes a comprehensive practice test students can take before the final.) The Instructor's Manual includes notes and suggestions for each chapter.

We are grateful for the invaluable assistance we received from a number of teachers at Mount Mary College in Milwaukee, Wisconsin. Special thanks go to Sister David Marie Mueller, S.S.N.D., who, in matters grammatical, certainly ranks among the world's great consulting detectives; to Sister Joan Cook, S.S.N.D., and Sister Mary Warner, S.S.N.D., who helped so much in classroom testing and provided unfailing encouragement; and to Richard A. Campbell, who lent us his considerable technical expertise in word processing. We're also indebted to many other teachers who contacted us with comments and suggestions based on their use of *Easy Writer* and to all the students who tested and retested our materials and offered many helpful suggestions. Of course, any shortcomings of the book are our responsibility and ours alone.

Once again, we're thankful for the encouragement of our sponsoring editor at Harper & Row, Phillip Leininger. Finally, very little of this work could have been completed without the loving cooperation of our families and the excellent child care provided by Kathy Kurtz and Grandma Evie Alivo.

Teaching basic writing is an important, demanding, and often exhausting job. Most students work with a textbook just once, whereas their teachers help new classes of students work through it again and again. With this in mind, we hope you'll enjoy the fresh material in this alternate edition.

Dianna S. Campbell
Terry Ryan Meier

To the Student

Before you begin the first exercise in *Easy Writer II*, you need to think seriously about how important it is to improve your basic writing skills. No matter what your college major or career goals may be, you know that there is very little you can do successfully in this world without basic competence in your own language. Learning to write well is nothing less than acquiring the power to succeed—in school and in the world that lies beyond school. Competence is power. Incompetence is a major handicap. It's as simple as that.

But before you can start to acquire competence in basic writing, you have to believe in your own potential. Some adult students are convinced that it's impossible to become a good writer. As teachers, we can tell you that it is certainly possible, but it takes a great deal of work. A halfhearted try will not be enough to make a real difference; you'll have to put your whole heart into your work in *Easy Writer II* if you want to see significant results. If you're not willing to devote a considerable amount of time and energy to the project, you have a very small chance of success. But with enthusiasm, consistency, and hard work, you have an excellent chance. Developing basic writing skills is not a matter of luck; it's a matter of pluck. It's not a matter of magic; it's a matter of mastery. To master any skill—whether it's racquetball, roller skating, or writing—you need confidence, hard work, and patience. We've taught many, many students who were amazed at how far they came in one or two semesters. They did it; you can do it, too.

We've tried to write a book that won't bore you. While you're working on problems such as run-ons, fragments, and subject-verb agreement, you'll be reading about world-class athletes who overcame tremendous physical handicaps, black musicians whose careers were affected by disc jockeys' decisions about which records to play in the early years of rock and roll, and pet psychologists who say mental problems in dogs can be avoided. Every topic will not appeal to every student, but we think you'll find most of them informative, amusing, or just offbeat and interesting.

In *Easy Writer II* we use simple terms and pared-down explanations of important rules and techniques. These are the products of years of experimenting to learn which explanations are the quickest and clearest, and some of the best suggestions have been made by our own students.

Here's the formula one more time: Believe in yourself, work hard, and work consistently. If you follow these guidelines, more power to you.

Dianna S. Campbell
Terry Ryan Meier

Chapter 1
Introduction to Sentence Structure

This chapter presents the most basic elements of sentence structure by focusing on the main components of simple sentences. If any chapter in the book should be taken slowly and reviewed frequently, this is the one. This chapter lays the groundwork for the rest of the book and tries to help you develop the tools for acquiring some of the most valuable basic writing skills.

UNIT 1: Overview of the Sentence Pattern

If someone asked you to define a *sentence,* do you think you could? Many people would say no, and yet the same people would immediately be able to pick out the *sentence* among the following choices:

(a)   At usually peaks, statistics a major according to league pitcher's 30 career age.

(b)   Major according to, usually peaks league statistics a career at pitcher's 30 age.

(c)   Career pitcher's major, statistics age according usually 30 league to peaks a at.

(d)   *According to statistics, a major league pitcher's career usually peaks at age 30.

Each one of the four sequences contains the same words, but only one makes *sense*—(d). It makes sense because the words are arranged in the form that we call a *sentence.* The fact that you can recognize the sentence so easily shows how natural the pattern is and how much intuitive language skill you already have. And for a writer, it is much more important to be able to recognize and produce good sentences than to be able to define them in the precise, meticulous way that linguists must.

But in order to make good sentences and avoid certain types of errors, we do need to develop a basic working definition of a *sentence.* That's what we want to accomplish in the five units of Chapter 1. Let's start by analyzing why (d) is a sentence.

Sentences are made up of clauses. In this chapter, we are concerned primarily with *simple sentences*—those that are made up of one clause. In the rest of the book, we will analyze and create sentences that contain more than one clause.

But for now, we need to define the word *clause*. A *clause* is *a subject plus a predicate.* The subject names something, possibly a person, an object, a place, or an idea. Then the predicate makes a statement about that subject. The predicate tells us something about that person, object, place, or idea.

Finding Key Parts of Simple Sentences

Most students find that the easiest way to analyze simple sentences is to look at the predicate first. The most important part of the predicate is the verb, and you probably remember that most verbs show some sort of action. So when you're analyzing a sentence, look for the verb first. Write *V* over the word that shows action in sentence (d):

According to statistics, a major league pitcher's career usually peaks at age 30.

Peaks is the word that shows action. It's the verb. Then you have to ask yourself, "What peaks? What comes to its peak or its highest point?" Obviously, it's *a major league pitcher's career* that peaks. *A major league pitcher's career* is the complete subject of the verb *peaks*. The key word in the complete subject is *career*. *Career* is the most important part of the complete subject, so we call it the key word in the subject. *Peaks* is the verb, and that makes it the most important part of the predicate.

A Note about Complements

Before you do the first exercise, there is one more thing you should know about the predicate of a sentence. Its most important element is always the verb, but some verbs don't make sense or sound complete by themselves. They need a *complement*—a word to *complete* their meaning. For example, look at this sentence:

New York Mets pitcher Dwight Gooden won the 1985 Cy Young Award at the surprisingly young age of 20.

You can probably pick out the verb—*won*—right away, and there's no question about the subject. Who won? New York Mets pitcher Dwight Gooden won. So *New York Mets pitcher Dwight Gooden* is the complete subject. The name *Dwight Gooden* is the key word in the subject. But in this particular sentence, if you say *Dwight Gooden won* and stop there, you have a sense of incompleteness, don't you? You want to ask, "Dwight Gooden won *what*?" In this sentence the verb *won* raises a question that needs to be answered. Without an answer, you have a feeling of incompleteness. So the answer to the question raised by certain kinds of verbs is called a *complement*. (It's helpful to realize that the word *complement* is related to the word *complete*.) The complement of a verb may come in the form of one word or more than one word. In the sentence about Dwight Gooden the complement of the verb *won* is *the 1985 Cy Young Award*. The sentence would be labeled in this way:

S   V   C

New York Mets pitcher <u>Dwight Gooden</u> <u>won</u> the 1985 Cy Young Award at the surprisingly young age of 20.

In the first example sentence, we didn't mark a complement because the verb *peaks* doesn't require one. It doesn't need anything. The word *peaks* doesn't leave you hanging, does it? *A career peaks* makes sense by itself. No one would ever ask, "A career peaks what?" A career just peaks; it reaches its top point. That's all.

Exercise One

Directions: Here are ten simple sentences. Remember that they are called "simple" because each one contains only one clause. Please do the following:

(a) Draw one line under the key word in the complete subject and label it *S*.
(b) Draw two lines under the verb in the predicate and label it *V*.
(c) Read the *S* and *V* together to see if they make sense by themselves. If they don't make sense or if they give you a feeling of incompleteness, then find the word that completes the idea of the verb and mark it *C* for *complement*. (You will find that most of the sentences do have complements.)

1. A hypnophobic person hates bedtime.

2. The typical American husband stands six inches taller than his wife.

3. In 1809 Napoleon divorced Josephine.

4. In the words of Ernest Hemingway, the great American writer, the sun also rises.

5. President Teddy Roosevelt studied judo.

6. The Dutch dip their french fries in mayonnaise rather than in catsup.

7. Yellowstone became the world's first national park in 1872.

8. After a six-year reign, King Tutankhamen died at the age of 18.

9. Oxygen constitutes 89 percent of the weight of water.

10. After a mysterious two-year disappearance, the famous *Mona Lisa* reappeared in

    Florence, Italy, in 1913.

NOTE: If you had a perfect or nearly perfect score on Exercise One and if you found the work easy, you may skip Exercise Two. If you had any difficulty at all, please do the exercise below.

Exercise Two

Directions: Please follow the same directions you followed for Exercise One.

1. Plato, the great philosopher of the ideal, taught Aristotle, another classic thinker.

2. Even with no specific guidance or instruction, healthy human babies walk at some

   point within the first or second year of life.

3. Conchiferous animals always sport shells.

4. Sweden outlaws all physical punishment of children, even punishment by the children's parents.

5. In 1944 *Seventeen* magazine began.

6. According to the account of Matthew in the New Testament, Jesus Christ suffered in the garden of Gethsemane.

7. The Division of Fine Arts of the University of Southern California chose Ronald Reagan as the most nearly perfect male figure in 1940.

8. In his lifetime a typical man cuts 94 miles of his own whiskers.

9. President Harry S. Truman installed bowling lanes in the White House.

10. Ian Fleming, the popular spy novelist, wrote 13 James Bond books.

UNIT 2: The Subject

In this unit, we will take a closer look at the subject of the sentence—the naming part.

The key part of the complete subject always consists of nouns or pronouns. The key word or key words can be a single noun, a single pronoun, or any combination of nouns and pronouns. Here are some simple examples. Underline and write *S* over the key word or words in the subject of each sentence:

(a) Abraham Lincoln had a very complex personality.

(b) Mary Todd Lincoln was also an extremely complicated individual.

(c) Abraham Lincoln and Mary Todd Lincoln were husband and wife.

(d) He and she were an intriguing couple.

(e) Abraham Lincoln and she endured great tragedy together.

[*Answers.* The key words in the subjects are (a) the noun *Abraham Lincoln*; (b) the noun *Mary Todd Lincoln*; (c) the nouns *Abraham Lincoln* and *Mary Todd Lincoln*; (d) the pronouns *He* and *she*; and (e) the noun *Abraham Lincoln* and the pronoun *she.*]

Now that you know that a complete subject can have more than one key word, and that the key words in subjects are always nouns and pronouns, let's go into each category—nouns and pronouns—in more detail.

Nouns

You might remember learning that a noun is the name of a person, place, thing, or idea. Here are some examples of nouns in each of these four groups:

PERSON	PLACE	THING	IDEA
brother	classroom	bagel	thoughts
friend	day-care center	earrings	solution
ballerina	farmyard	hot dog	love
con artist	bar	dress	wealth
lawyer	Superdome	sports car	future
Tina Turner	Oregon	Pepsi	attitude

Nouns can be singular or plural. Some are capitalized, and some are not. All of them, except the capitalized nouns, can follow the words *a, an,* and *the,* which are called *noun markers* because they mark or signal the appearance of a noun. For instance, you can say *a friend, an attitude, the earrings.*

The "Subject Test"

But for many people, thinking of nouns as the names of persons, places, things, and ideas is not helpful. This traditional definition is particularly weak with regard to abstract or idea nouns. **One easy way of checking to see if a word is a noun (or at least if it can be used as a noun) is to try to make it the subject of a sentence.** If a word can be used as the subject of a sentence, it is either a noun or a pronoun. (A pronoun is simply a substitute for a noun; we will discuss pronouns shortly.)

Let's say, for example, that we want to see if *create* and *creation* are nouns. We can try to use each one as the subject of a sentence. For instance, we might try these:

(a)   The *create* was amazing.

(b)   The *creation* was amazing.

This little test very quickly shows us that *creation* is a noun and *create* is not.

Let's use the test again, this time to see if *color* and *colorful* are nouns. Here are our test sentences:

(a)   That *color* is perfect.

(b)   That *colorful* is perfect.

Again, the attempt to use each word as the subject of a sentence immediately makes it clear that *color* is a noun and *colorful* is not.

So a word that is a noun can be used as the subject of a sentence. That does not mean that it *has* to be used that way. It just means that it can be. Nouns can also appear in many other spots in sentences; for example, you have already worked with nouns as complements. ("I loved the *creation.*" "Red is the right *color* for the trim.")

You will also learn, as we work our way through the book, that a word that is a noun in one context may sometimes function as another part of speech in another context. But that's for later.

Exercise One

Directions: In each pair below, there is one word that can be used as a noun and one word that cannot. Use the test we have just described to determine which word is the noun; in other words, on the lines provided, try to use each word as the subject of a short sentence. Circle the noun; that's the word that passes the subject test.

1. deny _____

   denial _____

2. organize _____

   organization _____

3. management _____

   manage _____

4. beauty _____

   beautify _____

5. warns _____

   warning _____

6. harass _____

   harassment _____

7. grew _____

   growth _____

8. purpose _____

   purposely _____

9. suggest _____

   suggestion _____

10. appearance _____

    appear _____

Correct Exercise One and, if you need more practice, do Exercise Two.

Exercise Two

Directions: Follow the same directions as in Exercise One to find the noun in each pair.

1. knowledge _____

   know _____

2. performance _____

   perform _____

3. confuse _____

   confusion _____

4. approval _____

   approve _____

5. justify _____

   justification _____

6. legality _____

   legally _____

7. announce _____

   announcement _____

8. define _____

   definition _____

9. belief _____

   believe _____

10. operate _____

   operator _____

A Note on Idea Nouns

Most of the nouns you identified in Exercises One and Two are "idea nouns." Notice how often idea nouns have the same suffixes (word endings). These five are very common noun suffixes: *-ance*, *-ity*, *-ment*, *-ness*, and *-tion*. If you watch for these word endings, you'll find it easier to identify many abstract nouns.

A Reminder

Before we move on to the next topic, let us remind you once more that nouns can be used in all parts of sentences. For example, we can say, "Her rich *imagination* fascinated me" or "I was fascinated by her rich *imagination*." The word *imagination* is a noun in both sentences. But it is the key word in the subject only in the first example. The noun's ability to perform as the key word in the subject of a clause is our major concern in this unit.

Pronouns

Pronouns are words that take the place of nouns. We use them to avoid repeating a noun over and over. Here are some examples of *nouns* [in the (a) sentences] being replaced by *pronouns* [in the (b) sentences]:

1. (a) According to legend, *Daniel Boone* discovered Kentucky.
   (b) According to legend, *he* discovered Kentucky.

2. (a) *The novel Billy Budd* was discovered in author Herman Melville's attic 20 years after Melville's death.
   (b) *It* was discovered in author Herman Melville's attic 20 years after Melville's death.

3. (a) *The years 400 to 1500* are often called the Middle Ages.
   (b) *They* are often called the Middle Ages.

As usual, we are highlighting the subject position even though pronouns, like nouns, can appear anywhere in sentences.

There are many different types of pronouns, but there are three main groups that can be used as subjects of sentences, and these are the pronouns that we are concerned about here. These pronouns in their three categories are the following:

PERSONAL	DEMONSTRATIVE	INDEFINITE
I	this	anybody
you	that	anyone
he	these	anything
she	those	everybody
it		everyone
we		everything
they		nobody
		no one
		nothing
		somebody
		someone
		something

The names of each group are not terribly important, but the knowledge that these words can function as subjects of sentences *is* very important. In fact, if you, like so many students, happen to have a problem with run-on sentences, this bit of information —that pronouns can be subjects of clauses—will be a key factor in the improvement of your basic writing skills. We'll go into that in more detail in Chapter 2.

Exercise Three

Directions: Write ten simple sentences, each one having a pronoun as its subject. Choose pronouns from each one of the three groups. Use your own paper, please.

UNIT 3: The Predicate

In this unit, we examine in more detail the part of the clause that makes a statement about the subject, and that part is called the *predicate*. We'll look at verbs first, then complements.

Verbs

You might remember learning that a verb is a word that shows action. That definition is true for many verbs, but it is not true for some of the verbs that we use most often. There are actually four main kinds of verbs, and we'll take them one by one.

1. Visible Action Verbs

Visible action verbs are the typical ones that we all remember easily—words such as *skip, chew, type, blink,* and *drive.* They represent actions that we can picture. They are the "visible action verbs."

2. Invisible Action Verbs

Invisible action verbs are slightly more difficult because they call to mind actions that can't be seen. They usually describe actions that go on inside one's mind. Some examples are *enjoy, wonder, predict, care,* and *forget.*

3. Linking Verbs

Linking verbs don't show an action, but they do help to make a statement about a subject by *linking* the subject to a complement. In these examples, notice how the linking verb, which is italicized, makes a statement about the subject by linking it to a complement:

He *is* funny.

She *was* serious.

They *are* comfortable.

The leaves *were* red.

My mother *appears* happy.

My father *seems* ready for retirement.

4. Helping Verbs

A verb is the only type of word in the English language that changes in any way in order to communicate differences in time. Sometimes it changes form and yet remains one word; for example, I *give*, the present tense, changes to I *gave*, the past tense. Other times, helping verbs are added to show changes in time (also called "tense"). Here are some of the verb phrases that can be made by using helping verbs with *give*:

I *am giving.*	I *can give.*
I *have given.*	I *could give.*
I *have been giving.*	I *may give.*
I *was giving.*	I *might give.*
I *had given.*	I *should give.*
I *had been giving.*	I *would give.*
I *will give.*	I *must give.*
I *will be giving.*	I *may have given.*
I *will have been giving.*	I *would have given.*
I *will have given.*	I *did give.*

All of these verb phrases are made by adding helping verbs to the base verb *give*, which sometimes changes form and becomes *giving* or *given*. (You may notice that some verbs, for example, *am, is, are,* and *were,* work in both groups 3 and 4. Sometimes they act as linking verbs, and other times they act as helping verbs.)

Exercise One

Directions: Choose one of these verbs: *talk, hope, smile, drive,* or *eat.* Then, on your own paper, write out all the different forms of that verb, using our workout with *give* as your model. Although at first glance this might seem to be nothing more than busywork, for most students it's the easiest and fastest way of becoming familiar with the helping verbs that make up verb phrases. And as you work through the rest of this chapter, you'll see how important it is to be familiar with helping verbs in order to have a good, basic sense of sentence structure.

If you need more practice, write out all the forms of the remaining verbs from the group of five above. But for the maximum effectiveness of the exercise (and for the preservation of your own sanity), spread the assignment out over a few days.

A Note on Multiple Verbs

In the last unit, you learned that more than one noun or pronoun can act as the key words in the subject of a sentence. It is also true that more than one verb or verb phrase can be used in the predicate of a sentence. Look closely at these examples:

(a)   **At seven feet seven, Washington Bullets' center Manute Bol dunks the ball and blocks shots with ease.**

In (a), *Manute Bol,* the subject of the simple sentence, does two things: he *dunks* something, and he *blocks* something. Find and underline the two verbs in example (b):

(b)   **John Steinbeck traveled across America with Charley, his dog, and wrote a famous account of their journey.**

Again we have one subject that is seen as doing—or having done—two things: John Steinbeck *traveled* and *wrote*.

Both the (a) and (b) examples contain two verbs, but you could actually have any number of verbs in a simple sentence—just as long as they all went with the same subject.

Exercise Two

PART A

Directions: Below is a series of simple sentences, a collection of facts about the Marx brothers and their early days. The information is based on material in *The People's Almanac #3* by David Wallechinsky and Irving Wallace. Please do the following:

(a) Draw a line under the key word or key words in the subject and use the label *S.*
(b) Draw two lines under the verb or verb phrase in the predicate and use the label *V* or *VP.*
(c) Label the complement, if there is one, with *C.*

1. The famous Marx brothers grew up on East 93d Street in New York City.

2. Without a doubt, their childhood and home life can be called unique.

3. The noisy Marx apartment housed several people besides the immediate family.

4. Grandpa and Grandma Schoenberg had come from Germany.

5. Grandpa Schoenberg had been a traveling magician in the old country.

6. Grandma Schoenberg played the harp.

7. The Marx brothers' mother was the legendary Minnie.

8. Minnie's husband was called "Frenchie."

9. Frenchie Marx was a so-so tailor and a great cook from French-speaking Alsace.

10. A homeless cousin and other stray relatives also shared quarters with the so-called castaways on East 93d Street.

Please stop and correct your answers before continuing on to the next part.

PART B

Directions: Please continue to follow the directions for Part A of this exercise.

1. Groucho, Harpo, Chico, Zeppo, and Gummo spent their early years in a fairly lively environment.

2. Without their nicknames, by the way, they would have been Julius, Adolph, Leonard, Herbert, and Milton.

3. Minnie Marx relentlessly promoted her sons and other relatives and friends on the vaudeville circuit and eventually enjoyed great success for her efforts.

4. She could never control her boys' zany antics on stage.

5. But the matriarch of the Marx family did try.

6. In one attempt Minnie stood in the wings and hissed "Greenbaum!" at her sons.

7. A Mr. Greenbaum had held the mortgage on the Marx family's first home.

8. After the start of vaudeville's decline during World War I, the Marx brothers toured the country in *I'll Say She Is,* with Groucho as Napoleon, and received rave reviews.

9. Just before the 1924 Broadway opening of that musical revue, Minnie Marx broke her ankle.

10. The indomitable Mrs. Marx would not have missed her sons' moment of triumph for anything and arrived at the theater on a stretcher!

This is all we're going to do with verbs for now because our intention here is to help you develop a strong sense of basic sentence structure. But verbs are complicated, and special problems concerning them are taken up in the first three units of Chapter 6. For now, let's continue building a basic understanding of what makes up the clauses that make up sentences. That will make your later work much easier.

Complements

Because our language is so complex, it is very difficult to explain anything in a direct and straightforward manner without stopping every once in a while and saying, "But there's an exception to this rule" or "This pattern has many variations, and what we're showing you is only a starting point." And yet, we want to keep these interruptions to a minimum so that you can get a clear, firm grasp of what's basic.

When it comes to *complements*, we'd like you to have a good general understanding of what they are. So far, we've tried to stick to sentences in which the complements are fairly simple and clear. But even with these short, simple sentences, you may already have had questions, and that's why we have to go into more detail here.

Let's take two sentences. One is crystal clear; the other is not. In (a) mark the key word or words in the subject, the verb or verb phrase, and the complement, if there is one:

(a) **On an average day, the "Strawberry Fields Forever" memorial in New York City's Central Park attracts John Lennon fans by the hundreds.**

It's easy to see that the key word in the subject is the noun *memorial*. The verb is clearly *attracts*. But *attracts* leaves you with a sense of incompleteness, so you ask, "attracts what?" or "attracts whom?" and the natural answer to that question is *fans*. So *fans* is the complement of the verb *attracts*. Example (a) is simple and clear cut.

But now mark the key parts of sentence (b):

(b) **Halley's comet appears once in the lifetime of the average person.**

Halley's comet (or just the word *comet*) is obviously the key word in the subject, and *appears* is the verb. But if your writing teacher asks how many people in your class marked a complement, you're likely to see some differences of opinion. Did "Halley's comet appears" strike you as complete? Or did you want to ask, "Halley's comet appears when?" And then did you answer "once" and go on to mark *once* as the complement of the verb *appears*? Either way, you can be considered correct. There are simply two different ways of looking at sentence (b). One student might have the opinion that it's an S-V sentence, whereas another student might believe it's an S-V-C sentence. Both views are valid; they both make a certain kind of sense. When it comes to complements, there is often room for individual judgment, so relax; some of your answers may vary from those of other students and still be correct. (The same *cannot* be said about identifying key words in subjects and finding verbs and verb phrases. When you're talking about subjects, verbs, and verb phrases, there should be general agreement among all students.)

In addition to this little bit of ambiguity about whether certain sentences even have complements, there is another issue: complements come in a number of different forms. Let's look at some examples of the most important types so that you'll be able to recognize them quickly.

1. **Nouns and Pronouns as Complements**

(a) I like my **neighbors.**

(b) I like **them.**

(c) I sent **money.**

(d) I sent **it.**

Sometimes you'll use a combination of two nouns and a pronoun. For example:

(e) I handed **Sam** the **lasagna.**

(f) I handed **him** the **lasagna.**

From earlier English courses, you might remember that *lasagna* is the *direct object,* whereas *Sam* and *him* are the indirect objects of the verb *handed.* For our purposes it is enough for you to see that both the direct object and the indirect object in a sentence complete the idea of the verb. So sentences that have both a direct and an indirect object can be labeled in this way:

```
S      V            C
I handed Sam the lasagna.
```

2. Adjectives, Adverbs, and Prepositional Phrases as Complements

We'll discuss adjectives, adverbs, and prepositional phrases in more detail in the next unit, but for now, just look at the examples.

(a) She is **excited**.   (adjective)

(b) She is **talented**.   (adjective)

(c) She sings **soulfully**.   (adverb)

(d) She daydreams **often**.   (adverb)

(e) She appeared **at the front door**. (prepositional phrase)

(f) She went **on a cruise**.   (prepositional phrase)

3. "To + Verb" as Complement

When the word *to* is used before a verb, an *infinitive verb phrase* is created. An infinitive verb phrase often acts as the complement of the verb that it follows. Here are some examples:

(a) He likes **to paint**.

(b) He tried **to cooperate**.

(c) He prefers **to work**.

In (a), for example, the subject of the sentence—*He*—is not actually painting. We don't see the subject doing the action of painting; we see him *liking* something. And what is it that he likes? In another sentence, it might be a noun or a pronoun: He likes *chocolate cake*. He likes *it*. But here—in (a)—the complement is an infinitive verb phrase: He likes *to paint*.

Sometimes you'll have a two-part complement: an infinitive verb phrase complement followed by another type of complement. For example: Suzanna loves *to write short stories*. With this sentence, you might ask yourself, "Suzanna loves what?" And the obvious answer would be "to write." So *to write* is the complement of the verb *loves*. But does Suzanna love to write in a general sort of way? Does she love to write any old thing? Is that what the writer of the sentence intends? No. Suzanna loves to write something in particular, and that's *short stories*. So *to write* is the complement of *loves*, and *short stories* is the complement of *to write*. This sounds complicated, but it's really not. Just mark the sentence this way:

S   V   C
Suzanna loves to write short stories.

Now try to label this one:

She also wants to try poems.

4. **Clauses as Complements**

An entire clause can be a complement. Analyze this example:

> They forgot **that they owed money to Henry.**

You know that *they owed money to Henry* is a clause—with *they* as its subject, *owed* as its verb, and *money* as its complement. That clause answers the question, "They forgot *what?*" So the entire clause in italics above is the complement of the verb of the *main* clause, and that verb is *forgot.* It's the complement of *forgot* just as a noun or a pronoun could be the complement in these examples:

> They forgot **the tickets.**
>
> They forgot **them.**

When a clause is a complement, it is usually connected to the verb before it by the word *that.* (Sometimes the word *that* is simply omitted.) But the important thing is to see the whole clause as completing the idea of the verb in the main clause and to mark it like this:

> S   V   C
> <u>They</u> <u>forgot</u> that they owed money to Henry.

A Final Note

In conclusion, a complement can be almost anything. It's whatever it takes to answer the questions "What?" or "Whom?" that are often raised by verbs and verb phrases. Just keep in mind the *American Heritage Dictionary*'s definition of a *complement:* "*Something that completes, makes up a whole, or brings to perfection.*" It's a good basic definition, and it applies well to the complements in sentences.

There's an exercise on the various types of complements at the beginning of Unit 5, but that work will be easier for you if we stop and look at modifiers in more detail before you try it.

UNIT 4: The Modifiers

The Kernel

Up to this point in Chapter 1, we have been focusing on the elements that form what you might call *the kernel of the clause.* Any central image would probably work; you could talk about the *kernel* or the *heart* or the *core* of the clause. At any rate, **the kernel is made up of the key word or words within the complete subject, plus the verb or verb phrase and the complement, if there is one.** Taken together, they form the kernel of the clause. (It helps some students to look at it in another way and say that these words make up the bare bones or the skeleton of the clause.)

So that's what we've been looking at so far—the kernel, the S-V or S-V-C of the clause. Now we're going to turn our attention to the words that modify the different parts of the kernel. The word *modify* in this case means "describe." The easiest modifiers are adjectives and adverbs, so we'll start with them.

Adjectives

Adjectives are words that are used to describe nouns and pronouns. In English, adjectives most commonly precede the nouns that they describe. For example:

1. (a) This is a *crazy* plan.
   (b) She had an *unusual* idea.
   (c) It is an *expensive* sound system.

But adjectives can also follow the nouns and pronouns they describe, and then they are usually in the complement position. Look at these examples:

2. (a) This plan is *crazy*.
   (b) Her idea was *unusual*.
   (c) The sound system is *expensive*.

Exercise One

Directions: Circle the adjectives in the phrases below.

1. an underrated young hockey team

2. spicy pizza and ice-cold Seven-Up

3. good childhood memories

4. an old-fashioned tree with red ribbons and bubbling electric candles

5. a slow-growing benign tumor

6. broken promises

7. an elegant party with interesting guests

8. hot cornbread

9. rude comments and nasty looks

10. the national political scene and its real relationship to local affairs

Please correct this exercise before you do Exercise Two.

Exercise Two

Directions: Circle the adjectives in the phrases below.

1. smooth, cold silk

2. an unexpected lesson about family relationships

3. rich egg noodles and crispy fried chicken

4. optimistic world leaders

5. an experienced coach and untested rookies

6. the advertised specials at a high-priced store

7. great expectations for a dream vacation

8. lemon cake and herbal tea

9. an aggressive, well-prepared reporter

10. a record-setting performance in an official event

NOTE: You probably noticed that a word that is normally thought of as a noun, such as *lemon*, can sometimes be used as an adjective; for instance, in item 8 of Exercise Two, we are obviously not talking about a lemon; we are talking about lemon flavoring. We are using the word *lemon* as an adjective, not a noun. What word in item 3 of Exercise Two is normally a noun but is here used as an adjective to describe something else?

_____

Adverbs

We usually think of adverbs as words that modify verbs and end in *-ly*. Many adverbs do. But adverbs don't have to end in *-ly*, and they can describe other modifiers—both adjectives and other adverbs. Here our focus is on basic sentence structure, so we are concerned only with how adverbs modify verbs.

Adverbs can appear almost anywhere in a sentence. Here are some examples of adverbs modifying verbs:

1. (a) The puppy *playfully* chased its tail.
   (b) One chubby toddler smiled *confidently*.
   (c) *Later* they bought the farm.
   (d) She spends a lot of money *here*.

Most adverbs describe *how* an action is done. For example, in (a) *playfully* describes *chased*; it tells how the puppy chased its tail. In (b) *confidently* describes *smiled*; that's how the toddler smiled—confidently.

Some adverbs tell not how but *when* an action takes place. For instance, in (c) the word *later* describes the verb *bought*; it tells when they bought the farm.

Adverbs can also tell *where* an action takes place. In (d) *here* describes *spends*; it tells where she spends a lot of money.

Exercise Three

Directions: Fill in the blanks with other adverbs.

2. (a) The puppy _____ chased its tail.

   (b) One chubby toddler smiled _____ .

(c) _____ they bought the farm.

(d) She spends a lot of money _____ .

Adverbs in the Middle of Verb Phrases

That's just about all we're going to do with adverbs because they don't have a great bearing on basic sentence structure. The only thing you want to watch out for is the way adverbs often appear in the middle of verb phrases. Look at the two examples below. Draw two lines under the verb phrases and circle the adverbs:

(a) The U.S. Postal Service has finally assigned Santa Claus his own zip code.

(b) Letters to that jolly old soul should really include it. (It's 99701.)

In sentences like these the adverbs are not considered to be part of the verb phrase. You might say that they describe the action, but they are not part of the action.

Phrases

The next two types of modifiers are phrases. A phrase is a sequence of two or more words that form a unit that does less than a clause. In other words, a phrase might contain the necessary elements for a subject *or* for a predicate, but not for both. There are many types of phrases, but there are two that are especially important: *appositives* and *prepositional phrases*. We'll look at appositives first.

Appositives

Appositives are noun phrases that follow and describe other nouns. Although they can appear after any noun, they often follow the key word in the subject of a clause, and that is why we're paying close attention to them in this chapter. Here are some examples:

(a) James Brown, *the godfather of soul*, debuted with "Please, Please, Please" in 1956.

(b) Tiffany's, *the famous jewelry and china store on Fifth Avenue in New York*, means elegance and good taste to millions.

(c) George Washington, *our first president*, proclaimed Thursday, November 26, 1789, as the first official national celebration of Thanksgiving.

(d) Illiteracy, *a largely hidden tragedy*, affects about 60 million American adults.

You can see that each phrase in italics is an appositive; in other words, each one is a noun phrase that describes another noun. In (a), for example, the noun *godfather* is the cornerstone of the appositive or noun phrase, and the phrase that is built upon that cornerstone describes the noun before it—*James Brown*. In (b) the noun *store* is the cornerstone of the appositive, and the appositive describes the noun *Tiffany's*.

Please complete these sentences:

In (c) the noun in the appositive is the word _____ , and the appositive describes the noun _____ .

In (d) the noun in the appositive is the word _____ , and the appositive describes the noun _____ .

(In all four of our examples the noun that is described by the appositive also happens to be the subject of the sentence, but appositives can be used to describe nouns that are in other positions in clauses, too.)

You probably noticed that each appositive in examples (a) through (d) is set off from the main clause of the sentence with two commas. But don't be concerned with punctuation at this point. For now, look at sentence structure. You'll do a lot of work with those commas soon enough—in Chapter 3.

Exercise Four

Directions: Here is a collection of miscellaneous facts from *The People's Almanac #3* about assorted historical figures. Please do the following:

(a) Draw one line under the key word or words in the subject and use the label *S*. Remember, the key word or words in the subject will not be in an appositive.
(b) Draw a wavy line under the appositive in each sentence.
(c) Draw two lines under the verb or verb phrase and use the label *V* or *VP*.
(d) Label the complement, if there is one, with *C*.
(e) Write out the kernel of each clause on the line provided. *(The kernel is defined at the very beginning of Unit 4 on page 15.)*

TWO IMPORTANT NOTES: First, when you write out the kernel of each sentence in this exercise, you may either include or drop words such as *a*, *an*, and *the*. Second, keep in mind that the kernel does not always contain the basic meaning of the longer sentence. It shouldn't be surprising that meaning often changes considerably when you drop out all the extras—the modifiers. Remember that the kernel is equivalent to the skeleton, the structural basis of the longer sentence. Now you're ready to start.

1. John Adams, a lifelong hypochondriac, lived longer than any other president of the

   United States. (He died at the age of 90.)*

   Kernel: _____

2. Briton Hadden and Henry Robinson Luce, two friends from their undergraduate

   days at Yale University, rented one floor of a house in New York for $55 a month

   and planned out *Time* magazine there in the house's parlor in the winter of 1922.

   Kernel: _____

*You do not need to label and analyze the sentences that are within parentheses. They're just little extra tidbits of information or clarification.

3. Marcel Proust, author of *Remembrance of Things Past,* described life among the elite circles of Parisian society in the years before World War I.

   Kernel: _____

4. Vasco Núñez de Balboa, a bankrupt planter and later an explorer in the New World, was beheaded and thrown to the vultures because of a trumped-up murder charge in 1519.

   Kernel: _____

5. Woodrow Wilson, a former president of Princeton University, enjoyed grapefruit juice and two raw eggs almost every morning during his tenure in the White House.

   Kernel: _____

6. Queen Victoria, a carrier of hemophilia, transmitted the disease in its active form to one son and in its passive form to two daughters. (In other words, the son became a hemophiliac; the daughters were carriers like their mother.)

   Kernel: _____

7. Cuba's Fidel Castro, a left-handed pitcher at Havana University in his younger days, was once given a tryout by the Washington Senators baseball team.

   Kernel: _____

8. Anne Frank, the heroic author of *The Diary of Anne Frank,* died at Bergen-Belsen Concentration Camp at the age of 15.

   Kernel: _____

9. Ronald Wilson Reagan, the former actor and governor of California, became America's first divorced president.

   Kernel: _____

10. Groucho Marx, a seventh grade dropout, wrote and published several books, including a volume of his correspondence with people such as Harry Truman, James Thurber, and T. S. Eliot.

Kernel: _____

Other Modifying Phrases

There are other types of modifying phrases that can follow the key word in the subject, but appositives (or noun phrases, as they are also called) are by far the most common in the writing of most people. Here are examples of two other types. Example (a) shows an adjective phrase, and example (b) shows an adverb phrase:

(a)   The book, *spicy and slanderous,* seemed a natural for the best-seller list.

(b)   The young man, *hesitantly at first,* began his ascent up the mountain.

You'll run into these again when you work with punctuation in Chapter 3.

Prepositional Phrases

Prepositional phrases may be the most challenging modifiers to learn because there are so many prepositions. Before we define anything, let's look at an example. If you were asked to underline the modifier or modifiers in this phrase, what would you do? Give it a try:

the increased cost of textbooks

You probably underlined *increased* without any difficulty because that word is obviously an adjective that describes the noun *cost.* But what kind of cost are we talking about? The cost of frozen dinners? The cost of designer clothing? No, we're talking about the cost *of textbooks.* So when you really stop to think about it, that phrase—*of textbooks*—also modifies the word *cost.* It describes what kind of cost we're talking about. That little phrase that follows the noun *cost* is a modifier just as the adjective that precedes it is.

Here is an example of a prepositional phrase that acts as an adverb:

The woman made the decision *in a state of complete confusion.*

The prepositional phrase *in a state of complete confusion* modifies the verb *made.* It tells how the woman made the decision.

Look at this example:

He finished his first novel *at a seaside hotel.*

Again, the prepositional phrase acts like an adverb, doesn't it? What is the verb that it describes? _____ What does it tell about the verb? Does it tell *how* the action was done? Or *when* it was done? Or *where* it was done? _____

Here is a list of the most common prepositions. We're showing them to you in the context of prepositional phrases so that you can see how they work. Notice that each preposition is followed by a noun or a pronoun. Again, that's what a prepositional phrase is—a preposition followed by a noun or pronoun. You'll notice that most of the prepositions can be thought of as "direction" or "relationship" words.

about the introduction	*above* his head
across the border	*after* the recess
against his principles	*among* ourselves
around the city	*at* the time
before the meeting	*behind* the picture
below the surface	*beneath* the covers
beside her mother	*between* two slices
beyond tomorrow	*by* the haystack
down the path	*during* the first minute
except you	*for* my children
from his grandmother	*in* the spirit
inside his mind	*into* the grocery store
like a winner	*near* her heart
of the joke	*off* the top
on the dresser	*outside* the solar system
over the pasta	*past* his house
since her graduation	*through* the middle
to my office	*toward* the future
under a stone	*until* Christmas
up the steps	*upon* her entrance
with love	*within* your lifetime
without regrets	

Exercise Five

Directions: Choose ten prepositional phrases from the list above and use each one in a short sentence. Underline the prepositional phrase and circle the word that the phrase modifies. Use your own paper, please.

Why are prepositional phrases so important? The answer to that question is this: *The key word or key words in the subject of a sentence will never be found in a prepositional phrase.* And if you're not able to identify the key word or words in the subject, there is an important basic writing error that will result—subject-verb disagreement. (There are other problems that can result, too.) So we're going to practice finding prepositional phrases and crossing them out or setting them off in parentheses. What, for example, is the key word in the subject of this sentence?

(a)   One piece of cherry pie equals about 350 calories.

If you labeled *piece* as the key word in the subject, you're right. *Cherry pie* can't possibly be the key word in the subject because it's in a prepositional phrase. It's the noun that follows the preposition *of.* Either cross out the prepositional phrase or set it off within parentheses ( ).

Let's take one more example. Use *S* to label the key word in the subject of this sentence:

(b)   Plans for a long autobiographical poem were incomplete at the time of E. B. White's death in 1985.

This time, *Plans* is the key word in the subject. The word *poem* can't be the key word because it's in a prepositional phrase (the one that begins with the preposition *for*). What other prepositional phrases are in (b)?

1. _____

2. _____

3. _____

Exercise Six

Directions: Find *all* the prepositional phrases in these simple sentences, whether they occur in the subject part of the sentence or anywhere else. Cross them out or enclose them within parentheses. Then do the following:

(a) Draw a single line under the key word or key words in the subject and use the label *S*.
(b) Draw two lines under the verb or verb phrase and use the label *V* or *VP.*
(c) Mark the complement, if there is one, with *C*.
(d) Write the kernel on the line provided.

SPECIAL NOTE: We've tried to build as many prepositional phrases as possible into these sentences in order to give you a good workout. But you'll find that the use of so many prepositional phrases makes some of the sentences sound a little odd. So please consider these as sentences to be analyzed, not necessarily imitated.

1. A period of five years is called a lustrum.

   Kernel: _____

2. The average human being on a typical day loses a half pint of fluid through perspiration of the feet.

   Kernel: _____

3. The uniforms of the soldiers in the Swiss Guard at the Vatican in Rome were designed in the sixteenth century by Michelangelo.

   Kernel: _____

4. The tragic deaths of singer Rick Nelson and several members of his band in a fiery plane crash on December 31, 1985, resurrected sad memories of the deaths under similar circumstances of several other figures in the history of popular music, figures like Buddy Holly, Jim Croce, Patsy Cline, and Otis Redding.

   Kernel: _____

5. A fortress city of the ancient Incas was discovered by American Hiram Bingham in 1911.

   Kernel: _____

6. In the words of the tenth verse of the sixth chapter of the first letter of Paul to Timothy in the New Testament, the love of money is the root of all evils.

   Kernel: _____

7. Some 3000 dreams occur in the life of the average person during any two-year period.

   Kernel: _____

8. In 1930 one of the 52 covers of *Time* magazine featured the face of the notorious Al Capone.

   Kernel: _____

9. The color of lemon popsicles is usually white. (The ones with the yellow tint are banana-flavored.)

   Kernel: _____

10. The captain of the United States' gold medal–winning women's basketball team at the 1984 Summer Olympics in Los Angeles became the first female player for the Harlem Globetrotters within a short time after her wide public exposure in the Olympic games. (She's Lynette Woodard.)

    Kernel: _____

If you noticed how often *of* is used in comparison with other prepositions, it's not an accident. *Of* does seem to be the most frequently used preposition in our language. And *of* certainly causes more problems in subject-verb agreement than any other word, so it's important to keep an eye on it. (You'll work on subject-verb agreement, if you need to, in Chapter 6.)

UNIT 5: Summary and Cumulative Exercises

These are the most important things you've learned in Chapter 1:

1. Sentences are made up of clauses. A sentence can be one clause or a combination of clauses. A sentence that contains only one clause is called a simple sentence. If you learn what makes up a simple sentence, you have the tools for developing the most important basic writing skills.

2. A clause is made up of a subject and a predicate. The key part of the complete subject is always a noun, a pronoun, or any combination of nouns and pronouns. The subject is the naming part of the clause.
    The predicate is the second part of the clause. It makes a statement about the key word or words in the subject. The predicate contains a verb or verb phrase and sometimes a complement.

3. The essential parts of the clause are the words you label *S*, *V* or *VP*, and sometimes *C*. When we take them together as a whole, we call them the **kernel** of the clause. The parts of the kernel can be described by a variety of modifiers, including adjectives, adverbs, appositives, and prepositional phrases. These modifiers add a lot of interest and meaning, but in terms of sentence structure, they are secondary. The kernel is primary.

The rest of this unit consists of exercises to help you remember and reinforce what you have learned in Chapter 1.

Exercise One

This is an exercise for people who would benefit from more practice on some of the basic parts of speech. Each word in the columns below can be used in at least two of three ways—as a **noun**, a **verb**, or an **adjective**. Some of the words can be used in all three ways. Our students have found this kind of exercise very helpful because it shows how sometimes the exact same word can be a noun in one context, a verb in another, and an adjective in a third. Here is an example of how the word *love* can function in these three different ways:

(a) *Love* is a precious commodity. (Here *love* is a noun.)

(b) The kids *love* raspberries and cream. (Here *love* is a verb.)

(c) Everybody should receive a *love* letter now and then. (Here *love* is an adjective.)

Directions: First, if you need to, review the introductory material on nouns, verbs, and adjectives earlier in Chapter 1. Then look at the choices listed below. Each word can be used in at least two different ways, and some can be used in three different ways. Choose five words and write two or three sentences for each of the five words you picked; in your sentences, show how the word can be used as a noun in one context, a verb in another context, and an adjective in still another. Use your own paper, please.

work	crack	team
pecan	wrinkle	marriage
swim	plan	color
worry	action	rest
radio	bread	pink
paint	stretch	complete
laugh	exercise	bite

Exercise Two

This is an exercise for people who would benefit from more practice on the different types of complements.

Directions: First, review the section on complements that begins on page 12. Then do the following:

(a) Underline the complement of each sentence.
(b) Identify the complement as one of the following on the blank provided: *noun, pronoun, adjective, adverb, prepositional phrase, clause, infinitive verb phrase,* or *infinitive verb phrase plus additional complement.*

1. We remembered the joke. _____

2. We remembered it. _____

3. We remembered in an instant. _____

4. We remembered that she had told it before. _____

5. We remembered without any problem. _____

6. We remembered quickly. _____

7. We remembered the garden. _____

8. We remembered to eat. _____

9. We remembered that your birthday is today. _____

10. We remembered to take the medicine. _____

Please correct Exercise Two before doing Exercise Three.

Exercise Three

Directions: Please continue to follow the same directions.

1. We remembered to wave. _____

2. We remembered before breakfast. _____

3. We remembered perfectly. _____

4. We remembered that you were always so sweet. _____

5. We remembered his moodiness. _____

6. We remembered you. _____

7. We remembered that. _____

8. We remembered later. _____

9. We remembered to gargle. _____

10. We remembered to call Madonna. _____

Now that you've reviewed parts of speech and complements, you're ready to begin to do a few final exercises on picking out the kernels of simple sentences.

Exercise Four

PART A

Directions: Below is a series of simple sentences. Please do the following:

(a) Draw a line under the key word or words in the subject and use the label *S*.
(b) Draw two lines under the verb or verb phrase in the predicate and use the label *V* or *VP*.
(c) Label the complement, if there is one, with *C*.
(d) Do whatever else is helpful to you—crossing out or enclosing prepositional phrases, drawing wavy lines beneath appositives, and so on.
(e) Write out the kernel on the line provided.

1. According to an article in *Psychology Today,* even three-year-old children can learn pain control.

   Kernel: _____

2. The techniques of biofeedback do work with very young human beings.

   Kernel: _____

3. This conclusion is supported by work at the Minneapolis Children's Medical Center.

Kernel: _____

4. Karen Olness, the director of behavioral pediatrics and research at the center, says that the possibilities for self-regulation by children are fantastic.

Kernel: _____

5. In fact, researchers have conducted several studies of children's abilities in this area.

Kernel: _____

6. In many research projects and experiments an unexpected degree of control over physical functions was found among kids.

Kernel: _____

7. Youngsters from six to ten years of age actually outperformed adults in one study of control of skin temperature.

Kernel: _____

8. Many of the potential beneficiaries of these mind-body procedures are children with asthma, hemophilia, diabetes, fecal incontinence, and cancer.

Kernel: _____

9. The physical benefits and the psychological rewards for children with chronic illnesses can be great.

Kernel: _____

10. They include a reduction of symptoms, freedom from pain, increased self-confidence, and a sense of independence.

Kernel: _____

PART B

Directions: **Please continue to follow the same directions.**

1. Through education in biofeedback techniques, seriously ill children often learn to control physiological factors such as pulse, temperature, and muscle response.

   Kernel: _____

2. The children's level of ability with these techniques often eliminates symptoms and creates an entirely new and more positive attitude toward the disease itself.

   Kernel: _____

3. According to researchers, some young patients make a leap of faith and begin to believe that recovery is possible.

   Kernel: _____

4. One study of children with migraine headaches has been especially encouraging to researchers in the field.

   Kernel: _____

5. In it the use of both biofeedback techniques and relaxation exercises stopped pain and reduced the frequency of symptoms to at least the same degree of effectiveness as the drug propranolol.

   Kernel: _____

6. Another successful experimental study involved young hemophiliacs.

   Kernel: _____

7. Bleeding in the joints can cause tremendous pain for these children.

   Kernel: _____

8. But fortunately it can be managed through biofeedback and relaxation regimens.

   Kernel: _____

9. These mind-body processes may seem complicated and even frightening to very

   young children, especially to two-and-a-half- to four-year-olds.

   Kernel: _____

10. However, medical personnel have successfully used several teaching tools, such

    as dolls, stuffed animals, and the example of slightly older children, in their work

    with the youngest ones.

    Kernel: _____

Exercise Five

PART A

Directions: Below is a series of simple sentences about early rock and roll trivia. A source for much of this information is *Dick Clark's The First 25 Years of Rock & Roll.* Please do the following:

(a) Draw a line under the key word or words in the subject and use the label *S*.
(b) Draw two lines under the verb or verb phrase in the predicate and use the label *V* or *VP.*
(c) Label the complement, if there is one, with *C*.
(d) Again, use whatever additional labeling helps you.
(e) Write out the kernel on the line provided.

1. Little Richard Penniman, one of the pioneers of early rock and roll, was a star in

   his own right and a benefactor to several other rising stars.

   Kernel: _____

2. One of Little Richard's concert tours in Europe in the 1960s included the then-

   unknown Rolling Stones.

   Kernel: _____

3. The Beatles, the most popular group in the world for many years, were once Little

   Richard's opening act on a tour through Germany.

   Kernel: _____

4. For two years Jimi Hendrix, one of rock and roll's greatest guitarists, played backup guitar in Little Richard's band.

   Kernel: _____

5. One of Elvis Presley's first big hits was a creation of Carl Perkins, one of the less widely known founding fathers of rock.

   Kernel: _____

6. Perkins, a young man from a poor family in Lake County, Tennessee, woke up in the middle of the night and wrote "Blue Suede Shoes" on a potato sack.

   Kernel: _____

7. Like Little Richard, Carl Perkins also had a transcontinental influence on the development of rock and roll.

   Kernel: _____

8. On a 1963 British tour with Chuck Berry, Perkins met the Beatles and became good friends with the "Fab Four."

   Kernel: _____

9. At the time, the lads from Liverpool were famous in Europe and unknown in America.

   Kernel: _____

10. They knew that Carl Perkins represented the roots of rock and roll and wanted his coaching on their renditions of three of his songs.

    Kernel: _____

11. The specific songs in question were "Everybody's Trying to Be My Baby," "Honey Don't," and "Matchbox."

    Kernel: _____

12. Both the lyrics and the performances of many early rock and roll recordings were labeled obscene.

    Kernel: _____

13. Everybody, for instance, knows that Elvis Presley was not shown below the waist on Ed Sullivan's variety show.

    Kernel: _____

14. That performance, however, was not Presley's first on television.

    Kernel: _____

15. Presley's first tryout on national television was his appearance on the *Tommy and Jimmy Dorsey Stage Show* on CBS on January 28, 1956.

    Kernel: _____

PART B

Directions: **Please continue to follow the same directions.**

1. According to one history of the early days of rock and roll, the young man from Mississippi "twisted, shook, leered, and swung his pelvis at the camera."

   Kernel: _____

2. All those verbs infuriated the parents, sponsors, and networks of the 1950s.

   Kernel: _____

3. But they pumped up the ratings like crazy.

   Kernel: _____

4. Ratings mean money.

   Kernel: _____

5. And money talks.

   Kernel: _____

6. Only a fool would fail to predict the next chapter in the story.

   Kernel: _____

7. Soon the networks were experiencing mixed feelings about rock and roll.

   Kernel: _____

8. They wanted to capture the teenage audience and still pacify the adults.

   Kernel: _____

9. Steve Allen's invitation to Jerry Lee Lewis, another Southerner and a very influential

   figure in the history of rock and roll, was a breakthrough.

   Kernel: _____

10. With Allen's blessing, Jerry Lee Lewis gave a wild and uncensored performance of

    "Whole Lotta Shakin' Going On" on *The Steve Allen Show* and became an over-

    night sensation in the United States.

    Kernel: _____

    (Lewis was so grateful for the big break that he named his first son Steve Allen

    Lewis.)

Chapter 2
Sentence Combining: Basic Strategies and Common Problems

Up to this point, we have been analyzing the single clauses of simple sentences, but now we are going to turn our attention to *combining* clauses. You probably know that if you rely too heavily on simple sentences in your writing, you produce a choppy, disconnected effect. But it's not difficult to combine clauses, and in fact, most or all of the sentence-combining techniques that we will present in Units 1 through 3 of this chapter are already part of your set of automatic language patterns. But the important thing is to become *conscious* of the process of combining sentences. If you are successful in this attempt (and you almost certainly will be if you work carefully through this chapter and later ones), you will have a number of options for making smooth, logical connections between thoughts, and you will have the variety you need for college-level writing.

Two common sentence structure problems—*run-ons* and *fragments*—are a result of missteps in the process of sentence combining, so they will be taken up in this chapter, too.

UNIT 1: Compound Sentences

One of the easiest ways to combine clauses is to link them with a conjunction. The easiest conjunctions to work with are the *compound conjunctions*. Traditionally, seven words are listed in this category, but two of them—*nor* and *for*—are used rather infrequently, so we're going to be working with five compound conjunctions in this unit:

and
but
or
so
yet

Please memorize this list of conjunctions, at least for the time being. Here are some examples of *compound sentences*:

(a) Ernest Lawrence Thayer wrote "Casey at the Bat," **and** the San Francisco *Examiner* first published it on June 3, 1888.

(b) Al Capone eventually made his name as a gangster, **but** he started out as a bouncer at Coney Island.

(c) According to M. Scott Peck, M.D., in *People of the Lie*, evil people attack others, **yet** they rarely face their own failures as human beings.

Label the sentences above, using *S, V* or *VP*, and *C*, so that you see clearly how each one is made up of two clauses. The clauses are *independent*, which means that they can stand on their own. Each one could be written as a simple sentence, which is actually one independent clause. (We will take up dependent clauses in the next unit.) In a compound sentence, two independent clauses are joined with one of the compound conjunctions.

Notice also that a *comma* is used in a compound sentence. It is placed after the first clause, just before the conjunction.

This does not mean that a comma is always used before *and, but, or, so,* and *yet*. For example, look at these sentences:

(a) Orange **and** green are two of the secondary colors.

(b) New college graduates are often excited **but** apprehensive about the next phase of their lives.

No comma is used in either sentence because in these cases *and* and *but* are not used to connect clauses. What is *and* used to connect in sentence (a)? _____
What is *but* used to connect in sentence (b)? _____

[*Answers.* In (a) *and* links two nouns that are used as subjects; in (b) *but* links two adjectives that function as complements.]

Exercise One

Directions: All of the sentences below are compound sentences, so you'll see that each one has two clauses. Label both clauses of each sentence, using *S, V* or *VP*, and *C*. Circle the conjunction that connects the clauses; then insert a comma before the conjunction.

1. On the average, Mexican-Americans have larger families than any other ethnic group in the United States and they can also claim the lowest divorce rate of all.

2. In the fifteenth century, French gardeners wanted the sweetest possible melons so they watered them with sugar water and honey.

3. Facial tissues are great for cold sufferers but those thin little sheets were actually invented for the removal of cold cream.

4. Both Bill Wilson, a New York stockbroker, and Robert H. Smith, an Ohio surgeon, had a drinking problem so they joined forces and started Alcoholics Anonymous in 1935.

5. Most people keep their New Year's resolutions for no more than a few weeks or they don't make them in the first place.

6. At a glance quilting might seem a nonpolitical activity but Susan B. Anthony gave her first suffrage speech at a quilting bee.

7. In the matriarchal society of elephants the oldest female in a herd usually leads the herd and the other females are ranked just under her in order of age.

8. Fifteen percent of women between the ages of 15 and 45 have some degree of endometriosis yet many have never even heard of this mysterious and often destructive disease.

9. Brookside Gardens in Wheaton, Maryland, was designed especially for the blind but even seeing visitors can enjoy the fragrance of the garden's waist-high flower beds, the tastes of its many herbs, and the sounds of its birds and fountains.

10. You can have a fried egg, two slices of toast without butter, and a cup of skim milk for breakfast and stay under 350 calories or you can enjoy a cup of oatmeal with a little milk, a sweet roll, and four ounces of orange juice and still remain within your limit.

Exercise Two

Directions: Choosing from the suggestions below, create five or more of your own compound sentences. For example, if you choose the first suggestion in category 2, you might create a sentence such as this one: *For several years the Milwaukee Brewers had great hitting,* **but** *their pitching was pitiful.* Please write your sentences on your own paper and remember to insert the comma.

1. Suggestions for clauses that are linked with **and:**

   —two things that you like about a particular television show

   —two hopes that you have for a child or a younger person you know

—two qualities that you admire in your favorite aunt or uncle

—two things that someone could learn from you

—two improvements that your town or city should make as soon as possible

2. Suggestions for clauses that are linked with **but** or **yet:**

—one strength and one weakness of a particular sports team, school, or radio station

—one thing that you have already accomplished and one thing that you have not yet been able to accomplish

—one thing that you love about a certain person's cooking (your mother's or father's, for instance) and one thing that you do not like about it at all

—one course that you find easy this term and one course that you find more difficult

—one point on which you agree with a particular political candidate and one point on which you don't agree

3. Suggestions for clauses that are linked with **or:**

—two possible theories about why a relationship with a certain person did not succeed

—two explanations that students sometimes give about why they were late for class

—two things a person could do to get in shape

—two topics on which you would be interested in writing

—two different theories about why you developed a certain interest or skill

4. Suggestions for clauses that are linked with **so:**

—two things: first, a hope or a goal (learning to dance or play a certain sport or a position on a team; breaking a pattern of negative thinking; starting to take better care of yourself; making more friends; or earning higher grades); second, a

course of action that will help you reach the goal

IMPORTANT NOTE: As you've learned, the compound conjunctions are usually used to connect two independent clauses, but they can also be used to connect more than two clauses within one sentence. Analyze and punctuate the following example, using *S, V* or *VP*, and *C*. Circle the conjunctions that connect the clauses and insert a comma before each:

At the age of 23, Frank Church of Idaho learned of his incurable cancer but he lived

another 36 years and in that time he became one of the century's most powerful

and effective liberal Democratic U.S. senators.

You can see that *three* independent clauses have been connected by compound conjunctions in the sentence about Sen. Frank Church. This is a useful option for combining clauses, but, of course, you wouldn't want to overuse it because you know that variety in sentence structure is a mark of good, lively writing. Three or four clauses combined with compound conjunctions would probably be the limit within one sentence. Keep in mind that the standard and most common use of the compound conjunction is simply to bring together two clauses.

UNIT 2: Complex Sentences

Complex sentences are another easy technique of sentence combination, and they provide even more variety in your writing because most of them can be presented in two different sequences. In a complex sentence the conjunction can be placed between the clauses, just as in a compound sentence. For example:

(a)   The mandrill of western Africa is often called the most colorful mammal in the world **because** it has a brilliant crimson nose and bright blue cheeks.

Or the conjunction (the word *because*) can be placed before the first clause in a complex sentence. For example:

(b)   **Because** it has a brilliant crimson nose and bright blue cheeks, the mandrill of western Africa is often called the most colorful mammal in the world.

In both the (a) and (b) sentences, the clause that comes right after the conjunction is called the *dependent clause.* It's called dependent because it depends upon more information. It can't stand alone. *Because it has a brilliant crimson nose and bright blue cheeks* doesn't make sense by itself. It needs something else, namely an independent clause. Once it is attached to an independent clause, such as *the mandrill of western Africa is often called the most colorful mammal in the world,* the two clauses work together to make a perfectly good sentence—a *complex* sentence. Remember, in both the (a) and (b) sentences, it is the word *because* that is the conjunction. That's the word that joins the clauses.

Make a complex sentence in both of its possible word orders. The dependent clause is already given to you; you create the independent clause. Again, we're using the conjunction *because*:

(c) _____

_____ because I've been working too hard lately.

(d) Because I've been working too hard lately, _____

_____ .

A Note on Punctuation

If you're especially observant, you may already have noticed that a comma is used in the examples above only when the conjunction appears at the start of the first clause; then a comma is placed between the dependent clause and the independent clause. A comma is not generally used in a complex sentence when the conjunction appears before the second clause; in other words, you don't use a comma when the conjunction is in the middle of a complex sentence. Here is another way to say this:

Dependent clause first → comma between clauses

Independent clause first → no comma

There are exceptions to this rule, and later you might want to learn about them and about some other fine points, but in this book, we are concerned with the basics, and this punctuation rule is correct for the vast majority of complex sentences that you will write.

15 Complex Conjunctions to Memorize

So far, we've looked at just one of the complex conjunctions, but there are others. These are the most commonly used 15:

after	if	when
although	since	whenever
as	though	where
because	unless	wherever
before	until	while

Please memorize these 15 complex conjunctions. Some students copy the list from the book and tape it to the bathroom mirror or the refrigerator door for a week or two. Then they read the list aloud whenever they get a chance, and they recopy it or test themselves on it occasionally. Students do the same with the five compound conjunctions: *and*, *but*, *or*, *so*, and *yet*. The point is certainly not that you're going to have to recite these lists in class; the point is that you need to be able to recognize both compound and complex conjunctions when you see them in sentences.

We call this *temporary memorization*, and we ask our students to do it whenever it's going to help them. The ones who give it a try tend to go through the course without getting unnecessarily confused by different groups of words and their functions. Students who don't make an effort to memorize the complex conjunctions, to cite one particular example, have the most trouble with another list that's coming up shortly; that list includes words and phrases that are often used with semicolons.

Now you should be ready to try some exercises.

Exercise One

Directions: Label the two clauses in each complex sentence, using *S, V* or *VP,* and *C.* (If you did very well spotting kernels in Chapter 1, your teacher may have you label only a few of these sentences.) Circle the conjunction that connects the clauses. Then follow the punctuation rules for complex sentences.

1. When you lick a postage stamp you consume one tenth of one calorie.

2. The birth of the Dionne quintuplets in 1934 created an enormous sensation because no other set of identical quintuplets had ever survived.

3. Although Pretty Boy Floyd was originally known for his string of bank robberies he gained even greater fame for his uncanny knack of avoiding police traps.

4. Eight thousand people must live in a community before the U.S. government calls it a city.

5. If F. Scott Fitzgerald had been able to complete the work before his death in 1940 at the age of 44 *The Last Tycoon* might have been a major American novel.

6. Although dogs generally have good vision they see only various shades of gray.

7. Male arrow poison frogs carry fertilized eggs on their backs until the eggs hatch into tadpoles and are released into the water.

8. If you are a typical American man you spend four hours a year tying your necktie.

9. While he was serving in Vietnam Rocky Bleier suffered severe injuries to his right leg and foot.

10. Bleier later became an outstanding member of the Pittsburgh Steelers' backfield after he had struggled through years of exercise and rehabilitative therapy.

Exercise Two

Directions: Take sentences 1, 2, 5, 9, and 10 from the exercise above and rewrite each of them below in reverse order. In other words, if a sentence began with the dependent clause in Exercise One, rewrite it below with the independent clause first. Adjust your punctuation accordingly, please.

1. _____

_____

_____

2. _____

_____

_____

5. _____

_____

_____

9. _____

_____

_____

10. _____

_____

_____

A NOTE ON OTHER SWITCHES: If you try to switch the clauses in some of the other sentences from Exercise One, you'll see that they don't all work out equally well unless you also make some other small changes; for instance, sometimes you need to switch the placement of a noun and a pronoun. Sentences 3 and 4 are good examples. The order of the clauses can certainly be reversed, but if they are reversed, it's going to be helpful to switch the placement of *Pretty Boy Floyd* and *he* in sentence 3 and *community* and *it* in sentence 4. Obviously, this is because it's usually easier for your reader to follow you if you use a noun first and then replace it with a pronoun.

Exercise Three

Directions: This is an exercise to do in class. Our students usually find it fun and useful. Pick out five complex conjunctions and write five dependent clauses. Then exchange papers with another student in your class and complete his or her sentences by adding an independent clause to each. Another student will do the same to your dependent clauses. The student who completes the sentence makes the decision to add or not add a comma. Exchange papers again so that you get back your own original work. Check the complex sentences that have been created from your dependent clauses; see if they're correct in terms of both logic and punctuation. Discuss any interesting combinations, problems, or special cases in class.

A Final Note

You may have noticed that some of the complex conjunctions were listed earlier as prepositions. Don't let this confuse you. Some words can be used as both parts of speech. Label these *conj.* or *prep.*:

1. (a) Wendy went to the Halloween party *after* school.

   (b) She had to go back for her broom *after* she left the party.

2. (a) I'd like to see you *before* the spring break starts on Monday.

   (b) I'd like to see you *before* the spring break.

3. (a) Daniel wasn't completely at home in Detroit *until* his third year there.

   (b) *Until* Daniel had been in Detroit for three years, he wasn't completely at home in the city.

UNIT 3: Embedded Sentences

Another very valuable strategy for combining sentences is *embedding*. At first this might seem less familiar to you than the process by which you form compound and complex sentences. But if you look at a large sampling of your own writing, you're sure to find examples of embedded sentences. You are already creating them, so it's just a matter of becoming more conscious of how the process works and learning the fine points of punctuation.

This process does not involve conjunctions. It involves what we are going to call *embedding words,* and these are the most important ones:

who
whose
which

(The word **that** can also be used for embedding, but we'll deal with it in Chapter 3 because it involves a different punctuation rule.)

Let's say that you wanted to combine these two sentences:

(a) **Eudora Welty is a major Southern writer.**

(b) **She was born in Mississippi in 1909.**

If you try to combine clauses (a) and (b) to make a compound or a complex sentence, you'll find that none of the conjunctions seems quite right. Sure, you could probably say, "Eudora Welty is a major Southern writer, and she was born in Mississippi in 1909," but doesn't that sentence have a weak, flat sound to it?

The process of embedding, on the other hand, works well with clauses (a) and (b). The first thing we have to do is change the subject of the second clause to an embedding word. Here's what we do:

who
(b) ~~She~~ was born in Mississippi in 1909.

Then we insert the new clause (b) between the subject and predicate of the (a) sentence. Now this is what we have:

Eudora Welty **who was born in Mississippi in 1909** is a major Southern writer.

As a finishing touch, we'll add two commas—one before and one after the clause we have embedded. And here's our final product, an embedded sentence:

Eudora Welty, who was born in Mississippi in 1909, is a major Southern writer.

The commas set the *embedded clause* off from the *main clause*, making the whole sentence much easier to read.

The embedding word *which* is used to replace nonhuman subjects. Use *which* to make an embedded sentence of these two clauses. (If you need to, go through the various steps on your own paper, please.)

1. (a) *Losing Battles* takes place at a family reunion in Mississippi.
   (b) It is one of the funniest of all American novels.

   _____

   _____

   _____

The word *whose* is the possessive embedding word. When *whose* is used, you'll find that you're not really replacing the subject of the second clause; you're replacing the possessive pronoun—a word such as *her* or *his*—that appears just before the subject. Use *whose* to combine these two simple sentences into an embedded sentence:

2. (a) Eudora Welty was very much influenced by her mother's love of reading.
   (b) Her early life is beautifully described in *One Writer's Beginnings*.

   _____

   _____

   _____

Most students don't need to be taught when to use a particular embedding word. But as you do the following exercises, if you have any questions about the appropriateness of *who, whose,* or *which*, just ask your writing teacher.

Exercise One

Directions: Combine these sets of sentences by using the embedding process. Remember to insert commas around the embedded clause. (Again, the embedding words are *which, who,* and *whose*.) These little bits of information are found in *The Presidents, Tidbits & Trivia* by Sid Frank and Arden Davis Melick.

1. (a) Thomas Jefferson was broke when he died.

   (b) He was certainly one of America's most brilliant presidents.

   _____

   _____

   _____

2. (a) Monrovia was founded in 1822 and named after President James Monroe.

   (b) It is the capital of the West African nation of Liberia.

   _____

   _____

   _____

3. (a) Herbert Hoover was supposedly worried that King Tut was becoming too attached to other people.

   (b) He once gave an order that no White House staffers were to pet his dog.

   _____

   _____

   _____

4. (a) James Buchanan was the only president to remain a bachelor.

   (b) His 23-year-old fiancée broke off their engagement and died mysteriously a short time later.

   _____

   _____

   _____

5. (a) Grover Cleveland's duties as a sheriff in New York State resulted in his partici-

      pation in the execution of two convicted murderers.

  (b) They included serving as one county's official hangman.

_____

_____

_____

6. (a) Every day Chester A. Arthur placed a bouquet of fresh flowers next to a

      photograph of his late wife Ellen.

  (b) He entered the presidency as a widower.

_____

_____

_____

7. (a) Richard Nixon once worked as a barker for the wheel of chance at the "Slip-

      pery Gulch Rodeo" in Prescott, Arizona.

  (b) His ill-fated presidency was the only one to end in resignation.

_____

_____

_____

8. (a) William Howard Taft threw out the first ball in a game between Washington

      and Philadelphia in 1910.

  (b) He was the first president to open a baseball season.

_____

_____

_____

9. (a)   The very first assassination attempt on the life of a U.S. president occurred in

1835.

(b)   It happened to be directed against Andrew Jackson.

_____

_____

_____

10. (a)   Richard Lawrence shot at President Jackson because Lawrence believed that

Jackson was preventing him from becoming the "King of America."

(b)   His two pistols misfired at close range.

_____

_____

_____

Be sure to correct your embedded sentences for Exercise One before continuing.

Exercise Two

Directions: Combine these sets of sentences by using the embedding process. Remember to insert commas around the embedded clause. (Again, the embedding words are *which, who,* and *whose.*) These facts, which concern presidential wives, mothers, and daughters, are also from *The Presidents, Tidbits & Trivia.*

1. (a)   All throughout her widowhood Sarah Polk left her home only to go to church.

(b)   She outlived her husband by 42 years.

_____

_____

_____

2. (a)   Woodrow and Ellen Wilson exchanged approximately 1400 love letters dur-

ing their various separations.

(b)   Their 29-year marriage lasted until her death.

_____

_____

_____

3. (a) Alice Roosevelt Longworth once called Warren Harding "a slob" and Dwight

Eisenhower "a nice boob."

(b) She was Teddy Roosevelt's outspoken daughter and a favorite of Washington

reporters.

_____

_____

_____

4. (a) Eleanor Roosevelt frequently joked about her own cooking and once served

hot dogs to the king of England.

(b) She undoubtedly thought she had better things to do.

_____

_____

_____

5. (a) The U.S. Senate conducted an investigation that cost $2000.

(b) It was infuriated with Dolley Madison's purchase of an imported $40 mirror

for the White House.

_____

_____

_____

6. (a) Knox Taylor became the bride of Jefferson Davis, later the president of the

Confederacy.

(b) Her father was President Zachary Taylor.

_____

_____

_____

7. (a) Abigail Fillmore refused to move into the White House until it had indoor

plumbing.

(b) She was born in 1798.

_____

_____

_____

8. (a) *Statesmen's Dishes and How to Cook Them* was written by Caroline Harrison,

the wife of President Benjamin Harrison.

(b) It was published in 1890.

_____

_____

_____

9. (a) Mary Ball Washington did not attend the inauguration of the first president of

the United States.

(b) Her relationship with her son George was always strained.

_____

_____

_____

10. (a) Jacqueline Kennedy had also lost an infant son less than four months before

the tragic trip to Dallas.

(b) She lost her husband on November 22, 1963.

_____

_____

_____

Two Variations of Embedded Sentences

Some of the embedded sentences that are made with the words *who* and *which* can be reworked in two ways. Knowing how to create these two variations will give you a little more flexibility in your writing.

Look at this example. First, we will combine two sentences by embedding, just as you have done in the last two exercises. We'll use these two simple sentences:

(a) **Flashlight fish blink their lights to attract their prey.**

(b) **They are equipped with glowing pockets of bacteria beneath each eye.**

When they are combined by embedding, we have:

1. Flashlight fish, which are equipped with glowing pockets of bacteria beneath each eye, blink their lights to attract their prey.

Sentence 1 is the type of sentence you've been creating in the last two exercises, but we're going to start calling it a "full embedding" or a "fully embedded" sentence.

Now we're going to make the first variation. We simply drop the embedding word *(which)* and the helping or linking verb *(are)*. Please circle the words *which are* in sentence 1, and with what we have left, we make a "reduced embedding":

2. Flashlight fish, **equipped with glowing pockets of bacteria beneath each eye,** blink their lights to attract their prey.

Now we're going to try the other variation. All we do is take the words that appear between the commas in sentence 2 and use them as an introductory phrase. This is what we'll have:

3. **Equipped with glowing pockets of bacteria beneath each eye,** flashlight fish blink their lights to attract their prey.

Sentence 3 is the "moved embedding." Notice that we haven't changed any wording when we went from 2 to 3. All we did was change the order of the words. Also notice that the reduced embedding takes two commas. The moved variation takes only one.

To review, please go back and write the following notes in the lefthand margin next to sentences 1 through 3 above:

1. fully embedded → two commas

2. reduced → two commas

3. moved → one comma

Exercise Three

Directions: Below are five fully embedded sentences. Practice working out the two variations for each. The facts are from the National Wildlife Federation's *Incredible Animals, A to Z.*

1. A quetzal, which is unable to take off into the air like other birds, has to jump off a tree branch backward to avoid snagging its 24-inch tail.

    Reduced: _____

    _____

    _____

    Moved: _____

    _____

    _____

2. Male narwhals, which are nicknamed "unicorns of the sea," sport a single nine-foot-long tusk.

    Reduced: _____

    _____

    _____

    Moved: _____

    _____

    _____

3. Some biologists, who are puzzled by the hump on the back of the thorny devil, speculate that the lizard can push the hump up to create the illusion of a second head when it wants to confuse its enemies.

    Reduced: _____

    _____

    _____

Moved: _____

_____

_____

4. A sloth, which is blessed with three very efficient curved claws on each foot, normally hangs from a tree for its daily 18-hour snooze.

Reduced: _____

_____

_____

Moved: _____

_____

_____

5. One scientist, who was curious about the basic color of the zebra, conducted a study and concluded that zebras are actually black with white stripes, not white with black stripes.

Reduced: _____

_____

_____

Moved: _____

_____

_____

Exercise Four

Directions: Combine each pair below to make a fully embedded sentence. Then create both variations—reduced and moved. Please use your own paper. More about these bits of information can be found in *The People's Almanac #2,* a book by David Wallechinsky and Irving Wallace.

1. (a) Philippe, the Duke of Orleans, was brought up as a girl so that his brother, the

   future Louis XIV, would not have a male rival.

   (b) Philippe was born in 1640.

2. (a) Vladimir Ilyich Lenin ended up ordering the execution of hundreds of thousands

   of peasants.

   (b) He was theoretically opposed to the oppressive use of authority.

3. (a) Barry Tarshis wrote an intriguing reference book called *What It Costs.*

   (b) He was hoping to profit from the average person's curiosity about the price of

   this and that.

4. (a) Director John Ford banned the use of makeup, artificial lighting, and special

   camera effects while filming *The Grapes of Wrath.*

   (b) He was attempting to stay true to the gritty, realistic nature of Steinbeck's novel.

5. (a) The Christian monk Telemachus threw himself between opponents and was

   beaten to death by spectators.

   (b) He was horrified by the gladiatorial contests in Rome.

ONE LAST NOTE: Some students tell us that some of the variations, although correct, just don't "sound right." If that's also true for you, it may be because you're not used to making these kinds of sentences. They're not part of spoken language patterns as much as compound and complex sentences are. Embedded sentences and their variations are patterns that we read more often than we hear.

Also, please remember that not every embedded sentence can be reworked into the two variations. But where the variations do work, you now have two more options for flexibility and variety in sentence combining.

UNIT 4: A Sentence-Combining Approach to the Problem of Run-Ons

Up to this point in Chapter 2, you have been working with various methods of combining sentences. Now we're going to turn our attention to two different types of errors that can easily occur during the process of sentence combining.

The first is the problem of *run-ons.* Even if run-ons have always been a feature of your writing, you now have some good sentence-combining techniques to use in solving them. In later chapters, you'll learn even more techniques.

What exactly is a run-on? It's actually a very simple sentence structure error. **A run-on is a series of two or more unconnected independent clauses.** Here is an example:

The Daughters of St. Crispin was founded in 1869 in Lynn, Massachusetts, it was

the first national organization of trade union women.

Label the example with *S, V* or *VP,* and *C* so that you can clearly see the two clauses. Then write *RO* where one sentence "runs on" into the other.

If we saw this sentence in a student's writing, we'd know that our student had been attempting to combine clauses. We'd know it from the placement of the two clauses between one capital letter and period. But the two clauses are *not* combined or connected. Instead, they are running into one another.

How can you solve the run-on? The comma after the word *Massachusetts* cannot join the clauses. Commas have many valuable uses, but they're not considered strong enough to join clauses. You *can* solve the run-on in a number of ways, using the techniques you've learned in this chapter. Below are four solutions. Notice that one is a compound sentence, one is complex, one is embedded, and so forth. In other words, the solutions are types of sentence combinations we've been studying in the preceding three units. Here are four possible solutions for the run-on:

(a) The Daughters of St. Crispin, which was the first national organization of trade union women, was founded in 1869 in Lynn, Massachusetts.

(b) The Daughters of St. Crispin was founded in 1869 in Lynn, Massachusetts, and it was the first national organization of trade union women.

(c) When the Daughters of St. Crispin was founded in 1869 in Lynn, Massachusetts, it was the first national organization of trade union women.

(d) Founded in 1869 in Lynn, Massachusetts, the Daughters of St. Crispin was the first national organization of trade union women.

As you can see, (a) is a fully embedded sentence, (b) is compound, (c) is complex, and (d) is a variation of an embedded and reduced sentence that we produced after juggling the parts of the sentence a bit. These are all good techniques for solving run-ons, and as we mentioned, you'll learn more strategies later.

Combining, Not Breaking Up

Notice that we did not solve the run-on about the Daughters of St. Crispin by breaking apart the two clauses and making two separate sentences, each with its own capital letter and period. Breaking run-ons up into separate sentences is probably a good technique to use in the early grades, but for adult writers, it is usually inappropriate. You *should* be combining clauses, but you have to do it correctly. There are only two times when you should break up a run-on: (1) when your run-on is long enough so that it might be difficult for your reader to follow your writing and (2) when you want to write a short, perhaps choppy sentence for a strong, simple, or dramatic effect. But for most students, those two cases are the exception. In the great majority of cases, run-ons should be corrected by combining clauses, not by separating them.

Three Things to Realize about Run-ons

There are three important things to remember about run-ons. First of all, they aren't necessarily long. These are all run-ons:

(a) He walked she ran.

(b) The vegetables were fresh they were great.

(c) Dogs bark cats meow.

(d) Nancy loved antiques, she disliked most modern things.

(e) The picnic was postponed, it rained.

(f) The first semester was hard, the second one was a little better.

Notice that the first three examples do not contain a comma between the clauses, and the last three examples do. Examples (d) through (f) are technically called *comma splices,* but they are a sentence structure error so similar to run-ons that we are going to call both types of mistakes *run-ons,* just to keep things simple. Try to solve each of the six errors above, using the sentence-combining techniques that you know.

The second important fact about run-ons is that the second clause often begins with a pronoun. Go back and see how many examples in our discussion show this pattern. If you watch for this tendency in your own writing, you'll prevent a lot of run-ons right there. Let's suppose you wrote, "Christopher wants to eat, he is starved." That's a run-on. When you produced "he is starved," you wrote an independent clause, which somehow has to be connected to the clause before it. The fact that *he* refers to *Christopher* in the first clause does not mean that the two clauses are already connected.

Here's the third point. Remember in Chapter 1 we told you that the word *that* can attach one clause to another clause as a complement. (Turn back to page 15 if you need to.) So the examples below are *not* run-ons. They are perfectly acceptable sentences because the word *that* makes the second clause the complement of the first clause. The clauses are connected by the word *that.* Label the key parts:

(a) Charlene knew that Mike was right.

(b) The managers of both stores thought that they could solve their problems alone.

(c) Mary Ann and Bobby hoped that their baby would be on time.

A Note on the Exercises

Now you're ready for some exercise. For many students, finding run-ons in their writing is actually harder than rewriting them. So please take your time. We'll start with individual items, and then after you're warmed up, we'll move on to essays in which run-ons appear in the context of a piece of writing.

Exercise One

Directions: Label each sentence *OK* or *RO*. Mark the spot where one sentence runs on into the other. Then rewrite the run-ons, using sentence-combining techniques. Please use your own paper for the rewrites for this exercise and all the other exercises in this unit.

1. _____ Diamonds have a certain mystique about them this has been true for over 2700 years.

2. _____ The first diamonds were discovered along riverbeds in south central India, they were found about 800 B.C.

3. _____ South central India was the primary source of diamonds for about 2000 years, then South America became the major source, later South Africa did.

4. _____ Although South Africa is the location of the best diamond mines in the world, diamonds are also found in many other places, including other parts of Africa, Australia, the Soviet Union, and the United States.

5. _____ In the United States, there are 19 diamond mines, most are around the border between Colorado and Wyoming.

6. _____ According to Lloyd Jaffe, the president of the American Diamond Industry Association, most of the diamonds that are found in the United States are small stones that are used for industrial rather than decorative purposes.

7. _____ In view of the fact that diamonds are simply crystallized carbon, why are they so highly valued?

8. _____ The answer goes beyond the beauty of the gems, it also involves a carefully controlled world market.

9. _____ The market is controlled by DeBeers, a company that buys and sells about 80 percent of the uncut diamonds in the world.

10. _____ In one recent year DeBeers was holding $1.86 billion worth of diamonds in storage, that enormous inventory, of course, keeps diamonds relatively rare and expensive.

PART B

Directions: Label each sentence *OK* or *RO.* Mark the spot where one sentence runs on into the other. Then rewrite the run-ons, using sentence-combining techniques.

1. _____ How do you know a good diamond when you see one?

2. _____ Diamonds are judged on the basis of the three C's, the three C's are carats, cut, and clarity.

3. _____ The word *carat* comes from the Greek word *keration*, which means "carob seed," carob seeds were used to measure the weight of diamonds long ago in India.

4. _____ In the modern world of diamond dealing, a carat is a more standard measure it represents $1/142$ of an ounce.

5. _____ The largest diamond ever found was 3106 carats, that equals about 1.3 pounds.

6. _____ It was found at the Premier Mines in South Africa, and it was named the Great Star of India.

7. _____ The cut of a diamond is also very important in determining its value, much of its brilliance comes from its cut.

8. _____ A diamond is cut with special grinding wheels and saws, and diamond dust is used as an abrasive.

9. _____ A fully faceted stone has 58 facets, some smaller diamonds have only 19 facets.

10. _____ If a diamond is to receive the top grade for clarity, it must have no visible flaws when it is magnified ten times, then it can be labeled "flawless."

PART C

Directions: Label each sentence *OK* or *RO*. Mark the spot where one sentence runs on into the other. Then rewrite the run-ons, using sentence-combining techniques.

1. _____ Diamonds are big business, but they are also the stuff of legends.

2. _____ Marilyn Monroe contributed to the rich history of diamond lore, she said, "Diamonds are a girl's best friend."

3. _____ One of the earliest bits of lore goes back to the Roman Empire, it is attributed to Pliny.

4. _____ Pliny was a Roman poet who claimed that diamonds could ward off insanity.

5. _____ Pliny also made another claim for diamonds, he said that they could be used as an antidote to poison.

6. _____ King Louis XVI of France gave thousands of diamonds to a certain lady, a lady by the rather famous name of Marie Antoinette.

7. _____ The emperor Charlemagne was known to wear diamonds often.

8. _____ Diamond Jim Brady presented his lady friend Lillian Russell with a bicycle it was studded with diamonds.

9. _____ The first time a diamond was given to symbolize an engagement was when Archduke Maximilian of Austria gave one to Princess Mary of Burgundy.

10. _____ According to legend, diamond engagement rings are put on the third finger of the left hand because of an ancient Egyptian belief, the Egyptians thought that a "love vein" ran directly from that finger to the heart.

Exercise Two

PART A

Directions: Label each sentence *OK* or *RO.* Mark the spot where one sentence runs on into the other. Then rewrite the run-ons, using sentence-combining techniques.

1. _____ *Newsweek* recently announced, "Arctophiles have come out of the closet—and brought furry friends with them," the magazine was referring to the ever-growing teddy bear craze.

2. _____ People all over the world love teddy bears, Americans are no exception.

3. _____ In the 1970s Americans spent about $40 million a year on teddy bears, by the mid-1980s the annual sales figure rose to an even more amazing $125 million a year.

4. _____ That's an awful lot of money to spend on stuffed animals, there is also an enormous amount spent on items such as teddy bear pajamas and nighties, teddy bear towels, teddy bear stationery and notebooks, and teddy bear cups and saucers.

5. _____ Where did it all start, when did the teddy bear phenomenon begin?

6. _____ The name "teddy" undoubtedly refers to Theodore Roosevelt, who refused to shoot a black bear on a hunting trip in 1902 because of conditions that were less than sporting.

7. _____ Other members of the presidential hunting party had tied a 235-pound bear to a tree, they wanted to make Roosevelt's outing a success.

8. _____ Naturally, he refused to shoot an animal that was at such a disadvantage.

9. _____ This incident became famous after it was depicted in a cartoon

the editorial cartoonist was Clifford Berryman.

10. _____ The bear was later killed with a knife, but according to *News-*

week, that fact usually goes unreported.

PART B

Directions: Label each sentence *OK* or *RO.* Mark the spot where one sentence runs
on into the other. Then rewrite the run-ons, using sentence-combining techniques.

1. _____ Supposedly, Morris Michtom, a Russian immigrant who had

settled in New York, was very impressed with President Roosevelt's humanitarian-

ism, and Michtom asked his wife to sew up a few little bears to display in the

window of their candy shop in Brooklyn.

2. _____ Later, Morris Michtom wrote to Roosevelt, asking if he could

use the president's name.

3. _____ Roosevelt is supposed to have answered that his name proba-

bly wouldn't mean much in the toy business but that Michtom could certainly use

it if he wanted to.

4. _____ Michtom did use Teddy Roosevelt's name for his stuffed bears,

and he went on to start his own toy company, it was the Ideal Toy Corporation.

5. _____ While the Michtoms were stuffing their first teddy bears in the

United States, a woman in Germany was making stuffed animals as part of a

rehabilitation program, she was Margarete Steiff, she was a victim of polio.

6. _____ Steiff's nephew also tried his hand at making a stuffed bear

several samples were shown at a trade fair in 1903.

7. _____ A toy buyer from the United States saw them and purchased

3000, some were used as decorations at the wedding of Alice Roosevelt, the

daughter of Theodore Roosevelt.

8. _____ According to the story, a guest at the wedding asked what the

decorations were called, and someone answered, "Teddy's bears."

9. _____ This event gave the name to a fad that has captured the hearts

of millions, but apparently Teddy's own daughter was not among them.

10. _____ Many years later she was offered an antique bear in exchange

for posing for a photograph, she asked, "What does a 79-year-old doll want with

a 60-year-old teddy bear?"

Run-ons in Context

If you have been successful in catching on to run-ons when they are presented as
individual items, then it's time to move on and start looking for them in context. This
is an important skill that you have to transfer to your own writing. The next five
exercises should help.

Exercise Three

Directions: Write *RO* at each spot where one sentence runs on into another. Then
rewrite the run-ons on your own paper, using a variety of sentence-combining
techniques.

Are you a coffee drinker? If you are one of the millions of people around the world who 1

can't get going in the morning without a few sips of that aromatic elixir, here are some 2

facts that might interest you. 3

Did you know, for instance, that the English word *coffee* comes from the Italian 4

caffe? The Italians got their word from the Turks, the Turkish word for it is *kahve*. The 5

Turkish term comes from the Arabic, the Arabs call it *qahwah*. 6

Most people who drink coffee every day don't know where it comes from it is 7

actually the fruit of an evergreen tree. Coffee berries look quite a bit like cherries, but 8

it's the seeds that are roasted and used for making coffee. The part that looks like a 9

cherry is thrown away. 10

Before coffee was used in the liquid form that we know today, it was first prepared 11

as a food. In some parts of Africa, ripe coffee berries were crushed in stone mortars, 12 then the crushed berries were mixed with animal fat. Sounds tempting, doesn't it? 13

Finally, the crushed coffee and fat were formed into balls these balls were eaten on war 14

parties. One can speculate that the caffeine in the coffee-fat balls might have provided 15

that little extra stimulus to go out and do battle. 16

When coffee was first used as a drink, it was an alcoholic beverage. The Africans 17

made wine with the fermented juice of the coffee berry, they also added cold water. 18

The first use of the coffee seed to make a hot beverage goes back to the Arabs, who 19

first boiled coffee around 1000 A.D. 20

Exercise Four

Directions: **Write *RO* at each spot where one sentence runs on into another. Then rewrite the run-ons, using a variety of sentence-combining techniques.**

Saving up for your dream car? Well, before you buy it, in addition to thinking about 1

performance, gas mileage, color, and trade-in value, you might want to consider how 2

likely it is to be stolen right out from under you. Recently, the National Highway Traffic 3

Safety Administration released a list of the cars that are most likely to be stolen, it was 4

based on the Federal Bureau of Investigation's (FBI's) statistics on car theft. 5

In one recent year, for example, the most frequently stolen model was the Buick 6

Riviera, which has been described as a "top-of-the-line specialty sedan." The theft rate 7

for the Riviera was over 16 cars per 1000 vehicles. In other words, out of every 1000 8

Buick Rivieras that came off the assembly line, between 16 and 17 were ripped off by 9

car thieves. The Riviera's place at the top of the list is not hard to understand, according 10

to Lt. Richard McQuown, he is a member of the Kentucky State Police and a recent 11

president of the International Association of Auto Theft Investigators. He explains that 12

car thieves want what the general public wants, they go after models that they'll be able 13

to get rid of profitably, either as complete cars or stripped-down parts. Ranked just 14

behind the Buick Riviera were the Toyota Celica Supra, the Cadillac Eldorado, the 15

Chevrolet Corvette, the Pontiac Firebird, the Chevrolet Camaro, the Mazda RX-7, the 16

Porsche, the Oldsmobile Toronado, and the Pontiac Grand Prix, these formed the top 17

ten. 18

Fourteen of the top 20 were General Motors (GM) cars, prompting some to wonder 19
if GM cars are easier to steal. "No," replied a General Motors engineer and spokesper- 20
son, he quipped, "People like our cars." The Corvette has been so sought after by car 21
thieves that GM now offers a sophisticated antitheft alarm, this is offered as standard 22
equipment on the Corvette. 23

At the bottom of the list were the Mercury Grand Marquis, the Honda Civic and 24
Accord, the Chevrolet Cavalier, the Oldsmobile Firenza, the Pontiac Phoenix, and some 25
Volvo models. Several rare automobiles were also at the bottom of the list, three 26
versions of the Rolls Royce were included among them. These, of course, would not 27
be so easy for a thief to unload. 28

Almost one million cars and trucks are stolen annually in the United States. Accord- 29
ing to experts in the insurance industry, ten years ago about half of all stolen cars were 30
eventually recovered now only about 15 percent are ever returned to their owners. 31

Exercise Five

Directions: Write *RO* at each spot where one sentence runs on into another. Then
rewrite the run-ons, using a variety of sentence-combining techniques.

One of the hottest looks in fashion is over 130 years old, it's Levi's shrink-to-fit 501 1
jeans. They're the world's original blue jeans, the jeans that were created by Levi 2
Strauss as work clothes for miners, cowboys, and loggers. 3

Manufactured first in the rugged American West, Levi jeans have been around 4
since 1853, the 501 jeans that were resurrected in the 1980s haven't changed a bit. 5
Each pair has a button-fly front, that front was a feature of the first 501 jeans, too. Just 6
like the originals, each pair today has copper rivets and a watch pocket. The back 7

pockets are sewn with a double arc design, and the right-hand back pocket sports a red   8

tab. They are still made from 100 percent cotton denim, the cloth is always pure white,   9

then it is dyed. In fact, the dye that is used in making Levis is about the only thing that   10

has really changed. Now you see a lot more than indigo blue you see practically every   11

color in the rainbow, from true red to neon yellow.   12

Although they've been around for well over a century, 501 jeans were not often   13

found outside the West until the late 1930s. But during the Great Depression, many   14

of the Western ranches, in order to make ends meet, began trying to attract so-called   15

dudes from the East, these were folks who wanted a "real" taste of the Old West and   16

were willing to spend part of their vacations in bunk beds to get it. During their stay,   17

they often bought 501 jeans for ranch work, and later they took their jeans back home   18

with them. Consequently, the popularity of Levi jeans spread across the nation, from   19

the West to the East.   20

Exercise Six

Directions: Write *RO* at each spot where one sentence runs on into another. Then
rewrite the run-ons, using a variety of sentence-combining techniques.

Three psychologists at the University of Kansas were interested in the subject of   1

hypochondria, they were Suzanne C. Perkins, Timothy W. Smith, and C. R. Snyder. They   2

chose to study the phenomenon in women, so they assembled two groups. One group   3

was composed of women who, according to the psychologists, could be described as   4

hypochondriacs, they showed a heightened concern about the way their bodies func-   5

tioned, often made general complaints about their health, and were thought to over-   6

react to actual illness. The other group of women showed no signs of hypochondria.   7

The women in both groups were to take a test on interpreting the behavior of   8

others and acting in appropriate ways. But before they took the test, half of the women   9

in each group were told that their performance on the test would not be evaluated   10 individually. In other words, they were told that the only thing that mattered was the ₁₁ big picture, the profile of the group that would emerge. The women in the other half ₁₂ of each group were told that their individual performances *would* be judged, the test ₁₃ would determine each woman's "social IQ." ₁₄

Then the psychologists who conducted the testing subdivided the groups again, ₁₅ this time telling half of the women in each group that poor health would not affect their ₁₆ performance on the test and telling the other half that poor health would disrupt their ₁₇ performance. This may all seem a bit complicated, but the results of the study were ₁₈ clear. The hypochondriacs reported more symptoms of illness after they were told that ₁₉ their individual performances would be judged and that poor health would affect their ₂₀ performance on the test. The women who were not judged to be hypochondriacs did ₂₁ not follow any similar pattern, they did not report more illness when they thought their ₂₂ performances were being judged individually or when they thought that illness would ₂₃ excuse a poor outcome on the test. ₂₄

The psychologists concluded that hypochondria has a secret payoff, it protects a ₂₅ person's self-esteem. Perkins, Smith, and Snyder called hypochondria a form of "self- ₂₆ handicapping," a way of protecting oneself when threatened by evaluation. In other ₂₇ words, a hypochondriac says, "Of course, I could do better, but I'm sick." Hypochon- ₂₈ driacs put up a barrier between themselves and any true test of their abilities. This ₂₉ strategy can be a conscious process, it's probably more often unconscious self-decep- ₃₀ tion. Hypochondria may protect a person's ego, but at the same time, it has a very ₃₁ negative effect this effect is to keep a person from ever really knowing his or her true ₃₂ strengths. ₃₃

Exercise Seven

Directions: Write *RO* at each spot where one sentence runs on into another. Then rewrite the run-ons on your own paper, using a variety of rewrite techniques.

Just before midnight on April 14 and in the early hours of April 15, 1912, one of the most dramatic and certainly the most famous of all maritime disasters occurred. When the *Titanic* was finally located more than 13,000 feet below sea level 500 miles south of Newfoundland by a joint U.S.-French mission in 1985, some of the public's 73-year-old questions were answered, but others were not and probably never will be.

The majestic ocean liner was on its maiden voyage from Southampton, England, to New York City, it was the largest and the most luxurious ship afloat at the time. Before it made its first trip, the 46,000-ton White Star liner was already well known for its double-bottomed hull, which was divided into 16 supposedly watertight compartments. The *Titanic* was considered "unsinkable" four of the 16 compartments could be flooded without threatening the ship's buoyancy.

But minutes before midnight on April 14, while the *Titanic* was sailing at 22 knots, which was too fast for prevailing conditions, the ship collided with a gigantic iceberg. Floating about 95 miles south of the Great Banks of Newfoundland, the iceberg slammed into the left side of the ship, the force ruptured five of the 16 watertight compartments. The great *Titanic* sank at 2:20 A.M., April 15. There were slightly over 2200 persons aboard, the death toll has been estimated at 1503 to 1513.

Could the iceberg have been avoided? Could rescue attempts have been more successful? The iceberg was partly hidden in haze, and its dark side, rather than its white side, faced the ship, making it even harder to spot. The ship had two lookouts, and according to one who survived the disaster, no officer on the ship saw the iceberg until it was only about 500 yards away, a distance that the ship would travel in 37 seconds. The rescued lookout was asked if perhaps there had been enough time to maneuver around the iceberg, he answered, "Half a minute more would have been enough to avoid it."

One awful chapter in the story involves a radio operator he had fallen asleep on ²⁶ duty when the *Titanic*'s call for help came over the wireless. He was a radio operator ²⁷ on an ocean liner called the *Californian,* which happened to be less than 20 miles away ²⁸ all through the night that the *Titanic* sank. Help did arrive from the *Carpathia* about 20 ²⁹ minutes after the *Titanic* went down, it was 58 miles away when the distress call came ³⁰ in. But many of the 1513 victims who died in the icy waters probably could have been ³¹ saved if the *Californian* had responded promptly. ³²

As is often the case, a number of good things emerged from the tragedy. New rules ³³ required ships to employ enough radio operators to keep a 24-hour watch without ³⁴ exhausting any one individual. The first International Convention for Safety of Life at ³⁵ Sea, which was held in London after the accident, mandated that every seagoing vessel ³⁶ have lifeboat space for each person who embarks the *Titanic* was short 1046 spaces. ³⁷ Finally, in order to prevent the horrible confusion that prevailed that night, ocean liners ³⁸ were subsequently required to have lifeboat drills during every voyage. ³⁹

One interesting footnote is the fact that a radio operator who was stationed on top ⁴⁰ of the John Wanamaker department store in New York City gained a great deal of ⁴¹ favorable attention from the episode. During the time that the airwaves were cleared ⁴² by order of the government, this young operator spent long hours at his post, coordinat- ⁴³ ing the efforts of rescue ships and compiling a list of survivors. The operator was David ⁴⁴ Sarnoff, he was soon named commercial manager of American Marconi. Later he ⁴⁵ became president and chairman of the board of RCA, RCA owns the NBC television ⁴⁶ network. ⁴⁷

UNIT 5: A Sentence-Combining Approach to the Problem of Fragments

Another problem that can be solved by sentence combining is that of *fragments.* In the last unit, you learned that run-ons are not always long, and in this unit, you'll learn that fragments are not always short.

What is a fragment? As you might expect from the name, it is a *piece* or a *part* of something. A fragment is only part of a sentence, but it's "pretending" to be a whole sentence. In what way does it pretend to be a sentence? It does this in the sense that a fragment starts out with a capital letter and ends with a period.

Here's a formal definition: **A fragment is a group of words that is set up between a capital letter and a period even though it does not meet all three of the requirements of a sentence.** To be a sentence, a group of words must have three things:

1. a subject
2. a predicate
3. a sense of independence

In other words, a fragment might have one or two of these ingredients, but it doesn't have all three. If it did, it would be a sentence, not just part of one.

The problem of fragments is not one that all students have. In fact, many more students have a problem with run-ons. But when adult writers do have a hard time with fragments, their fragments usually take a number of different forms, and that fact, of course, makes working with fragments a bit of a challenge. We're going to take a look at the four types of fragments that appear most often in the work of college students.

Type 1: Dependent Clause Set Up as a Sentence

A type 1 fragment is the simplest type of fragment, and it should be especially easy to spot now that you've worked with complex sentences. This fragment has a subject and a predicate, but it does not have a sense of independence. It lacks that because a conjunction has been attached to it. When we say that it lacks a sense of independence, we mean that it can't stand on its own as a unit of communication. The conjunction makes the reader expect to be told more than the information in the dependent clause. Here are some examples of dependent clause fragments:

1. **Because** goldfish were supposed to bring love and harmony to an Egyptian household in ancient times.

2. **If** the color red really does scare witches away.

3. **Although** the word *bride* comes from an Old English word for "cook."

Items 1, 2, and 3 are perfectly good clauses, but they are not whole sentences, are they? That's why they cannot be set up between a capital letter and a period. Once you add a complex conjunction to the beginning of a clause, that clause has been "marked" for combination with another clause. Then you have two choices: You can combine the dependent clause with an independent one, which will give the sentence its sense of independence. Or you can remove the conjunction and leave it as a simple sentence. Take one of the fragments and solve it in the two ways just described:

Solution one: _____

_____

_____

Solution two: _____

_____

_____

If you know that dependent clause fragments show up frequently in your writing, write two solutions for the remaining two fragments on your own paper, please.

SPECIAL NOTE: Whenever you start a sentence with one of the 15 complex conjunctions, you can be sure that if the sentence has only one clause, you've got a fragment. But you do not always have a fragment if you start a simple sentence with one of the compound conjunctions. Sometimes those five—*and, but, or, so,* and *yet*—are used as transition words at the beginning of a simple sentence.

For instance, there's no fragment here: "I told him never to come here again. *And I meant it.*" *And I meant it* has been written as a separate sentence to give it strong emphasis, and that's fine. If the writer did not want the emphasis that comes from a new sentence, he or she could have written, "I told him never to come here again, *and I meant it.*" Either way, it's acceptable.

Type 2: Fragment Involving an *-Ing* Verb

A type 2 fragment may look less familiar, but it's not difficult to understand. This type also has a subject and a predicate and lacks a sense of independence. But this time there is no conjunction involved. Here the problem is an *-ing* verb used alone in a sentence of one clause. For example:

1. Peacock feathers **bringing** bad luck into a family's home.

2. The tradition of Easter eggs **having** its roots in early Germanic custom.

3. The pearl **being** an essential ingredient in many love potions.

Each of these three fragments has a subject and a predicate, but the *-ing* verb used alone robs each one of its sense of independence.

To solve this type of fragment, you can use three different approaches. One is to add a helping verb. For example:

1. (a)   Peacock feathers **were bringing** bad luck into a family's home.

We added the helping verb *were.*

Another method is to change the *-ing* verb to a different verb form. For example:

2. (a)   The tradition of Easter eggs **had** its roots in early Germanic custom.

We changed *having* to *had.*

A third solution calls for treating the *-ing* verb and the words after it as a phrase that describes the subject. Then you add an entirely new predicate to the sentence. For example:

3. (a)   The pearl, being an essential ingredient in many love potions, **was highly valued by superstitious romantics.**

We added the predicate *was highly valued by superstitious romantics.*

Solve the problem of the following *-ing* fragment, using each of the three solutions we've outlined above:

Carole Potter collecting facts about folklore and superstitions.

Solution one: _____

_____

Solution two: _____

_____

Solution three: _____

_____

A NOTE ABOUT *BEING:* The word *being* is often the culprit in this type of fragment. If you have a fragment with *being* in it, you need to know that *being* is a form of the verb *to be.* So *being* should be changed to another form of the verb *to be*—a word such as *is, am, are, were,* or *will be.*

Type 3: Fragment Related to Embedding

Another type of fragment comes from a slipup in the embedding process. Here are three examples:

1. The superstition **that** amethysts prevented drunkenness. Was widely believed by people in ancient times.

2. A person **who** spills pepper. Is probably going to get into an argument with a good friend.

3. Tattoos, **which** some sailors considered protection against drowning. At one time were also thought to prevent smallpox.

After all the work you've done with embedding, these fragments should be crystal clear. Each numbered item really contains two fragments, doesn't it? Each contains a subject that is set up as a full sentence and a predicate that is set up as a full sentence. To correct them, all you have to do is change capitalization and punctuation. You can correct fragments 1 through 3 by making those changes in the copy above; you don't have to write out your solutions.

Another kind of fragment is a variation of this type. It begins with an embedding word, and it describes the complement (or last noun or pronoun) of the sentence before it. For example:

The pepper was spilled by Pat. **Who any minute might find himself in an argument with his best friend John.**

To solve it, all you do is change the period to a comma and make the capital *W* on *Who* a lowercase letter.

Questions

Another way to avoid fragments that involve embedding words is simply to keep this rule in mind: *The only sentences that can begin with embedding words are questions.* These, for example, are perfectly fine. They're not fragments:

Who wrote *Jitterbug Perfume?*

Whose size 13 shoes are these?

Which pasta recipe works best?

Type 4: Cutoff Modifier

The last type of fragment involves a modifying phrase that is cut off from the sentence it describes. Here are some examples:

1. **Used to cure headaches and insomnia.** Opium was extracted from poppies in Persia and Asia Minor for centuries before it was discovered in other parts of the world.

2. **Hoping to keep a friendship from breaking up.** Some people whisper "bread and butter" whenever anything, such as another person, a tree, or a child on a bike, momentarily separates two friends out for a stroll.

3. The ancient Greeks valued thyme highly. **Believing that the herb's fragrance restored one's energy.**

Again, you can see how easily these would be solved. Once more, it is just a matter of making changes in capitalization and punctuation. Please make those changes in the examples above. These fragments could also be solved in a variety of other ways. Choose any fragment and solve it in some way other than changing capitalization and punctuation:

Solution: _____

_____

_____

Now you should be ready to do some exercises. If you want to read more about any of the folklore, customs, or superstitions referred to above, check out Carole Potter's fascinating *Knock on Wood: An Encyclopedia of Talismans, Charms, Superstitions & Symbols.*

Exercise One

Directions: Label each item *OK* or *F*. Then rewrite the fragments, using a variety of sentence-combining techniques. Please do the rewrites for all the exercises in this unit on your own paper.

Also, if fragments are difficult for you, label each fragment you find:

type 1—dependent clause set up as a sentence
type 2—fragment involving an -ing verb
type 3—fragment related to embedding
type 4—cutoff modifier

You can use the space in the left margin to identify the fragment type.

1. _____ *The Statistical Abstract,* which is produced annually by the U.S.

Commerce Department. Fills almost 1000 pages.

2. _____ In one recent year *The Statistical Abstract* offered a number of

interesting tidbits of information about the 50 states in the union.

3. _____ Massachusetts, for example, being the state with the highest

number of doctors per 100,000 people.

4. _____ The fact that New York has more lawyers per person than any

other state.

5. _____ The state with the highest percentage of people over the age

of 65 is, not surprisingly, Florida.

6. _____ Florida also having the most crimes per 100,000 persons.

7. _____ Because New Jersey has the most people per square mile.

8. _____ The state that has the highest percentage of high school gradu-

ates is Alaska.

9. _____ Alaska can also boast of the highest average per capita income.

10. _____ Louisiana has the highest expenditure of energy per capita.

According to *The Statistical Abstract.*

Exercise Two

PART A

Directions: Label each item *OK* or *F.* Then rewrite the fragments, using a variety of techniques. Here's more material about superstition and folklore; much of the research is from an interesting, fun book by Alvin Schwartz and Glen Rounds.

1. _____ *Cross Your Fingers, Spit in Your Hat,* which is a book about superstitions and folklore.

2. _____ The most interesting superstitions being the ones about love and marriage.

3. _____ Here is a sampling of a few especially quirky ones.

4. _____ If you pull a hair from the head of someone you love, he or she will love you back and love you deeply.

5. _____ The object of your desire will also love you if you give him or her a bowl of soup. Which is flavored with three drops of your blood.

6. _____ A glass of lemonade with a few of your clipped toenails having the same effect.

7. _____ Some people are curious about whether or not they will ever marry.

8. _____ According to one superstition, you certainly will not marry. If you kiss someone with a mustache and end up with a hair in your mouth.

9. _____ You might eat the point of a piece of pie before you eat the rest. Suggesting to the superstitious that you are destined for the single life.

10. _____ The belief that you will marry if you dream of taking a bath or if the lines in the palm of your hand form the letter *M.*

PART B

Directions: **Label each item *OK* or *F.* Then rewrite each fragment on your own paper, using a variety of techniques.**

1. _____ If a woman who wishes to marry wants to see what her future husband will look like. She should sleep with a mirror under her pillow.

2. _____ The woman may get the same result by counting nine stars each night for nine nights in a row.

3. _____ The woman who wears her nightgown inside out. May also see her future spouse in her dreams.

4. _____ Another woman might be more interested in his name than in his face.

5. _____ She might soak a shoelace in water and toss it at the ceiling. Believing that it will leave a mark resembling his initial.

6. _____ She might also run around the block three times with her mouth full of water, and the first person that she sees when she stops will have the same name as her future husband.

7. _____ The idea that a person can succeed with any marital prospect if he or she is willing to eat 100 chicken gizzards in one sitting.

8. _____ An easier route might be to eat the raw heart of a chicken, but according to the superstition, it must be swallowed whole.

9. _____ If all this is successful and a wedding takes place, superstition holds that a bride should wear a veil to protect herself from any jealous person. Who might try to give her the evil eye.

10. _____ A wedding must also include a maid of honor, a best man, and other attendants who are dressed in formal attire. Because they help to prevent the evil spirits from figuring out who the bride and groom are.

Exercise Three

PART A

Directions: **Label each item** *OK* **or** *F*. **Then rewrite each fragment, using a variety of techniques.**

1. _____ Alan Beck is the director of the Center for Interaction of Animals and Society.

2. _____ It is located at the University of Pennsylvania's School of Veterinary Medicine.

3. _____ Dr. Beck recently pointing out some good news and some bad news about pets.

4. _____ The good news being the animals' effect on people who are sick or anxious.

5. _____ Because studies have shown some amazing things.

6. _____ For example, there is a better survival rate for heart attack victims if they happen to be pet owners.

7. _____ In one experiment, blood pressure and signs of stress were reduced in children. When a dog was present in the laboratory.

8. _____ Simply by watching fish in an aquarium, people can reduce their level of tension.

9. _____ Parents who allow their children to have pets. Have always known that the children can become more loving and responsible as a result.

10. _____ Children, especially city kids, often develop a much greater love of nature once they become acquainted with a bunny, a dog, a cat, or a newt.

PART B

Directions: Label each item *OK* or *F.* Then rewrite each fragment, using a variety of techniques.

1. _____ But the pet picture is not completely rosy.

2. _____ For one thing, pets often cause a number of health problems. Especially in urban areas.

3. _____ Dog feces, which are one of the most common transmitters of disease, are also the most common breeding ground for flies. Which are notorious disease carriers.

4. _____ The fact that one fecal deposit from a dog produces an average of 144 houseflies.

5. _____ Although "pooper scooper" laws may seem amusing. It is obvious that they are important, and studies have shown that they really do help to reduce disease.

6. _____ Pets can also be problematic in other ways. According to animal psychologists.

7. _____ Yes, there really are at least a dozen or so highly trained pet psychologists in the United States.

8. _____ Pet psychologists claim that most mental problems in animals are a result of their environment and their owners' ignorance rather than anything inborn.

9. _____ Dogs and cats, for instance, are often cooped up all alone in a house or apartment for eight hours or more a day.

10. _____ When a pet's owner gets home at five or six in the afternoon after a hard day's work. The pet's natural exuberance and its understandable need for attention are sometimes seen as just one more demand on a person who already feels exhausted.

Fragments in Context

Now you will be going on to work with fragments in context, which naturally will be more difficult but which will also be a good bridge between success in the workbook exercises and improvement in your own writing.

Exercise Four

Directions: Underline and correct each fragment, using a variety of sentence-combining techniques. More on this topic can be found in *The Encyclopedia of Sports* by Frank G. Menke. (Please continue to use your own paper for rewrites.)

In almost every American family, there is at least one person. Who pulls out the sports ₁ section of the newspaper as soon as it's delivered every day. But there hasn't always ₂ been a sports section to pull out. In fact, it wasn't long ago that a sports promoter had ₃ to take out a classified ad. If advance notice of a sports event was desired. According ₄ to *The Encyclopedia of Sports* by Frank G. Menke, for many years a person who wanted ₅ to sell tickets to a sporting event was in the same category as a person who wanted ₆ to sell rat traps or hair tonic. ₇

But in 1819 the *American Farmer* was founded. The *American Farmer* being the ₈ first sporting journal. Sponsored by John Stuart Skinner, the postmaster of Baltimore, ₉ Maryland, the *American Farmer* sold advertising space, printed stories about sporting ₁₀ events, and had very little to do with farming, in spite of its name. The *American Farmer* ₁₁ gave rise to the *American Turf Register* and several other imitators and successors, ₁₂ including *The Spirit of the Times* and *Police Gazette*, but sports events were rarely ₁₃ mentioned in general interest newspapers until quite a while after the Civil War. For ₁₄ a long time, newspaper people held that sports was a business. Insisting that it deserved ₁₅ free advertising no more than any other business. ₁₆

Eventually, however, editors and publishers realized that they were missing an ₁₇ opportunity for increased circulation by not printing sports stories. So where did the ₁₈ first sports stories come from? Boxing stories were usually supplied by fight referees. ₁₉ Baseball stories coming from retired players. Racing stories often came from anyone. ₂₀ Who hung around the track and was able to write a simple sentence. These refs, ₂₁ retirees, and race fans became the nation's first sports editors when the papers eventu- ₂₂ ally expanded their coverage. Which many did when the first World Series baseball ₂₃ games were played in 1905. That, according to sports historians, marked the beginning ₂₄ of consistent coverage of sports as news. ₂₅

Exercise Five

PART A

Directions: Underline and correct each fragment, using a variety of sentence-combining techniques.

As Americans, we take justifiable pride in our love of freedom and our concern for ^{1} individual rights. But it's important to take note of our lapses, too. One shocking lapse ^{2} involved the only people who were really native to this country—the American Indians. ^{3}

According to dance historians Reginald and Gladys Laubin in *The Dance Encyclo-* ^{4} *pedia,* for the Indians of North America, life was dancing, and dancing was life. In Indian ^{5} culture, men, women, and children were actually performing a dramatization or panto- ^{6} mime of the actions of the spirits. When they danced. Dance involved every aspect of ^{7} life. Ranging from the social to the religious to the political. Indians danced for peace, ^{8} for war, for joy, for sorrow, and for a celebration of all the stages in the life cycle. The ^{9} fact that in some Indian languages the word for "dance" and the word for "ceremony" ^{10} are the same. ^{11}

But to many and perhaps most white Americans, Indians danced only one dance. ^{12} That being the war dance. Indian dance was, therefore, viewed as threatening. In spite ^{13} of Americans' guaranteed constitutional freedoms, Indian dancing was actually prohib- ^{14} ited for years. The ban was finally lifted in 1934. ^{15}

Characterized by a bent-knee stance, a straight back, little arm movement, and ^{16} quite a lot of head movement. Native American Indian dances involve very complex ^{17} patterns that are often hard to see by those with an untrained eye. Subtle shifts of ^{18} weight are another hallmark of Indian dance. With its movements governed by percus- ^{19} sion instruments, authentic Indian dancing is very vigorous. It is often said that the ^{20} movements seem to increase rather than decrease the dancers' power.

PART B

Directions: Underline and correct each fragment, using a variety of sentence-combining techniques.

Some experts in the history of dance claim that there is an Indian step to correlate with 1 every step of every other known form of dance. Those who worry that this original 2 American art form could pass into oblivion. Point out that the Sioux, for example, once 3 danced 35 different dances. Now they dance only part of one. The reason for this being 4 not only the ban but also such factors as the disappearance of the buffalo and, of 5 course, the changing life-style of the modern American Indian. 6

   Indian dance, however, has enjoyed a rather strong revival. An interesting footnote 7 concerns a revival among the Crows of Montana. Over 40 years ago they experienced 8 a renewed interest in the sun dance. Although they had lost their own version of it. 9 Because it had not been danced since 1874. The Crows, therefore, went to the Sho- 10 shones of Wyoming to learn their sun dance. Which is simpler than the Crow sun dance 11 but also beautiful and powerful. The Crows of Montana first danced the sun dance in 12 August 1941. Repeating it the following summer as a prayer for victory in World War 13 II. Each year that the war continued, the Crows repeated this ritual, and the year after 14 the war ended, the Crows danced the sun dance again in thanksgiving and celebration. 15 The Crows attribute to the sun dance the fact that not a single Crow was killed in 16 combat in World War II. Although Crows were involved in some of the bloodiest battles 17 on all fronts. 18

Exercise Six

Directions: Underline and correct each fragment, using a variety of sentence-combining techniques.

Can you imagine spending $250 million for boxer shorts, key rings, beer mugs, and 1 backpacks that display your school's colors or insignia? That's what college students 2 do—every year. There's said to be a rebirth of the old school spirit in America. A rebirth 3 of school spirit, of course, means big bucks. College stores in the United States repre-   4

sent a $4.5 billion market. There are about 100 college or university stores. That   5

altogether boast of annual sales of over $3 million. The largest such enterprise is the   6

Harvard Coop in Cambridge, Massachusetts. Reporting $47 million in sales in one   7

recent year.   8

This phenomenon was discussed by G. F. Distelhorst. Who recently served as   9

director of the National Association of College Stores and who spoke at the group's   10

annual trade fair in San Antonio, Texas. Although students are buying more college   11

paraphernalia, sales to nonstudents are growing also. Because colleges and universities   12

get so much more national exposure than ever before through televised sports events.   13

In addition, alums are shelling out more money in order to advertise their alma mater.   14

The fact that many college stores have published four-color alumni catalogs in the past   15

few years. Is partially responsible for this increase. Simple nostalgia certainly plays a   16

part, too.   17

The traditional college T-shirts and sweatshirts still being the hottest-selling items.   18

But college stores also report that there is an increased demand for so-called upscale   19

products. Reflecting the baby boom and the emergence of the well-heeled Yuppies.   20

Included among upscale souvenirs are such items as insulated wine bottle jackets, baby   21

car seats, and pillow cases. All these items invariably displaying a college or university's   22

logo.   23

So while the students are yelling, "Rah, rah!" The manufacturers of school spirit are,   24

too.   25

Exercise Seven

PART A

Directions: Underline and correct each fragment, using a variety of sentence-combining techniques.

According to *Newsweek* magazine, "if the 1980s have taught us anything, it is how to make a virtue out of vanity." The subject was the surprising increase in the number of Americans who have plastic surgery every year. People who have dieted, lifted weights, bicycled, run, stayed at the spas, and who are still not satisfied with the results. Apparently, they don't think that their hard, smooth bodies deserve to be topped off by soft, crinkly faces.

The American Society of Plastic and Reconstructive Surgeons (ASPRS) announced in a recent report that the number of operations in the field rose 61 percent between 1981 and 1984. Indicating that plastic surgery is one of the fastest-growing medical specialties in the United States. In one recent year plastic surgeons performed over 1.3 million reconstructive procedures. These procedures including the rebuilding of breasts after a mastectomy and the treatment of burn victims. But plastic surgeons also performed close to 500,000 optional or "aesthetic" procedures. These numbers are conservative estimates. Because there are many plastic surgeries that are performed by specialists in other fields, such as dermatology. There are also quite a few that are performed by physicians who are not certified in plastic surgery, so they are not included in the ASPRS's numbers, either.

What are these optional operations that seem so necessary to those who are willing to go under the knife to beat the clock? Surprisingly, the most frequently performed aesthetic plastic surgery is breast augmentation. Almost 100,000 such surgeries were performed in one recent year. The second most popular procedure is blepharoplasty. Which usually means an eye tuck. Following close behind is rhinoplasty, which is the technical term for a nose job. Suction lipectomy, which is fat removal, and that old classic, the face-lift, are also each performed over 50,000 times a year.

PART B

Directions: Underline and correct each fragment, using a variety of sentence-combining techniques.

What's behind the boom in plastic surgery? Actually, several factors can be cited. The

most obvious being a new federal ruling. The government decided in 1979 that doctors

could advertise for patients. This change benefited plastic surgery far more than any

other branch of medicine. Bringing in patients who previously wouldn't have given

more than a passing thought to having their face lifted or their tummy tucked.

Another factor is the trend toward social acceptance of the male's concern with

his appearance. Which, of course, is also reflected in the physical fitness craze and in

the successful marketing of cosmetics and jewelry for men. About ten years ago men

accounted for approximately five percent of plastic surgery patients. Now they consti-

tute about 20 percent.

Men not only want to look better; they also want to look younger. The increase in

the number of male plastic surgery patients is also tied up with the coming of age of

the baby boomers. There are simply way more young people in the work force now.

The age of the average doctor, lawyer, businessperson, teacher, or computer specialist

is simply quite a bit younger than it used to be. There seems to be a natural, although

not very noble, human tendency to want to move toward the norm, and the norm is now

more a matter of the twenties and thirties than the forties and fifties.

This concern with youth is certainly part of the picture. Although it is not by any

means the whole story. One of the most interesting reasons for the increase in the

number of plastic surgeries is the decline in occupations that have nothing at all to do

with one's appearance. Farming is one good example. Wheat and corn rarely grow

faster. Because a farmer is handsome or confident looking. But unfortunately, nowa-

days fewer and fewer people can make a good living at farming. More and more new

occupations require a certain kind of look. A look that says, "I know what I'm doing."

Management consulting, advertising, and public relations all being good examples.

What used to be undisguised vanity is now viewed by some as a business investment. 26

Women have always constituted the biggest market for plastic surgery, but now 27
some have new reasons for wanting to change their appearance. Traditionally, most 28
women who wanted to alter their looks. Were interested in emulating a classically 29
beautiful movie star or television celebrity. But this is not so true any longer. Many 30
women who visit plastic surgeons now want to achieve a more authoritative look. As 31
one plastic surgeon says, "The executive woman is in. The Debbie Reynolds look with 32
the cute turned-up nose is out the window." At least one plastic surgeon in New York 33
has begun altering noses. Transforming the sweet and cute into the handsome and 34
assertive. 35

One has to wonder, what next? 36

Chapter 3
Punctuating Sentence Combinations

A chapter on punctuation can be very valuable to you as a writer if you take an *active* approach to the subject. What's an active approach? Well, first let's say what it's not. It's not working through the material on semicolons, for example, and thinking, "Okay, if I ever happen to write this kind of a sentence, I'll put a semicolon in it." That's a *passive* approach. And that approach won't make much of a difference in your writing because you might never "just happen" to write a sentence that needs a semicolon.

On the other hand, you can take an active approach to the rules and conventions you'll be learning in Chapter 3. With that attitude, you'll work through the exercises on the semicolon knowing that they're going to provide you with another valuable sentence-combining tool. If you take an active approach to punctuation, you'll go out of your way every now and then to make sentences that call for semicolons.

Each punctuation mark you'll learn in the following units will give you more variety and flexibility in the sentence structures you'll be able to use. But in order to make these gains, you'll have to practice each new technique in your own writing. It won't be enough to complete the workbook exercises and leave it at that. In other words, when you learn what you can do with commas, semicolons, and colons, you are empowered to make new kinds of sentence structures that you haven't made before. But if you don't make a conscious attempt to create the new structures in your paragraphs, stories, and essays, it probably won't be very long before you've lost what you worked so hard to get. It's like they say—use it or lose it.

One more thing: *Try to start fresh.* What do we mean? If you are completely clear about a certain punctuation rule that you learned before working with *Easy Writer II*, that's fine. But if you're confused about what you've learned previously, then you'll do a lot better if you clear your mind and start over. Just forget all the "half-truths" and all the "never do this" and "always do that" punctuation rules that are left over from earlier experiences. Use only the rules you learn here. When you hand in a paper to your writing teacher, be prepared to explain any comma, semicolon, or colon you use in terms of the techniques and rules described in this chapter.

In other words, use a punctuation mark only if you can say why you're using it. Whatever you do, don't continue to let "pauses" be your guide; that favorite technique of so many students works correctly less than half the time. If all a literate person needed to know about punctuation was that you put in a comma wherever you wanted a little pause, we wouldn't have had to write this chapter.

UNIT 1: Using Commas in Compound and Complex Sentences (A Review)

As you already know, one use of the comma is to punctuate compound and complex sentences. In the last chapter, you worked with compound and complex sentences, but there we were primarily interested in the structure of those sentence forms. Here our emphasis is on the punctuation of compound and complex sentences.

Compound Sentences

Here again are the five most important **compound conjunctions:**

and	so
but	yet
or	

The basic rule is this: *In a compound sentence, you insert a comma before the conjunction that joins two clauses.* Your writing teacher might tell you that sometimes it's okay to leave the comma out if the clauses in a compound sentence are short and if there's no chance of confusion. That's true. But for the purpose of simplicity and for reinforcement of your knowledge of the basic rule, *we want you to insert a comma in all compound sentences* in this chapter. This is also the simplest rule to remember and use in your own writing.

Also remember that you don't put a comma before every *and* or *but* you see in a sentence. Make sure there's actually a clause both before and after the compound conjunction.

Should you insert a comma in this remark by Harry Truman? Is there a clause both before and after the word *and*?

"This administration is going to be cussed and discussed for years to come."

Complex Sentences

By now you know that these are the 15 most important **complex conjunctions:**

after	if	when
although	since	whenever
as	though	where
because	unless	wherever
before	until	while

Remember that a complex conjunction can join clauses in two different ways: the conjunction can be placed before the first clause or before the second clause. When the conjunction is placed before the first clause, you use a comma between the clauses. When the conjunction is placed before the second clause, you normally don't use a comma between the clauses. Another way to say this is:

Dependent clause first → comma between clauses

Independent clause first → no comma

Here's a review exercise on recognizing and punctuating compound and complex sentences.

Exercise One

Directions: Some of these sentences are compound, and others are complex. Please do the following: (1) Label each sentence *compound* or *complex.* (2) Circle the conjunction that joins the two clauses in each sentence. (3) Insert a comma if it is needed because a sentence is compound or because a sentence is complex with the dependent clause first. (Label subjects, verbs, verb phrases, and complements if you need to in order to see the two clauses in each sentence.)

1. _____ When it introduced box lunches on a flight to Paris in 1919

   Handley Page Transport of England became the first airline to serve meals in flight.

2. _____ Imperial Airways became the first airline to show an in-flight

   movie when it ran Arthur Conan Doyle's *The Lost World* in 1925.

3. _____ Most beer drinkers now buy their beer in cans but for 35 years

   bottled beer outsold canned beer.

4. _____ England's Queen Victoria dressed primarily in black for the

   remaining 39 years of her life after she lost her beloved husband Albert.

5. _____ Since Kahlil Gibran, the author of *The Prophet* and many other

   works, died in 1931 at the age of 48 the royalties from all posthumous sales have

   gone to the people of his impoverished native village of Bsharri in Lebanon.

6. _____ Emily Dickinson, a brilliant poet, spent most of her adult life in

   her second-story bedroom and only seven of her poems saw publication during her

   lifetime.

7. _____ Buster Keaton's *The General* is now considered the first com-

   edy epic and one of the great classic movies of all time but it received almost

   entirely negative reviews during Keaton's lifetime.

8. _____ Because novelist Willa Cather was angry about Hollywood's

treatment of *A Lost Lady* she stipulated in her will that no work of hers could ever

be adapted for stage, screen, radio, or television.

9. _____ The young Fidel Castro once allegedly threatened to burn

down his parents' house if they didn't send him to school. (They did, and he didn't.)

10. _____ The Reverend Charles Lutwidge Dodgson, a lecturer in mathe-

matics at Oxford, took the pen name Lewis Carroll after he wrote *Alice's Adven-*

tures in Wonderland.

Compound/Complex Sentences

Before we move on to other punctuation rules, we want to point out that some sentences are both compound and complex. They're called, not surprisingly, *compound/*
complex sentences. You'll see that in such a sentence a writer uses a compound
conjunction and a complex conjunction. Circle the conjunctions in these examples and
punctuate the sentences:

(a)   Octopuses occasionally eat other octopuses and if they are old or sick they
      sometimes nibble on their own arms.

(b)   Because Jesus Christ died on the cross many Christians assume that the symbol
      originated with Christ's death but actually the cross had been used as a reli-
      gious emblem for centuries before the crucifixion.

(c)   This was the favorite saying of the great American actor Spencer Tracy: "You
      only live once and if you work it right once is enough."

UNIT 2: Using Commas in Embedded Sentences

Like the unit you have just completed, this unit is partly a review of what you already
know from your work in Chapter 2, but it also introduces a new idea.

Earlier we were interested primarily in how to make embedded sentences. Now
we want to look at how to punctuate them.

Example (a) is typical of the kind of embedded sentence you've already been
dealing with. Punctuate it, please:

(a)   **Pierre-Auguste Renoir who was born in 1841 never wanted to be known as a**
      painter of modern life.

If you set off *who was born in 1841* with two commas, you're correct. This is the classic
embedded sentence. In sentences like example (a) you have a clear subject—*Pierre-*
Auguste Renoir—that is easily understood by the reader without the embedded information. In other words, *who was born in 1841* is just extra information. It's interesting
perhaps, but you don't need it in order to know what the subject of the sentence is; it's

clear that the subject is *Pierre-Auguste Renoir.* When you have embedded information that is extra, meaning that you don't need it in order to identify the subject of the sentence, then you always set off that extra embedded information with two commas.

But there's another kind of sentence in which the embedded information *is* necessary to identify the subject. Look at this example and draw a wavy line under the embedded clause:

(b) **All men who are irrationally and excessively submissive to their wives can be described as uxorious.**

If you want to figure out if the embedded information is merely extra and not needed to identify the subject of the sentence, just omit it for a moment. Then you'll have: *All men can be described as uxorious.* That's not true, is it? If this rather odd and interesting word *uxorious* means "irrationally and excessively submissive to one's wife," then certainly you can't describe "all men" as uxorious.

In other words, the subject in (b) is not simply *All men.* The subject is really *All men who are irrationally and excessively submissive to their wives.* It's a particular kind of man the writer is talking about. The embedded words are not just a little extra information that is added as an interesting aside after the subject. The embedded clause is so important that it can be considered part of the subject itself. Because of that, it should not be set off with two commas.

Here's another way to say this:

If the subject of the main clause is clear and easy to identify without the embedded information, surround the embedded clause with two commas.

If the embedded information is needed to make sense of the subject of the main clause, don't use any commas.

Try to study this concept as much as you can in the next few days. This isn't an easy pair of rules; it often takes a while for the rules to become clear.

Let's look at a few more examples before you do the exercises. Make a decision about each sentence below. Two commas or none? Take your time.

(c) **My parents who are worried about everything going just right should start planning their trip abroad as early as possible.**

(d) **Travelers who are worried about everything going just right should start planning their trip abroad as early as possible.**

(e) **My very best friend who loves to find old dishes at bargain prices would really go for this store.**

(f) **Anyone who loves to find old dishes at bargain prices would really go for this store.**

[*Answers.* Examples (c) and (e) each require two commas. Examples (d) and (f) should have no commas. It's important to realize that in (c) and (e) you're not using the embedded information to identify the subject of the main clause. In other words, it's not as if you have two or more sets of parents and you want to be sure that the reader knows you're referring to the particular set of parents who are going on a trip soon. The same goes for (e): No matter what he or she loves to find at bargain prices, you have only one very best friend. The subjects *My parents* and *My very best friend* are clear and specific without the embedded information that follows them.]

An Important Reminder

Remember, when you drop out the embedded information, you are trying to see whether it is needed or not needed in order to make sense out of the *SUBJECT*. You are not trying to see how important the embedded clause is in relationship to the overall meaning of the sentence. Keep your eyes on the *subject* of the main clause!

Here's the formula, one more time:

Extra embedded information → two commas
Necessary embedded information → no commas

Now you should be ready to try the exercises.

Exercise One

Directions: Draw a wavy line below the embedded clause in each sentence and write *S* over the subject of the main clause. Then make your decision to insert *two commas* or *none*.

1. St. Nicholas who was a fourth-century bishop in Asia Minor is the patron saint of children and sailors.

2. The dog who guarded the gates of Hades in ancient mythology was the three-headed Cerberus.

3. William Cummings who went by the nickname "Candy" is given credit for inventing baseball's curve ball in 1864.

4. The person who wrote the Oz books probably remains unknown even to many of the biggest fans of his work. (The Oz series was written by L. Frank Baum.)

5. The average child who is between two and three years of age does not really know how to play with other children.

6. The two eighteenth-century English artists who were responsible for editorial cartoons becoming an important part of newspapers were William Hogarth and Thomas Rowlandson.

7. Babe Ruth who accurately predicted the exact spot where he'd hit one out of the park in the 1932 World Series had been up against Cubs pitcher Charles Root.

8. Queen Elizabeth II who withdrew her racehorse Above Suspicion from England's Champion Stakes in 1959 was fined $140.

9. At present most people who suffer from acquired immune deficiency syndrome are homosexuals or bisexuals, intravenous drug users, or hemophiliacs.

10. Benjamin Harrison who was the president of the United States was the grandson of another president. The man who was Benjamin Harrison's grandfather was William Henry Harrison.

The Difference between *Which* and *That*

When a sentence contains an embedded clause beginning with *which*, it usually calls for two commas because *which* is normally used with extra information that is not needed to make the subject clear and specific.

When an embedded clause begins with *that*, the information in the clause is usually needed to understand the subject, so no commas are used. Please study these examples:

(a) Neverland, **which is often mistakenly called "Never-Never Land,"** is the place where the children in *Peter Pan* met mermaids, pirates, and Indians.

(b) The lines **that connect points of equal barometric pressure on a map** are isobars.

The Embedding Word *Whose*

The embedding word *whose* works the same way as *who*; in other words, *whose* is sometimes used with two commas and sometimes with none. It all depends upon whether or not the embedded clause is needed to make sense of the subject of the main clause.

In the first exercise, you worked with only the embedding word *who*. Now you'll begin to analyze sentences that have been made with *who, whose, which,* and *that*.

Exercise Two

Directions: Draw a wavy line below the embedded clause in each sentence and write *S* over the subject of the main clause. Then make your decision to insert *two commas* or *none*. This time you'll see a variety of different embedding words. (Remember to think about how important the embedded information is in relation to the *subject*—not in relation to the whole sentence.)

1. A person who was born under the sign of Taurus is supposedly stubborn and independent.

2. The person who founded Vassar College was a brewer. (It was Matthew Vassar.)

3. The U.S. Senate which has been called "the most exclusive club in the world" is never open to more than 100 members.

4. The grape that makes California's most successful white wine is the Chardonnay.

5. The abbreviation *lb.* which means pound comes from the Latin word *libra,* meaning "scales."

6. The Shakespearean character who "lards the lean earth as he walks along" is Falstaff.

7. Calamity Jane whose real name was Martha Jane Canary supposedly had 12 husbands and was buried next to Wild Bill Hickok in Deadwood, South Dakota.

8. The fruit whose name comes from the Nahuatl word for testicle is the avocado.

9. The second-oldest child in a family who usually does not receive quite as much discipline as the oldest often tends to be more daring and mischievous.

10. Leo Rosten once made this statement about W. C. Fields: "Any man who hates dogs and babies can't be all bad."

Please correct Exercise Two and discuss any problems with your writing teacher before continuing.

Exercise Three

Directions: Draw a wavy line beneath the embedded clause in each sentence and write *S* over the subject of the main clause. Then make your decision to insert *two commas* or *none.*

1. The *Enola Gay* which dropped the first atomic bomb on Hiroshima in 1945 was named after the mother of the B-29's commander, Col. Paul Tibbets, Jr.

2. The person who invented contract bridge while on a Caribbean cruise in 1925 was Harold S. Vanderbilt.

3. According to a recent survey, the thing that Americans fear more than anything else is speaking before a large group.

4. Abigail Adams whose request that women's rights be included in the Constitution was ignored is often considered the first prominent advocate of women's rights in the United States.

5. Manx cats which are unique for having almost no tail originally came from the Isle of Man.

6. The one singer who has performed with perhaps every major jazz musician is Ella Fitzgerald.

7. The oldest university that was established in the New World is the Universidad de San Marcos in Lima, Peru. (It was established in 1551.)

8. In a recent study the main regret that was reported by a number of very well paid businessmen and businesswomen was a lack of time to spend with their children.

9. Wyatt Earp whose brothers Morgan and Virgil accompanied him fought the Clanton and McLaury brothers in the famous shoot-out at the O.K. Corral in Tombstone, Arizona, in 1881. (Doc Holliday also fought with the Earps.)

10. A person who has superior knowledge or taste can be called a cognoscente.

Please correct and discuss Exercise Three before continuing.

Exercise Four

Directions: Here are ten pairs of sentences about figures in the history of popular music. Take each pair and embed the (b) sentence into the (a) sentence. (You learned to do this in Chapter Two, so check back to page 43 if you need to.) After you have combined the sentences by embedding, decide whether to add *two commas* or *none*. You will choose from the embedding words *who, whose, which,* and *that.*

1. (a) Chubby Checker worked as a chicken plucker in a poultry shop before he became famous for doing "The Twist."

   (b) His real name was Ernest Evans.

   _____

   _____

   _____

2. (a) Neil Sedaka made a comeback in the 1970s with the help of Elton John.

   (b) He had enjoyed a great deal of success as a songwriter and singer in the 1950s.

   _____

   _____

   _____

3. (a) Critic Jon Landau is responsible for the now somewhat famous line "I saw rock'n'roll's future, and its name is Bruce Springsteen."

   (b) He wrote a rave review after seeing "the Boss" in concert in 1974.

   _____

   _____

   _____

4. (a) Annie Mae Bullock changed her name to Tina Turner.

   (b) She married Ike Turner in 1958.

   _____

   _____

   _____

5. (a) The heart attack occurred while the famous soul singer was performing on stage in Cherry Hill, New Jersey, on September 25, 1975.

   (b) It left Jackie Wilson in a coma for the rest of his life.

   _____

   _____

   _____

6. (a) Aretha Franklin started her career by singing in the choir with her sisters, Carolyn and Erma.

(b)   Her father was the Reverend C. L. Franklin of the New Bethel Baptist Church

in Detroit.

_____

_____

_____

7. (a)   Stevie Wonder was the first Motown musician to have complete artistic con-

trol of his own work.

(b)   He composes, arranges, and plays a variety of instruments.

_____

_____

_____

8. (a)   The Cree Indian woman is Buffy Sainte-Marie.

(b)   She is known for combining elements of rock, classical, and Native American

music in her songs.

_____

_____

_____

9. (a)   The record producer was Phil Spector.

(b)   He created pop music's so-called wall of sound.

_____

_____

_____

10. (a)   Spector's wall of sound resulted from overdubbing various tracks.

(b)   It almost always involved several guitars, pianos, drums, tambourines, casta-

nets, and bells.

_____

_____

_____

Exercise Five

Directions: Draw a wavy line below the embedded clause in each sentence and write *S* over the subject of the main clause. Then make your decision and insert *two commas* or *none.* These facts can be found in *The Quintessential Quiz Book* by Norman G. Hickman.

1. The state that ratified the Constitution first was Delaware.

2. The word *laser* which is actually an acronym is made from the first letters of the words *light amplification by stimulated emission of radiation.* (The prepositions, of course, are excluded.)

3. *Walden* which was written by Henry David Thoreau is subtitled *Life in the Woods.*

4. The award that is given by the Mystery Writers of America for the best mystery of each year is the Edgar.

5. Dorothy Parker who was a great literary wit is reputed to have willed ten percent of her ashes to her agent.

6. Mt. Vesuvius which erupted in 79 A.D. covered Pompeii with ashes and cinders. (Pompeii was not, contrary to what many people think, covered with lava.)

7. The only woman who was part of the Lewis and Clark Expedition was the great Sacajawea.

8. A statement that criticized and chastised believers in astrology was issued by 18 Nobel Prize winners in 1975.

9. Thomas Crapper whose biography is entitled *Flushed with Pride* invented the valve-and-siphon system that made flush toilets possible.

10. Dr. Mary D. Leakey who happened to be the wife of one famous anthropologist and the mother of another discovered in Tanzania a hominid fossil that was over 1.7 million years old.

UNIT 3: Using Commas to Set Off Phrases

To understand the point of punctuation we'll discuss in Unit 3, you have to recall the difference between a *clause* and a *phrase*. Remember that a clause has both a subject and a verb. A phrase, on the other hand, is a sequence of words that has some sort of meaning but does not have both a subject and a predicate. A phrase might have a noun or a pronoun, or it might have some form of a verb, but it will not have a subject and a verb working together. A phrase might be short or long, but its function is less than the function of a clause. It does less grammatically.

Label each sequence of words *Cl* (for clause) or *P* (for phrase):

1. _____ this man loved his child

2. _____ loving his child

3. _____ the water is deep

4. _____ in a certain depth of water

5. _____ because the store will close in an hour

6. _____ closing the store soon

7. _____ devoted to the exploration of space

8. _____ the tragedy of the space shuttle *Challenger*

9. _____ if we expect to continue the quest

10. _____ expecting to continue the quest

[*Answers.* The clauses are items 1, 3, 5, and 9. The phrases are items 2, 4, 6, 7, 8, and 10.]

If you had trouble with the ten examples above, get help from your writing teacher or a good tutor before you continue.

Introductory Phrases

Please read this sentence aloud:

(a) **Not leaving a thing to chance one cookbook says that Grandma's "pinch" is**

really one eighth of a teaspoon.

If you're like most readers, this sentence cannot be read easily without a very short pause and a slight shift in vocal pitch after the word *chance*. Insert a comma after *chance* and read the sentence aloud again. It's clearer with the comma, isn't it?

Most writers would have inserted a comma after *chance* even if they knew very little about the formal rules of punctuation. You might say it's a common sense comma. The reason it's so helpful is that it separates what we're going to call an "introductory phrase" from the independent clause that follows it. Go back to the (a) sentence and draw a bracket over *Not leaving a thing to chance*; then write *introductory phrase* above the bracket. Finally, mark the main parts of the kernel in the independent clause in (a).

End Phrases

Now read this sentence aloud:

> (b) **Kurt Vonnegut has written some of the funniest and saddest books of the twentieth century repeatedly lamenting the exchange of kindness and love for progress and technology.**

Go back and insert a comma after the word *century*; then read the sentence aloud once more. Again, it's easier to handle with the comma, isn't it? With the Kurt Vonnegut sentence, we have an example of an "end phrase" (or a "concluding phrase," you could say). In this kind of sentence, we have the independent clause first. For the convenience of your reader the end phrase that follows the clause should be set off with a comma. Please label the end phrase in example (b) and also the key parts of the kernel in the independent clause.

Notes to Remember

Sometimes it's a matter of your own judgment whether or not to set off an introductory phrase or an end phrase from an independent clause. You'll do fine as long as you use this question as your guideline: *What will make my sentence easier to read?* That, of course, is the whole purpose of punctuation—making your writing easier for your reader to understand.

When a single word or a very short phrase appears before an independent clause, you can *usually* go either way. For example, you can insert a comma after the introductory phrase in each of these sentences, or you can leave it out:

> (c) In a minute she'll be ready.

> (d) Later he'll stop at the library.

> (e) Actually I don't know what to do.

Again, (c) through (e) are fine with or without a comma.

But there are times when you should definitely use a comma even though you might have only *one word* before the start of the independent clause. *Yes, No, First, Second,* and *Third* are good examples of single words that should be set off with a comma when they appear as the first word in a sentence. Another good example is a person's name in a sentence in which you are addressing that person. Add commas:

> (f) No he isn't scheduled to play tonight.

> (g) Yes she seems to be the front-runner.

(h)   First you must have the desire to write well.

(i)   Second a certain amount of time must be set aside for the effort.

(j)   Ann come here for a minute.

(k)   George do you think we'll have time for a short drive?

When in doubt, try reading aloud and let your reader's need for a pause be your guide.

Exercise One

Directions: Add commas to set off phrases where doing so makes the sentence easier to read. You might want to label the clauses with *S, V* or *VP,* and *C* to make your decisions easier.

1. In the lingo of the racetrack a maiden is a horse that has not yet won its first race.

2. First awarded in the American Revolution the Purple Heart is bestowed upon soldiers who are wounded in the line of duty.

3. The city of Leningrad has perhaps undergone something of an identity crisis through the years having earlier been known both as St. Petersburg and as Petrograd.

4. England adopted a national policy of women's suffrage in 1918 followed by the United States in 1920.

5. The word *khaki* comes from the Persian word *khak* meaning "dust."

6. Located in enormous cavities in its head a sperm whale's "sperm" is a waxy substance that was at one time commonly used in making candles.

7. Many pediatricians believe that mother's milk is the perfect food for infants providing most of the essential nutrients for at least the first few months of life.

8. Indicating a score of zero the word *love* in tennis is probably derived from *l'oeuf* the French word for "egg."

9. The universe is about 12 billion years old according to proponents of the big bang theory.

10. Confirming the suspicions of many juniors and seniors a sophomore is literally half wise and half foolish. (The word *sophomore* is derived from the Greek words *sophos,* which means "wise," and *moros,* which means "foolish.")

Please correct Exercise One before continuing.

Exercise Two

Directions: Add commas to set off phrases where doing so makes the sentences easier to read. Label the kernel of the clause if you find that helpful. The information in this exercise is based on a section of *The People's Almanac #3* that tells about athletes who overcame handicaps.

1. Lou Brissie had both of his legs severely mangled in World War II necessitating 23 operations within a two-year period. Despite his physical problems Brissie became a major league pitcher achieving a 14–10 record for the Philadelphia A's in 1948.

2. Paralyzed throughout his childhood Ray Ewry was confined at first to bed then to a wheelchair. After regaining the use of his legs through daily exercise Ewry went on to win ten Olympic medals in track and field between 1900 and 1908.

3. Like Ewry Wilma Rudolph started out with dismal prospects for success in track and field. Afflicted with scarlet fever and double pneumonia at the age of four Wilma Rudolph did not walk again until she was seven. Later she won three gold medals in the 1960 Olympics sprinting her way to an Olympic record in the 100-meter dash.

4. A gifted athlete with a good chance of becoming a major league baseball player Charley Boswell was blinded in World War II while trying to rescue a buddy from a tank that was under fire. After the war Boswell took up golf winning the National Blind Golf Tournament more than a dozen times.

5. Stricken with polio as a youngster Australian John Konrads overcame his disability and won a gold medal in freestyle swimming in the 1960 Olympics.

6. A victim of rickets in his youth O. J. Simpson had to wear braces on his legs for years. He went on to earn many honors in football including ownership of the all-time pro rushing record of 2003 yards in a single season.

7. Dave Stallworth was a two-time All-American and a first-round draft choice for the New York Knicks. Two years after suffering a heart attack at the end of his second pro season he made a comeback and played all 82 games for the Knicks in 1970.

8. According to *The People's Almanac #3* Lis Hartel suffered from a severe case of polio in her midtwenties. After months of rigorous and exhausting daily exercises this Danish horsewoman competed in the Scandinavian riding championships. Still paralyzed from her knees down Hartel placed second in the women's dressage. In the 1952 and 1956 Olympics she won the silver medal in the dressage.

9. Glenn Cunningham set a new world record in the mile in 1934 in spite of severe childhood injuries to his legs and feet. At the age of eight Cunningham had been badly burned in a fire at school losing all of the toes on his left foot.

10. Having lost his right hand in 1938 Karoly Takacs simply learned to shoot with his left. The Hungarian marksman claimed gold medals in both the 1948 and the 1952 Olympics.

Exercise Three

Directions: As you know, punctuation should be learned *actively* as a sentence-combining technique. For this exercise, which is to be done on your own paper, think of five statements about yourself, a family member, or a friend. Each statement should be written first as a compound or complex sentence. Then it should be rewritten as a sentence with an independent clause plus an introductory phrase or an end phrase. (You'll write ten sentences altogether.) Punctuate the sentences correctly.

Let's say you're a Sagittarius. Here's an example of what you could do:

compound: I was blessed with the honest and forgiving nature of the typical Sagittarius, so I am affectionate, open, and friendly.

phrase + clause: Blessed with the honest and forgiving nature of the typical Sagittarius, I am affectionate, open, and friendly.

or

phrase + clause: Honest and forgiving, I am as affectionate, open, and friendly as the typical Sagittarius.

Here's another example:

complex: I am going to the reunion because I hope to see Elaine Martin after all these years.

clause + phrase: I am going to the reunion, hoping to see Elaine Martin after all these years.

Phrases that Interrupt Clauses

We've been working with phrases that come before or after an independent clause, but a phrase can also appear in the middle of a clause. When it does, again you have to use your judgment to decide if it should be set off with commas. If you think that a pause and a shift in vocal pitch are required, then you'll use *two commas*—one before and one after the phrase. Using oral reading to guide your decisions, punctuate these examples:

(a) The new shopping district in spite of careful planning by the town council did not turn out to be much of a success.

(b) Your cousin with or without his Doberman pinscher is not welcome here today.

(c) The real reason for her actions will however become obvious by the end of the story.

(d) The hospital surprising everyone became the center for heart transplant surgery in the region.

UNIT 4: Using Commas in a Series

One of the most natural uses of the comma is for separating items in a series. The items might be three or more of almost anything—nouns, adjectives, verbs, prepositional phrases, or practically any other grammatical unit.

The comma before the *and* that joins the last two items in a series is optional, but it often makes a sentence easier to read if you put it in.

Exercise One

Directions: Add commas where they are necessary or helpful for separating items in a series. (Commas that are necessary for other reasons have already been added for you.)

1. Animals that form monogamous bonds between males and females include ducks swans geese eagles foxes wolves and mountain lions.

2. *Fly patterns flares bombs safety blitzes* and *flea flickers* are all part of the lingo known only to the true football fan.

3. The Arc de Triomphe in Paris is 164 feet high 148 feet wide and 72 feet thick.

4. In one of the many works written about him, the famous Faust exchanged his soul for 24 years of wisdom wealth power and pleasure.

5. Until recently, Ariel Miranda Oberon Titania and Umbriel were thought to be the only moons that revolved around the planet Uranus.

6. Arizona Colorado New Mexico and Utah all meet at what is known as the "Four Corners."

7. An order of champagne can come in a variety of sizes, including a split a half bottle a quart a magnum and a jeroboam.

8. People born under the sign of Aries are said to be self-reliant intellectual enthusiastic and bold.

9. Carbon hydrogen nitrogen and oxygen constitute about 90 percent of the human body.

10. American kids are used to calling Donald Duck's nephews Huey Dewey and Louie, but to cartoon lovers in Yugoslavia, they're known as *Vlaja Gaja* and *Raja.*

Please correct Exercise One before doing Exercise Two.

Exercise Two

Directions: Add commas where they are necessary or helpful. In this exercise, you'll be dealing with items in a series, but you'll also have to consider adding commas for other reasons. In other words, in some of these items, you might also find compound sentences, complex sentences, embedded sentences, sentences with introductory phrases or end phrases, and so on.

1. *The Rule Book* was written by Stephen M. Kirschner Barry J. Pavelec and Jeffrey Feinman. In it the authors list the rules for interpreting Irish omens. According to their list traditional Irish omens held that someone was going to die soon if crickets chirped at midnight if a patient improved on a Sunday if four magpies were seen together or if the corpse remained limp during a wake. On the other hand good luck was around the corner if the West wind blew on New Year's Eve if a garment had been put on inside out or if two magpies were seen together.

2. A pamphlet called "Helping Baby Grow" which was published by the City of Milwaukee Health Department suggests that some ideal toys for toddlers who are between 18 and 20 months are a toy telephone a shape-sorting box a carrying case cloth picture books and a record player that is kept out of reach when not in use.

3. Four good books on making a career change are *What Color Is Your Parachute? Where Do I Go From Here with My Life? What To Do with the Rest of Your Life* and *Self-Directed Search.*

4. In *Life-spans, Or, How Long Things Last* the reader can find the life expectancies for human beings in ages past. In the twentieth century we can expect to live into our 70s but it wasn't always so. The Neanderthals could expect to live to the age of 29 the Cro-Magnons to 32 the Greeks and Romans to 36 and the fourteenth-century English to 38. These estimates were calculated after careful study of skeletons gravestones legal papers and other records.

5. Modern methods of food processing and storage are fairly recent inventions. The process of canning was invented in 1809 the refrigerator in 1834 condensed milk in 1858 and the process of quick freezing in the 1920s.

6. Alice Roosevelt Longworth once said, "I have a simple philosophy. Fill what's empty empty what's full and scratch where it itches."

7. In *The Book of Firsts* Patrick Robertson describes the first time roller skates were worn in public. In 1760 Joseph Merlin a maker of musical instruments wore the first roller skates to a masquerade party at Carlisle House in Soho Square. When he rolled into the ballroom playing a violin he was unable to slow down or change direction. Robertson tells us that Merlin "impelled himself against a large mirror valued at over 500 pounds smashed it to atoms broke his instrument and wounded himself severely."

8. Toxemia which is also known as pregnancy-induced hypertension occurs in five to seven percent of expectant women. Some of the most typical signs of this potentially fatal condition are a sudden and unusually large increase in weight protein in the urine high blood pressure and swelling in the face hands and feet. Dizziness blurred vision and persistent headaches are sometimes present in the most severe cases.

9. Macaroon Kiss cookies as described in *Hershey's Chocolate Treasury* are made with butter sugar egg yolk almond extract orange juice flour baking powder flaked coconut salt Hershey's Kisses and cream cheese.

10. In *Anatomy of an Illness* and in *The Healing Heart* Norman Cousins describes how patients can sometimes help themselves recover from serious illnesses. He does not argue in favor of any substitute for a scientific approach to treating disease but he does maintain that medical treatment is most likely to succeed when the patient creates an environment in which the recovery can flourish. In *Anatomy of an Illness* the earlier of the two books he wrote a great deal about the role of laughter but in *The Healing Heart* Cousins explains that laughter was and is meant as a metaphor for an entire range of positive emotions. According to Cousins some of the emotions that have the strongest therapeutic value are love hope faith cheerfulness the will to live humor creativity confidence playfulness and great expectations.

Commas in Adjective Pairs

A related rule concerns the use of a comma between two adjectives that describe the same noun. Sometimes you insert a comma, and sometimes you don't. What's the rule? It's really very simple. Just ask yourself if you could put the word *and* between the two adjectives. If you could, then insert the comma. If the word *and* would sound odd between the adjectives, then leave out the comma.

With this guideline in mind, put a comma between the adjectives in *one* of these two sentences:

(a)   Peter is a **happy young** man.

(b)   Peter is an **enthusiastic energetic** man.

The comma should be inserted in sentence (b), right? You know that it's (b) because you might easily say, "Peter is an enthusiastic and energetic man," but you would never say, "Peter is a happy and young man."

This rule can be explained in another way, which you might find useful. Normally, if you can switch the order of the adjectives, then you put in the comma. If you can't switch the order, then you omit the comma. See if this rule works by rewriting (a) and (b), switching the order of *happy* and *young* in sentence (a) and *enthusiastic* and *energetic* in sentence (b):

(a)   _____

(b)   _____

When the adjectives in (a) are switched, the sentence—*Peter is a young happy man*—sounds odd, doesn't it? It's not a sentence you'd be likely to write. That tells you to leave out the comma. When the adjectives in sentence (b) are switched, the sentence sounds fine; that tells you to put in the comma.

To us, the first technique—trying to insert *and*—seems the clearer test in most sentences. But some students find it very helpful to try to switch the order of the adjectives. So use the rule that is easier for you.

Exercise Three

Directions: Underline the adjectives in each sentence. Then insert a comma between them where one is needed. In each set of sentences, one adjective pair will call for a comma, and one will not. Use one or both of the methods described above.

1. (a)   She was known for her quick little smile.

   (b)   She was known for her generous good-hearted smile.

2. (a)   This is a serious military affair.

   (b)   This is a ridiculous tragic affair.

3. (a)   The garden was bordered with perfect tea roses.

   (b)   The garden was bordered with delicate delightful roses.

4. (a) A creamy buttery soup was served in the cafeteria.

   (b) A delicious bean soup was served in the cafeteria.

5. (a) He was a skillful thoughtful sculptor.

   (b) He was a thoughtful Italian sculptor.

Please correct Exercise Three before doing Exercise Four.

Exercise Four

Directions: Follow the directions for Exercise Three.

1. (a) A blushing new bride walked into the reception hall.

   (b) A blushing embarrassed bride walked into the reception hall.

2. (a) We had to sign some lengthy inconsequential forms.

   (b) We had to sign the necessary legal forms.

3. (a) She brought the long wet worms in a bucket.

   (b) She brought the slippery squirmy worms in a bucket.

4. (a) You know that this is an essential unavoidable step in the process.

   (b) You know that this is an essential second step in the process.

5. (a) They were in unheated unattached rooms.

   (b) They were in separate hotel rooms.

UNIT 5: Cumulative Review of Commas

This unit is simply a series of exercises in which you use all the different comma rules you've learned in this chapter.

   Before you begin the exercises, please go back through the chapter and review the various rules, especially any that you might have found difficult. Then use these lines to write the comma rules from each unit in your own words.

Comma Rules

From Unit 1: _____

_____

_____

_____

_____

_____

_____

From Unit 2: _____

_____

_____

_____

_____

From Unit 3: _____

_____

_____

_____

_____

_____

From Unit 4: _____

_____

_____

_____

_____

_____

To the rules you've reviewed, you can add two that need very little explanation.

Commas to Set Off City from State

You normally use one comma between the name of a city and a state and another comma after the state. For example:

1. (a) The authors of *The Best* insist that **New York, New York,** is home to the best hamburgers in America.

2. (a) **New Haven, Connecticut,** is the city where they found the best pizza.

The only exception is when the city and state come right before another punctuation mark such as a period or a semicolon. In these examples, you use only the comma between city and state:

1. (b) The authors of *The Best* insist that the best hamburgers in America are served at the Campus Dining Room Restaurant and Bar in **New York, New York.**

2. (b) Peter Passell and Leonard Ross really liked the pizza at The Spot in **New Haven, Connecticut**; in fact, they called it the best pizza in the United States.

Commas in Dates

The rule for punctuating dates is similar. You use one comma between the day of the month and the year and another comma after the year. In other words, you normally set the year off with two commas, just as you usually set the state off with two commas. For example:

(a) The first use of videotape on television was on **October 23, 1956,** on *The Jonathan Winters Show.*

(b) **December 25, 1968,** was the day when the *Apollo 8* astronauts became the first human beings to see the far side of the moon.

The same exception applies here as applies to city and state; in other words, you use no comma after the year if another punctuation mark is used in that position.

Reminders

Remember, the way to get the most out of exercises on punctuation is to avoid guessing. Use a comma only when you can say why you're using it, according to the rules and suggestions in Chapter 3. If you go by hunches, you won't get much of a workout.

As usual, please correct each exercise and discuss any problems before going on to the next.

Exercise One

Directions: Add commas where they are necessary or helpful, according to the guidelines of Chapter 3. These unusual bits of information are from *The Quintessential Quiz Book* by Norman G. Hickman.

1. If you ever really want to go to Timbuktu you'll have to head out for Mali in northwest Africa. Timbuktu which was a famous center for trading in gold was settled by the Tuaregs in 1087.

2. The ice cream sundae now a classic American treat was supposedly created in a Wisconsin ice cream parlor and originally it was served only on Sundays.

3. September 1 1939 is an important date because it marks the beginning of World War II. (On that date Germany invaded Poland.)

4. For concocting the original Coca-Cola in 1886 John Styth Pemberton an Atlanta pharmacist will always be remembered and appreciated.

5. When fireflies light up they send sexual signals to one another. According to the experts male and female fireflies identify themselves and indicate sexual interest by the frequency and intensity of their flashes.

6. King Louis XIV of France who was a ballet dancer from the time he was 13 years old is credited with founding the Royal Ballet Company.

7. A desert rose is really not a rose at all. It's a rock that is made up of fused eroded grains of sand. Desert roses which are really flowers carved by the elements are not difficult to find in the Sahara.

8. The first person to be called the "father of his country" was Cicero not George Washington.

9. Totally unrelated to either sweets or bread a sweetbread is actually the thymus gland of an animal.

10. The longest heaviest snake in the world is the South American anaconda or python a typical specimen measuring 30 feet or more.

Exercise Two

Directions: Add commas where they are necessary or helpful, according to the guidelines of Chapter 3. Here's more information, mostly from *The Quintessential Quiz Book.*

1. Isadora Duncan a great American dancer of the early twentieth century has become almost as famous for her death as for her dancing. Duncan was riding in a car when her long scarf became entangled in a rear wheel. Her neck was broken and she died.

2. It was December 17 1903 when Orville and Wilbur Wright made their first controlled sustained flights in a power-driven airplane. These first flights of course took place near Kitty Hawk North Carolina.

3. On April 26 1977 Studio 54 which was to become closely associated with the disco phenomenon first opened its doors in New York New York.

4. Although he did not go to Antarctica Capt. James Cook is generally given credit as the first man to set foot on all the continents.

5. Corned beef which is beef preserved in salt got its name because salt used to come in little pellets that were called corns.

6. Many people think that the majority of forest fires are caused by the careless use of matches or negligent tending of campfires but most are actually started by lightning.

7. There is one thing that you'll seldom see in a gambling casino and that's a clock.

8. Manfred von Richthofen who was nicknamed "the Red Baron" because of the red planes he flew had shot down 80 Allied aircraft before he was killed in action in 1918. He was the top-ranked flying ace of World War I and he has become something of a legend through songs movies and even Snoopy cartoons.

9. A snake that sticks out its tongue is actually smelling.

10. Dr. Joseph I. Guillotin did not invent the guillotine but he did popularize it in France because he believed that it was a quick painless form of execution.

Now we'll try some exercises in context. These might appear more difficult, but just take the sentences one by one. The exercises require you to use only the comma rules that you've been studying, nothing new.

There are some items that include direct quotes, but the punctuation that is needed before a direct quote is already supplied for you. Within a direct quote, use a comma when it is appropriate. (You'll learn how to set up direct quotes in Chapter 4.)

Exercise Three

Directions: Add commas where they are necessary or helpful, according to the guidelines of Chapter 3. We hope you'll enjoy these items, which are based on material from the *Speaker's Treasury of Anecdotes about the Famous* by James C. Humes.

(a) The person who supposedly originated the coffee break was a young sergeant in the Civil War by the name of William McKinley. It was September 17 1862 and federal troops had crossed Antietam Creek and were moving toward Sharpsburg. Sergeant McKinley who was in charge of the commissary for an Ohio regiment carried a bucket of steaming hot coffee and a box of hot food to the men who were on the front lines and were encountering heavy resistance. At the site of this historic battle in western Maryland a tall granite monument to the first coffee break has been erected.

(b) When he was an old man Pierre-Auguste Renoir suffered terribly from arthritis especially in his hands. The great Renoir could still paint but he could do so only with great difficulty grasping his paint brush with just the tips of his fingers. One day Henri Matisse another great French artist and Renoir's dear friend asked Renoir why he continued to work knowing that he could paint only with great physical agony. Renoir answered, "The pain passes but the beauty remains."

(c) Robert Benchley the American humorist and critic took a course in international law while he was a student at Harvard University. When it came time for the final exam Benchley was asked to discuss the arbitration of an international fishing dispute between the United States and Great Britain and he was supposed to pay special attention to hatcheries protocol and dragnet and trawl procedure. Benchley who was not prepared for the examination began his essay by announcing that he knew absolutely nothing about the point of view of the United States with respect to any international fishing controversy and he also confessed that he knew nothing about the point of view that Great Britain might hold in such a matter. "Therefore," Benchley asserted in the introduction to his essay, "I shall discuss the question from the point of view of the fish."

Exercise Four

Directions: Add commas where they are necessary or helpful, according to the guidelines of Chapter 3. Here are more items based on anecdotes from Humes' collection.

(a) Phineas T. Barnum the great American showman and circus impresario was near death in 1891 when an editor of a New York newspaper contacted his agent inquiring as to whether or not Barnum would enjoy seeing his obituary published while he could still read it. Never one to refuse a little free publicity Barnum told his agent that he thought it was a fine idea. The next day P. T. Barnum read a four-column story about his own life and death and he loved it.

(b) Have you ever wondered why thin crisp bread is called Melba toast? Actually it was named after Nellie Melba a famous Australian soprano of the late nineteenth and early twentieth century. The prima donna was staying at the Savoy Hotel in London and was on a stringent diet. According to the story she was living on almost nothing but toast. Normally she was served her meals by Auguste Escoffier a famous French chef and author. But on one particular occasion the master chef was busy elsewhere so the great lady's toast had to be prepared by one of Escoffier's assistants. The assistant as you've probably already guessed bungled the job. When the unfortunate helper served the ruined toast to Nellie Melba the head steward rushed forward to offer his sincerest and most horrified apologies. But before Cesar Ritz the head steward could reach her the celebrated opera star exclaimed, "Cesar how clever of Escoffier! I have never eaten such lovely toast." Ever since then it's been

called Melba toast.

(c) The French philosopher Voltaire whose real name was François-Marie Arouet

predicted that within a century of his death the Bible would be a mere curiosity.

He believed that it would be found primarily in museums and would be largely

forgotten by the general public. Ironically 100 years after he died in 1778 Vol-

taire's former home was occupied by the Geneva Bible Society.

Exercise Five

Directions: **Add commas where they are necessary or helpful, according to the guidelines of Chapter 3. We continue with items based on anecdotes from James C. Humes' collection.**

(a) When Leopold Stokowski was once conducting the Philadelphia Orchestra in the

Leonore Overture no. 3 he was more than a little irritated about an offstage trumpet

call that had failed to sound on cue both times it had been expected. After the

performance was finished the famous British-born American conductor flew into

the wings fully prepared to rant and rave. But what did he find? He found the

gentleman who was responsible for the trumpet call struggling in the arms of a

well-built watchman. "I tell you, you can't blow that damn thing in here," Stokowski

heard the burly guard tell the trumpet player. "There's a concert going on!"

(b) Benjamin Franklin once said, "Money begets money and its offspring begets

more." Illustrating this axiom Ben Franklin left a legacy of $5000 to the city of

Boston stipulating that the interest from the money must be allowed to accumulate

for 100 years. Between 1791 and 1891 the fund grew from $5000 to almost

$400,000. After the first century was up the city of Boston built a school with part

of the money and reinvested the remaining $92,000. By the middle of the twen-

tieth century Ben Franklin's $5000 had grown to just under $1 million.

(c) Ignace Paderewski a Polish concert pianist and statesman was known to work at the piano six hours a day skipping practice for no man no woman and no reason. In view of his virtuosity at the piano some people wondered why he continued to practice so faithfully and they asked him. His answer reveals much about Paderewski and about who he thought held the highest standards. This is what he told them: "If I miss one day's practice I notice it. If I miss two days the critics notice it. If I miss three days the audience notices it."

UNIT 6: Using Semicolons

The basic function of the semicolon (;) is simple. A semicolon is used where you could use a capital letter and a period, but you'd rather not have such a strong break between your clauses. It's good for spots where you want to bring clauses together, but you don't want to use a conjunction.

In other words, **a semicolon is used between independent clauses that are not linked by a conjunction.** A semicolon is used when the information in the independent clauses is related or balanced. Here are five good examples for you to study carefully:

(a) Children between the ages of one and three need about 25 grams of protein a day; adults need 55 to 75 grams a day.

(b) The red parts of poinsettias are not flowers; the red parts are actually leaves.

(c) A female has two X chromosomes; a male has one X chromosome and one Y chromosome.

(d) The first president who didn't go to college was George Washington; the last was Harry Truman.

(e) It is against federal law to impersonate a 4-H Club member; it is also a federal offense to misuse the 4-H symbol in a fraudulent manner.

Label the kernels of the clauses in examples (a) through (e) if that helps you see that each sentence is made up of two independent clauses. Please note that the first word after the semicolon is *not* capitalized.

Exercise One

Directions: Insert one semicolon into each sentence. Label the clauses with *S, V* or *VP,* and *C* if you need to. (In this exercise and in other exercises in this unit, we're supplying any punctuation that is not related to the use of the semicolon. See sentences 4 and 7, for example.)

1. Mildred "Babe" Didrikson was voted the woman athlete of the year in 1932 for her accomplishments in track she received the honor for her achievements in golf in 1954.

2. The Eiffel Tower was not intended as a permanent structure it was built as a merely temporary attraction for the Paris Exposition in 1889.

3. The skeletons of sharks are not composed of bone they are made up entirely of cartilage.

4. According to a recent national survey by American Demographics, high school boys expect a starting salary of $18,500 for their first full-time job high school girls expect a starting salary of only $14,700.

5. In the 1870s the most admired American sports heroes were riflemen oarsmen were almost as popular with the U.S. public.

6. The linguistic origin of *Santa Claus* is Dutch the name is really a contraction of the words *Sint Nikolaas.*

7. In Louisiana you might eat both Creole and Cajun cooking. Paul Prudhomme, the great New Orleans chef, says that the two types of cuisine share many features but have very different histories. Creole is city food Cajun is country food.

8. American households with annual incomes of at least $25,000 receive an average of 25 pieces of mail a week households with annual incomes of $5000 or less receive about eight pieces a week.

9. The very first newspaper story about baseball appeared in New York's *Sunday Mercury* in April 1853 the article described baseball very simply as a new game with lots of followers.

10. A postcard needs a stamp a postal card has one already affixed by the post office.

Notice that each time you used a semicolon in Exercise One, strictly speaking, you could have used a capital letter and a period. (Many students find that to be a helpful guide.) So what's the difference? When you use a semicolon, you're *connecting* two independent clauses. When you use a capital letter and a period, you're *separating* two independent clauses.

An Introductory Word or Phrase for the Clause after the Semicolon

You know that semicolons are used when a writer wants to show a relationship between two independent clauses. (Sometimes it's actually independent *combinations* of clauses; for example, you might have a complex sentence on one side of a semicolon and a compound sentence on the other side.) Often a writer uses an introductory word or phrase at the beginning of the clause that follows the semicolon. *This word or phrase does not connect the clauses. The semicolon does that.* The introductory word or phrase simply makes the relationship between the clauses clearer and more explicit.

Here's a list of words and phrases that are often used in this way. They're divided into groups on the basis of similar or closely related meanings:

for example	therefore
for instance	consequently
	as a result
however	in fact
on the other hand	as a matter of fact
nevertheless	actually
also	then
furthermore	now
in addition	later
in other words	

If you have any difficulty understanding the meaning of any of these words or phrases, please consult a dictionary or ask your writing teacher.

Let's take a sentence you punctuated in Exercise One:

(a) American households with annual incomes of at least $25,000 receive an average of 25 pieces of mail a week; households with annual incomes of $5000 or less receive about eight pieces a week.

The sentence is perfectly fine the way it is. But it *can* be revised in a very small way so that the contrast it describes is more obvious. To see how this works, fill in the blank with an introductory word or phrase from the list above:

(b) American households with annual incomes of at least $25,000 receive an average of 25 pieces of mail a week; _____, households with annual incomes of $5000 or less receive about eight pieces a week.

If you chose *however* or *on the other hand,* you're correct. Either one helps to make the contrast between the clauses more apparent.

Notice that a comma is used after the introductory word or phrase in (b). This is the normal procedure: use a semicolon before the introductory word or phrase and a comma after it.

Exercise Two

Directions: This exercise calls for you to rewrite a selection of sentences from Exercise One on your own paper. Revise the items by adding an appropriate introductory word or phrase before the clause that follows the semicolon. Insert a comma after the word or phrase.

Use these items from Exercise One: sentences 1, 2, 3, 4, and 10. Work with introductory words and phrases from the six groups we presented. (There is often more than one workable option for a given sentence.)

Other Introductory Words and Phrases

The list we have given you is certainly not complete. It's just a good basic list of words that can be used in creating this particular sentence structure. But there are many other expressions that can serve as introductory words and phrases before a clause. You'll probably come up with a variety in your own writing. Look at these two examples:

(a) The manager of a professional baseball team can visit the pitcher on the mound only once; *after that*, he can't go out again unless he's going to call in a reliever.

(b) There are many legends about the Canary Islands; *according to one*, the islands are really the highest peaks of Atlantis, the lost continent.

Exercise Three

Directions: Write five sentences of your own, using semicolons and five different introductory words or phrases. Don't forget the comma after the word or phrase. You may select introductory words and phrases from our list, and you may also use some of your own making. Do the exercise on your own paper, please.

Exercise Four

Directions: Punctuate these sentences with semicolons and commas. Some sentences call for a semicolon only, and others call for a semicolon and a comma. (Label *S*, *V* or *VP*, and *C* if you need to.)

1. The largest lake or inland sea in the world is the Caspian Sea however the biggest freshwater lake is Lake Superior.

2. The familiar word *oriental* refers to the people and culture of the East the less familiar word *occidental* refers to the people and culture of the West.

3. Fyodor Dostoyevsky wrote a novel called *The Gambler* in fact the great Russian literary figure was himself a compulsive gambler.

4. North America is slowly moving westward at an annual rate of about three inches

consequently the Atlantic Ocean is now about 20 feet wider than it was when Columbus crossed it.

5. During the ninth-century reign of Alfred, King of the West Saxons, there was a specific punishment for practically every bodily injury for example if a person's thigh were pierced, he or she could collect a fine of 30 shillings from the injuring party.

6. A copyright stays in effect for the lifetime of the creator of the copyrighted work in fact it is valid for his or her lifetime plus 50 years.

7. In O. Henry's "The Gift of the Magi" a husband sells his watch in order to buy his wife a pair of combs for her beautiful hair the wife cuts off her long hair and sells it in order to buy her husband a fob chain for his watch.

8. Much of Humphrey Bogart's mystique came as a result of his wonderful perform-ance in *Casablanca* however few people know that Ronald Reagan was originally cast as Rick, the main character.

9. An amulet is an object that supposedly protects a person against bad luck a talisman is something that is thought to attract good luck.

10. A wolf's eye, a stone with a hole in it, and a horseshoe are examples of amulets a four-leaf clover and a rabbit's foot are examples of talismans.

Please correct Exercise Four and discuss any problems before continuing.

Exercise Five

Directions: Punctuate these sentences correctly. Some call for a semicolon only, and others call for a semicolon and a comma. Label the kernels if you need to in order to see the structure of the sentences.

1. At 43 John Kennedy was the youngest elected president in U.S. history however Teddy Roosevelt was only 42 when he was sworn in after the assassination of William McKinley.

2. King Edward VII originated the fashion of leaving the lowest button on a vest unbuttoned it is uncertain whether he did so because of carelessness or increasing girth.

3. Color is an important factor in marketing commercial products for example food in green containers sells faster than food in containers of other colors.

4. We earthlings might not be alone in fact some experts say that over one billion planets in the universe are capable of supporting life.

5. The calendar year starts on January 1 the fiscal year begins on July 1.

6. It was recently announced that McDonald's does better per capita business in Canada than anywhere else therefore it would not be surprising to see McDonald's expand its operations up north.

7. Dr. Ben Green was concerned about sun exposure for World War II pilots who had to bail out over the Pacific consequently he invented the product that is now known as Coppertone.

8. England's Queen Elizabeth enjoys many privileges however the right to vote is not among them.

9. George Orwell's *Nineteen Eighty-four* was a best-seller when it was published in 1949 it became a best-seller again in 1984.

10. The main goal of expressionism was heightened expression the artists in that school distorted natural proportions in order to achieve it.

Exercise Six

Directions: This is an exercise for students who might have difficulty with some of the introductory words and phrases. (*However* and *therefore* take some practice for many people.) Read the sentences very carefully and fill in each blank with one of the introductory words or phrases that we listed on page 117. For some items, there's more than one logical possibility.

1. Actors have some interesting superstitions; _____ , it is thought to be bad luck for anyone to say the word "Macbeth" in a theater right before a performance.

2. Milwaukee and St. Louis both have reputations as big beer-producing cities; _____ , Los Angeles actually brews more beer than any other American city.

3. A chromophobe is afraid of color; _____ , if a chromophobic person buys a television, it's likely to be black and white.

4. Before 1931 a baseball that landed in fair territory and bounced into the stands was a home run; _____ , the rule was changed so that now such a ball is considered a ground rule double.

5. Every increase of one number on the Richter scale represents a tenfold increase in the magnitude of the ground motions that are recorded by a seismograph; _____ , a reading of 8.5 on the Richter scale represents an earthquake that is ten times stronger than an earthquake that produces a reading of 7.5.

Correct this exercise and discuss any problems before continuing with Exercise Seven.

Exercise Seven

Directions: **Continue to complete the items by filling in logical introductory words or phrases.**

1. *The Muppet Show* might not strike most viewers as particularly political; _____ , it was once banned in Saudi Arabia.

2. Cardplaying must have been serious business in eighteenth-century England; _____ , anyone who forged an ace of spades risked execution.

3. *The Honeymooners,* starring Jackie Gleason and Art Carney, began as a skit on *Cavalcade of Stars* in 1951; _____ , it debuted as a series in its own right in the fall of 1955.

4. Washington, D.C., which was built on low, marshy ground, used to become in-

fested with malaria-carrying mosquitoes every summer; _____ , when

presidents left the capital to vacation elsewhere, they left with good reason.

5. Zoologists know that certain animals are attracted to specific colors;

_____ , frogs supposedly favor blue.

A Note of Caution

There's one bad habit that some writers fall into. They begin to assume that the words and phrases listed on page 117 are always used with semicolons and are never used in any other ways in a sentence. Of course, that's not true. These words and phrases are not used with a semicolon unless you have an independent clause (or an independent combination of clauses) both before and after. All these words and phrases can be used with semicolons, but they can all be used in other spots in sentences, too. Study these correct examples and then complete Exercise Eight:

1. (a) Craig always has something to complain about; *for instance,* he might be upset about lumpy mashed potatoes one night and the growing national debt the next.
   (b) Craig's complaints, *for instance,* cover everything from lumpy mashed potatoes to the growing national debt.

2. (a) The doctor predicted a good outcome for the operation; *as a matter of fact,* she almost guaranteed total recovery.
   (b) The doctor's prediction, *as a matter of fact,* was almost totally optimistic.

Remember, don't be guilty of a knee-jerk reaction to any particular word or phrase, or you will use semicolons where they don't belong. All of these "introductory words and phrases," as we're calling them, can be used in other ways in sentences. They don't always signal the need for a semicolon.

Exercise Eight

Directions: Punctuate the following sentences. Some sentences call for no punctuation, some for commas only, and some for a semicolon and a comma.

1. (a) Robert had a great idea.

   (b) His idea however was not immediately accepted by the group.

   (c) Robert had a great idea however it was not immediately accepted by the group.

2. (a) Christina was more than a passing acquaintance of Ben's in fact she was his

   closest friend.

(b) Christina was very close to Ben.

(c) She was in fact his best friend in the world.

3. (a) Mitchell wants to graduate with a degree in mechanical engineering at the end of his college days.

(b) This highly motivated young man is therefore going to have to work hard and play little during the next four years.

(c) Mitchell wants to graduate from college with a degree in mechanical engineering therefore he is going to have to work hard and play little during the next four years.

4. (a) The exact time that language skills emerge in children varies greatly among individuals.

(b) Language skills emerge at greatly varying times in the development of children for example some toddlers begin talking in short sentences around the age of two.

(c) Other completely normal youngsters for example speak very little until they're three.

5. (a) John and Marsha are debating whether they should go with periwinkle blue or China red for their new carpet.

(b) Marsha thinks periwinkle blue would be an elegant choice on the other hand John's afraid that blue might make the room seem cold.

(c) John on the other hand thinks that China red would be warm and lively.

UNIT 7: Using Colons

Occasionally, you might want to use a full colon (:) to set up a list. In order to do this, you need to create a sentence that contains a subject, a verb or verb phrase, and a complement or a word that functions like a complement.

First, let's look at what not to do. *Don't do this*:

(a)   The four major reasons for the landslide victory *were*: the candidate's personal popularity, the enthusiastic support of his party, his stand on budget issues, and the general mood of the nation.

What's wrong with it? The problem is that the colon follows a verb—in sentence (a) the verb *were*. You might see this type of sentence in a newspaper or a magazine, but it's not accepted in academic writing by most college teachers.

In academic writing, it is normally expected that a **complement or a word very similar to a complement should appear before the colon.** Write *C* over the complement in this example:

(b)   The four major reasons for the landslide victory were obvious: the candidate's personal popularity, the enthusiastic support of his party, his stand on budget issues, and the general mood of the nation.

If you identified the word *obvious* as the complement, you're correct. The addition of *obvious* in sentence (b) corrects the problem that exists in sentence (a).

Exercise One

Directions: On your own paper, revise the "setup" of example (a) in three or four other ways, using different complements each time. The *setup* means the part of the sentence that comes before the colon. You can change the setup in any way you want to, as long as you preserve the basic meaning, namely, that a certain candidate won an election by a big margin because of four factors. In other words, you have more options than simply replacing the word *obvious* from sentence (b). Discuss your revisions in class.

An Important Note about the Complement

Sometimes it's okay to use a word that isn't exactly a complement but that still gives the sentence something of a sense of completion before the items in the list begin. For example, let's look at this sentence:

The strange coincidences happened during each of these *years*: 1921, 1937, 1952, 1964, and 1986.

You know that the word *years* is not the complement of the verb *happened*. If something happened, it happened. We don't ask a question such as "It happened what?" So strictly speaking, *happened* is a verb that doesn't take a complement.

But the word *years* does help to give the first part of the sentence a sense of completion—a sense that now we've finished the setup, and we're ready to present the items in the list.

To keep things simple, we'll refer to this kind of word as the *complement of the setup*. In the majority of sentences—your own and ours—you'll be working with a true complement anyway, so this won't often be an issue.

The important thing is this: **You need a feeling of completeness in the setup, the part of the sentence that precedes the colon.** That sense of wholeness in the setup can be produced by using a **true complement** or a **complement-type word.**

Exercise Two

Directions: Punctuate the following sentences. Some call for a colon and commas, and others call for commas only. Label each setup with *S, V* or *VP*, and especially *C* to see if a colon is called for. Remember, if there's no complement in the setup, there's no colon.

(a) The six wives of Henry VIII were Katharine of Aragon Anne Boleyn Jane Seymour Anne of Cleves Catherine Howard and Catherine Parr.

(b) King Henry VIII had six wives Katharine of Aragon Anne Boleyn Jane Seymour Anne of Cleves Catherine Howard and Catherine Parr.

(c) The six wives of Henry VIII were the following Katharine of Aragon Anne Boleyn Jane Seymour Anne of Cleves Catherine Howard and Catherine Parr.

(d) King Henry VIII's wives included Katharine of Aragon Anne Boleyn Jane Seymour Anne of Cleves Catherine Howard and Catherine Parr.

(e) Henry VIII married a half dozen women Katharine of Aragon Anne Boleyn Jane Seymour Anne of Cleves Catherine Howard and Catherine Parr.

(f) The wives of Henry VIII numbered six Katharine of Aragon Anne Boleyn Jane Seymour Anne of Cleves Catherine Howard and Catherine Parr.

(g) At different times in his life King Henry VIII married Katharine of Aragon Anne Boleyn Jane Seymour Anne of Cleves Catherine Howard and Catherine Parr.

Correct Exercise Two and discuss any questions before continuing.

Exercise Three

Directions: Punctuate the following sentences with colons and commas. Some sentences might call for commas only. Label *S, V* or *VP*, and *C.* Pay close attention to complements. (We have already supplied any punctuation that is not related to using colons or separating items in a list.)

1. In *The Misunderstood Child,* Dr. Larry B. Silver says that the human brain goes through major growth spurts during five time periods. Those periods are the following between three and ten months between two and four years between six and eight years between ten and 12 years and between 14 and 16 years.

2. Santa's eight tiny reindeer are Dasher Dancer Prancer Vixen Comet Cupid Donner and Blitzen.

3. These are the seven wonders of the ancient world the Great Pyramid of Cheops the Hanging Gardens of Babylon the Tomb of King Mausolus at Halicarnassus the Temple of Artemis the Colossus of Rhodes the Statue of Zeus at Olympia and the lighthouse on the Isle of Pharos.

4. Most of us would probably call a flock of birds a flock of birds. But those who want to be more precise might use one of these terms a bevy of quail a muster of peacocks a charm of finches or an exaltation of larks.

5. Charles Blondin, the French acrobat and tightrope walker, crossed Niagara Falls in 1855 1859 and 1860.

6. If a person happened to be named Roy G. Biv, his name would be an acronym for all the colors in the spectrum red orange yellow green blue indigo and violet.

7. The United Kingdom includes England Scotland Wales Northern Ireland the Isle of Man and the Channel Islands.

8. Worcestershire sauce gets its flavor from three main ingredients anchovies soy and tamarinds.

9. Toyko, which is the capital of Japan and also one of the world's largest cities, has at various times been known by these other names Edo Yedo and Yeddo.

10. Martha Graham, one of the great American dancers of all time, choreographed "Primitive Mysteries," "Appalachian Spring," "Deaths and Entrances," and "Clytemnestra." One critic says that Martha Graham opened up three new areas of dance dance as technique for training the body dance as theatrical presentation and dance as philosophy.

Exercise Four

Directions: Choosing from the subjects suggested below, write *five* sentences demonstrating your understanding of the colon. Use your own paper, please. Remember that you need a complement before the items in the list.

(a) your most highly valued personal possessions
(b) your three or four favorite holidays
(c) your favorite television shows when you were a little kid
(d) the academic courses you're most looking forward to taking
(e) your own or someone else's bad habits
(f) your heroes
(g) improvements you want to make in your own life
(h) first names that are very popular now or were popular in your parents' day

Exercise Five

Directions: Turn back to Chapter 3, Unit 4, Exercise One (pages 102–103). Choose five sentences from Exercise One and rewrite them on your own paper, changing the wording so that a colon is appropriate.

A Common Error—Important!—Don't Skip

One very common error is to use a colon after the word *including* or after *such as.* These situations, however, do not call for colons. The word *including* or the expression *such as* is really better viewed as the start of an "end phrase" or, in other words, a phrase following a clause (see Chapter 3, Unit 3, pages 97–102). Look at these correct examples:

(a) J. B. Rhine of Duke University has conducted scientific studies of various aspects of parapsychology, **including** clairvoyance, extrasensory perception, psychokinesis, and telepathy.

(b) J. B. Rhine of Duke University has conducted scientific studies of various aspects of parapsychology, **such as** clairvoyance, extrasensory perception, psychokinesis, and telepathy.

You should *not* use a colon in (a) and (b). Try rewriting the sentence about J. B. Rhine so that a colon is appropriate. If this is still not quite clear to you, ask your writing teacher for more examples. Then punctuate sentences (c) through (f):

(c) These are the seven deadly sins anger covetousness envy gluttony lust pride and sloth.

(d) He committed each and every one of the seven deadly sins anger covetousness envy gluttony lust pride and sloth.

(e) She committed a number of the seven deadly sins including anger envy lust and sloth.

(f) Of the seven deadly sins, they had their own personal favorites such as gluttony lust and sloth.

[*Answers.* (c) sins: anger, covetousness, envy, gluttony, lust, pride, and sloth. (d) sins: anger, covetousness, envy, gluttony, lust, pride, and sloth. (e) sins, including anger, envy, lust, and sloth. (f) favorites, such as gluttony, lust, and sloth.]

Another Use for the Colon

There is another way to use the colon, but if you still have difficulty with *any* of the other rules of punctuation, you should skip this brief section. This is a low priority compared with the other rules, and it will *not* be included in the cumulative exercises in the next unit. But for many writers, it is a valuable sentence-combining technique, so that is why we are presenting it here.

The colon can be used in this way:

Stephen Potter's *Gamesmanship* has an interesting subtitle: *The Art of Winning Games Without Actually Cheating.*

Mark the clause before the colon with *S*, *V* or *VP*, and *C*. You see that we do have a complement—*subtitle*—just as we always have a complement when we are using the colon before a list. But here we're not setting up for a list; we're setting up for an *explanation of the word in the complement position*. The *subtitle* is explained by the words that follow the colon.

When you make this kind of a sentence, you don't capitalize the first word after the colon unless the explanation is a full sentence. If the explanation, the part after the colon, is a full sentence, you have the option of capitalizing the first word or leaving it lowercase.

Mark these sentences *S*, *V* or *VP*, and *C* and insert a colon where needed:

(a) We discovered one surprising fact there is more protein in a pound of peanuts than in a pound of steak.

(b) When the word *Shanghai* is not capitalized, it does not refer to a city. The word *shanghai* has another meaning to kidnap a person for forced service aboard a ship.

(c) Ann Landers and Abigail Van Buren have a lot in common they are twin sisters who both write advice columns.

(d) In common law, there is one basic difference between libel and slander libel is written, printed, or broadcast by television or radio, and slander is only spoken.

(e) The Chinese symbol for *crisis*, which is made up of two picture characters, reveals an intriguing understanding of the word one picture character means danger, and the other means opportunity.

(f) England's Queen Elizabeth enjoys two birthdays one is her real birthdate in April, and the other is the official celebration of the event in June, which is marked by a ceremony called the Trooping of the Colour.

(g) At a traditional church wedding, it is customary for the bride to take her father's right arm as she walks down the aisle. There is a practical reason for this the father is thus ensured of reaching the front pew on the left side, which is usually reserved for the bride's family and friends, without crossing his daughter's train.

UNIT 8: Cumulative Review of Commas, Semicolons, and Colons

This unit is a series of exercises that ask you to use all the information you've learned and all the skills you've acquired in Chapter 3.

Review all the rules and guidelines before beginning the exercises. As you did earlier, rephrase the rules from each unit here:

From Unit 1: _____

_____

_____

_____

_____

_____

From Unit 2: _____

_____

_____

_____

_____

_____

From Unit 3: _____

_____

_____

_____

_____

_____

From Unit 4: _____

_____

_____

_____

_____

_____

From Unit 5: (Cite the comma rules used in cities and states and in dates.)

_____

_____

_____

_____

From Unit 6: _____

_____

_____

_____

_____

From Unit 7: (Cite the colon rule for lists only. Remember, as we explained in Unit 7, the colon as it is used in explanations is not included in the following exercises.)

_____

_____

_____

_____

A Preliminary Exercise

Directions: Make up a sentence that has two "chunks" of information. For example, something like this compound sentence would do fine: *William went to the party, and he wore his best clothes.* Then see how many different ways you can rewrite it, using various forms of sentence combining and as many punctuation rules as possible from Chapter 3. For instance, you could create these sentences and many others:

(a) William went to the party, wearing his best clothes.

(b) Wearing his best clothes, William went to the party.

(c) William went to the party; he wore his best clothes.

(d) William, who went to the party, wore his best clothes.

(e) The man who was in the good-looking clothes was on his way to a party.

(f) Because he was going to a party, William wore his best clothes.

(g) William wore his best clothes because he was going to a party.

You could also add information to enable yourself to practice other rules. For instance, you might come up with something like this:

(h) William went to the party in Missoula, Montana, on November 7, 1986, dressed in his best clothes.

Although these sentences might seem a little simple, our students have found this type of exercise to be a very effective way of reviewing different sentence combinations and related punctuation rules.

If you need an idea for your two chunks of information, how about *Laura drove to the show in Birmingham and took all the kids in the neighborhood with her*?

A Few Important Words about the Exercises

In these exercises, you will be using *commas, colons,* and *semicolons.* Commas, of course, will be used most frequently because the comma has so many different functions. Not every exercise will call for all three punctuation marks. For example, you might go through an entire ten-sentence exercise without using a single colon. In another exercise, however, you might use two or three colons.

Some sentences will call for no punctuation.

Some sentences will lend themselves to more than one interpretation or more than one method of punctuation. These sentences should be discussed in class after you do each exercise.

If punctuation is needed to introduce a direct quote, it will already be supplied for you. As we noted earlier, you'll learn how to do it in the next chapter.

Use the labels *S, V* or *VP,* and *C* where labeling the key parts of the kernel is helpful to you.

Finally, *mark up the book*! Most often, if you take a look at the books of students who are really improving in their writing, you find that those books are completely marked up with notes, labels, underlinings, and symbols. The marks give testimony to a lot of hard work and show that those students are making the information their own. Develop a system—whether it's circling conjunctions, drawing wavy lines under embedded clauses, or whatever—and use it. And when you're stuck on a particular sentence, if you can't figure it out, put a question mark in the margin and move on.

As usual, to get the most out of the exercises, please correct each one (or each ten-item part) and discuss any questions before continuing.

Exercise One

PART A

Directions: Use *commas, semicolons,* and *colons* where they are needed.

1. *Sea of Slaughter* which was published recently by Atlantic Monthly Press was written by Farley Mowat.

2. Mowat who is a Canadian is a naturalist and a writer.

3. Focusing on the northern part of the Atlantic seaboard Mowat examines the history of man's relationship with wildlife since the first Europeans arrived on this continent.

4. Although Farley Mowat's research is limited to one geographical area his conclusions can be said to hold true for the entire continent of North America.

5. According to the author human beings have meant almost nothing but death for the mammals birds and fish of North America in fact Mowat estimates that the entire "biomass" has been reduced by perhaps as much as 95 percent through human destruction.

6. Animals have been "overkilled" basically for three reasons economic recreational and scientific.

7. Economic reasons include the killing of animals for meat hides and fur.

8. Some species have survived but they have survived only with great difficulty for example the wolf the Plains buffalo and the grizzly bear were depleted by the millions because of wanton slaughter by human beings.

9. Other animals such as the passenger pigeon the sea mink and the Eastern buffalo are gone forever driven into extinction by the planet's supposedly most intelligent creatures.

10. These are harsh tragic realities and they are not only a matter of history animals continue to die for sport for fashion for food and for experimentation.

PART B

Directions: Use *commas, semicolons,* and *colons* where they are needed.

1. *Sea of Slaughter* a substantial book of more than 400 pages points out that human beings destroy their own rich history when they destroy any part of the natural world.

2. Many people for example believe that the great auk was a myth.

3. Farley Mowat assures us that this fascinating bird which could dive to a depth of 300 feet and stay underwater for a quarter of an hour did exist.

4. While the great auk once numbered 100 million its natural enemies numbered only one.

5. That enemy of course was deadly it was man.

6. Mowat also reminds us that the whale once one of the most stable of all life forms is now in danger of disappearing from the planet.

7. The author sees only one animal that has succeeded in thriving against all odds and that is the coyote.

8. Mowat credits the coyote for being adaptable and for being just plain smart.

9. Lamenting man's role as a predator Mowat concludes that there is some hope for the future but the best hope lies in aware and sensitive individuals not in massive organizations.

10. Although books like *Sea of Slaughter* are rare they can make important headway in forming those sensitive aware human beings. As Robert W. Smith said in a review of Mowat's publication it "deserves to stand with Rachel Carson's *Silent Spring* as an outstanding indictment of man's stupidity in alienating himself from nature."

Exercise Two

Directions: Use *commas*, *semicolons*, and *colons* where they are needed.

1. When her father sued the local board of education Linda Brown was in the sixth grade in Topeka Kansas.

2. Her father the Reverend Oliver Brown brought suit against the Topeka Board of Education because he believed that his daughter was receiving an inferior education.

3. The neighborhood school was only four blocks from the Brown home but that particular school was for whites only.

4. Linda Brown however was not white she was black.

5. Because she was black Linda Brown was bused to a school two miles away.

6. Kansas like 16 other states at the time required racially segregated schooling.

7. These states did not simply allow a system of segregated education they actually required it.

8. In doing so these states were following an 1896 ruling of the U.S. Supreme Court that ruling affirmed the famous "separate but equal" doctrine.

9. Focusing on the issue of equality the Brown family argued that the school system for black children was clearly inferior to the system for white children.

10. On May 17 1954 the U.S. Supreme Court ruled in favor of the Brown family it declared that racially segregated public education was unconstitutional in the United States.

Directions: Use *commas*, *semicolons*, and *colons* where they are needed.

1. Earl Warren who was Chief Justice of the U.S. Supreme Court at the time wrote the landmark opinion.

2. In it Warren asked if the very notion of separate but equal was not bound to deprive black children of their rights even assuming that factors such as physical facilities could be equal.

3. Chief Justice Warren asked this question and he answered it in the affirmative.

4. Speaking for the Supreme Court Warren wrote that the act of separating black children from other children of similar age and qualifications "generates a feeling of inferiority as to their status in the community that may affect their hearts and minds in a way unlikely ever to be undone."

5. In other words the Court established the idea that educational systems could not be equal if they were separate therefore the Court ordered the Topeka schools to be desegregated "with all deliberate speed."

6. Although *Brown* v. *the Topeka Board of Education* was a landmark decision that has had an enormous impact on American education some people question the speed with which desegregation has been accomplished in Kansas and elsewhere across the nation.

7. Linda Brown who is now Linda Brown Smith recently told an interviewer, *"Brown* was a necessary victory but it was not the quick fix we thought it would be."

8. A woman of extraordinary persistence Linda Brown Smith was one of eight parents who petitioned to reopen the *Brown* case in 1979 a full quarter century after it began.

9. Brown the mother of two children and still a resident of Topeka claimed that nothing had really changed since the U.S. Supreme Court had ruled in her favor in 1954.

10. While the litigation continues an amazing symmetry takes shape. Linda Brown Smith and the other parents are currently represented by attorney Charles Scott,

Jr., whose father had represented Brown's father in the original case in 1954. Back then Charles Scott, Jr., was a little first-grader in an all-black Topeka school.

Exercise Three

PART A

Directions: Add *commas, semicolons,* and *colons* where they are needed below.

1. The man who eventually became the first president of the United States was an extremely wealthy individual.

2. George Washington accumulated a great deal of wealth by the fruits of his own labor he also happened to marry a very rich widow.

3. Martha Washington who later became the nation's original first lady was once married to Daniel Parke Custis.

4. After having established himself as one of the wealthiest planters in Virginia Daniel Parke Custis died in 1757 at the age of 45.

5. Although Custis left no will colonial law dictated how his personal property and his real estate were to be divided.

6. Martha Dandrige Custis as she was known at the time inherited one third of what had belonged to her deceased husband their two children John Parke and Martha Parke Custis inherited the remaining two thirds.

7. The three heirs of Daniel Parke Custis were Martha Dandrige Custis John Parke Custis and Martha Parke. Custis.

8. The heirs of Daniel Parke Custis included Martha Dandrige Custis John Parke Custis and Martha Parke Custis.

9. Daniel Park Custis had three heirs Martha Dandrige Custis John Parke Custis and Martha Parke Custis.

10. The widow's inheritance which amounted to 29,650 pounds in colonial Virginia currency would equal roughly $6 million today.

PART B

Directions: Add *commas, semicolons,* and *colons* where they are needed below.

1. That figure of $6 million however does not include the value of more than 17,000 acres of plantation land that she and her children also received as a legacy from Mr. Custis.

2. When the young George Washington began to court this well-to-do widow in her midtwenties she was the mistress of White House plantation on the Pamunkey River in New Kent County and one of the wealthiest people in the colony of Virginia.

3. All this information recently came to light when one of George Washington's ledgers was found in a vault at Washington and Lee University.

4. The faded discolored pages of the ledger created a great deal of interest especially for scholars and history buffs.

5. W. W. Abbot a University of Virginia historian and editor of *The Papers of George Washington* has said that this discovery is very important in fact he believes that it is the most important addition to information about George Washington to come along in more than a generation.

6. Before the ledger was put away for safekeeping at Washington and Lee it had been buried with other family treasures ever since the Civil War.

7. The document consisting of 36 leaves from an account book is a formal record of the way that the Custis estate was settled in addition it details Washington's assumption of guardianship over his stepchildren.

8. This documentation is important to scholars because the official legal papers that concerned these matters were burned at the end of the Civil War.

9. At the time of the discovery scholars were planning to take the ledger to the Center

for Conservation of Art and Historic Artifacts hoping to be able to make additional passages readable.

10. At the Center for Conservation of Art and Historic Artifacts which is located in Philadelphia Pennsylvania highly skilled experts in book conservation will attempt to eliminate some of the green and violet mold that makes certain passages in the ledger unreadable.

Exercise Four

PART A

Directions: Use *commas, semicolons,* and *colons* where they are needed.

1. Women who have strong relationships with their sisters are very fortunate.

2. According to experts in family dynamics these women share a special bond.

3. Dr. Stephen P. Bank a psychology professor and a coauthor of *The Sibling Bond* says that the strength of any relationship between siblings is largely determined by "access."

4. By the word *access* he means three things closeness in age mutual experiences and shared gender.

5. The "mutual experiences" might include attending the same schools having some of the same friends and sharing childhood hobbies or interests.

6. Although brothers can also be very close some experts have suggested that there is often a special quality about the bond between sisters.

7. Not surprisingly a certain degree of rivalry exists between some sisters but even difficult relationships often become smoother and more satisfying as time passes.

8. Dr. Victor G. Ciccerelli a psychology professor at Purdue University asked a number of middle-aged and elderly siblings to describe their relationships.

9. Sixty-eight percent of the siblings who were 30 to 60 years old classified their relationships as "close" or "very close."

10. Eighty-three percent of the siblings who were 60 or older however described their relationships in the same way.

PART B

Directions: Use *commas, semicolons,* and *colons* where they are needed.

1. Growing out of fixed childhood roles is a necessary step in building a good relationship with any sibling.

2. Some siblings never abandon early labels such as "the good-looking one" "the smart one" "the athletic one" or "the musical one."

3. Their relationships tend to become stuck in first gear because of the pain created by those labels.

4. According to experts from the field of psychology people who feel inferior to a sister or brother should increase their own self-confidence by developing their strengths.

5. If two people can relate as equals they are much more likely to find their relationship comfortable and beneficial.

6. *Sisters* which was written by Elizabeth Fishel and published by William Morrow includes fascinating material about celebrities and their sisters.

7. England's Queen Elizabeth for example is described as very supportive of her spirited younger sister the monarch has explained that she can tolerate in Princess Margaret certain emotions that she has to suppress in herself.

8. Margaret Mead the famous anthropologist recalled her younger sister as the only artist in a family of scholars and intellectuals and she told Fishel that she loved her sister because the younger woman's differences were a source of great delight.

9. The final word however may belong to the French actress Catherine Deneuve whose sister Françoise was killed in an automobile accident.

10. Deneuve said of herself and Françoise, "You will never truly know me until you understand my sister."

Exercise Five

PART A

Directions: Use *commas, semicolons,* and *colons* where they are needed.

1. If you are like most people you at least occasionally have the feeling that you are "faking it" or bluffing your way through a particular situation.

2. Some people however feel this way most of the time.

3. Pauline Rose Clance a psychologist at Georgia State University and Suzanne Imes who is in private practice in Atlanta Georgia have studied people who feel that they are faking it in their professional lives.

4. After interviewing more than 150 such people Clance and Imes coined the term *impostor phenomenon* to describe this condition.

5. People who suffer from the impostor phenomenon usually experience depression anxiety and frustration however they do not suffer from a low self-image in the usual sense.

6. They tend to be high achievers and they know that they command the respect and have the admiration of others.

7. In fact many self-accused "impostors" do give themselves credit for being successful worthy individuals in certain areas of their lives.

8. But these high achievers don't feel that they deserve the success they have experienced professionally consequently in the world of work they feel they are fakes.

9. Overlooking their own intelligence and professional skill they tend to focus on other explanations for their accomplishments.

10. "Impostors" often believe that they have achieved success through other means such as luck hard work good looks or well-developed social graces.

PART B

Directions: Use *commas, semicolons,* and *colons* where they are needed.

1. Psychologist Joan Harvey who is from the University of Pennsylvania School of Medicine has divided self-accused impostors into categories and these are four of the most important ones charmers shrinking violets workaholics and magical thinkers.

2. Charmers are physically attractive and well practiced in the social graces and they attribute their success to those superficial factors completely ignoring their own competence and hard work.

3. Shrinking violets afraid of appearing arrogant or "getting above themselves" criticize and undervalue their own work even when it's highly praised by their employers.

4. Viewing themselves as mediocre or even stupid workaholics attribute all their success to hard work and hard work alone.

5. Perhaps Harvey's strangest impostors are the magical thinkers because they superstitiously believe that fate will punish them if they enjoy their success or believe they're really responsible for it.

6. While some high achievers derive a great deal of pleasure from their professional success and believe they have a right to it others are not able to do so. Why not?

7. The psychologists who study this problem say that it seems to occur in successful people of all ages and both sexes but they have learned that it is especially prevalent among people who are extremely shy.

8. Although not all shy achievers are impostors those who experienced impostor

feelings most acutely were also the most introverted people among the research subjects.

9. Another cause might be inconsistent feedback for example a child might have been praised by teachers but criticized or ignored by his or her parents.

10. One other possible cause is that the impostor has achieved in areas that were not typical for his or her family in general for example a man whose family has been in the wholesale food business for generations might doubt his own worthiness and talent as a sculptor.

Exercises in Context

The five remaining exercises are opportunities to practice punctuation and recognition of sentence patterns in the context of larger pieces of writing. Please take your time because these exercises can help to form a valuable bridge from success in workbook exercises to improvement in your own writing.

Exercise Six

PART A

Directions: Use *commas, semicolons,* and *colons* where they are needed.

There was a time when plastic jewelry was out now it's back in. And what's most in 1

is bold vibrant jewelry that was formed from Bakelite the first entirely man-made mate- 2

rial. 3

   Bakelite is a tradename that was coined in 1908 by Dr. Leo H. Baekeland a 4

chemist. Bakelite jewelry is as a matter of fact an accidental by-product of an effort to 5

find a superior material for electrical insulation. Made from carbolic acid and formalde- 6

hyde this material will not remelt once it is formed. Unlike earlier plastics Bakelite is a 7

complex polymer that will not revert to a resinous state when it is subjected to heat 8

therefore it was considered the perfect material for the insulation of electrical wiring. 9

   Because it was such a strong plastic manufacturers of many types of products 10

found Bakelite to be extremely useful. It was molded into all kinds of things ranging from 11 steering wheels to teething rings. Telephone receivers were often formed of Bakelite   12

and thousands of other common household items were too.   13

But certainly the most famous product is Bakelite jewelry which can often be found   14

in bright shades of red black green and butterscotch yellow. (Pastel pieces exist but they   15

are very rare consequently they are also very expensive.) Bakelite jewelry which sold   16

for anything from a couple of quarters to a few dollars during the Great Depression and   17

the years immediately afterward has become a hot collector's item in the 1980s. Earlier   18

Gabrielle "Coco" Chanel the legendary French dress designer did much to popularize   19

Bakelite jewelry among the wealthy. Women who could easily have afforded much   20

more expensive jewelry started to buy and wear Bakelite necklaces bracelets and pins   21

when they saw similar items on Chanel's runway and magazine layout models. Before   22

Chanel showed her designs worn with obviously fake jewels couture clothing had   23

always been shown with precious gems such as diamonds emeralds rubies sapphires   24

and pearls. In fact if you would like to see an example of Bakelite jewelry here's what   25

you do. First go to the bound periodical section of your college or university library then   26

look up the April 28 1941 issue of *Life* magazine. The woman who's pictured on the   27

cover is wearing a large red Bakelite heart and key padlock pin on her wool jacket.   28

PART B

Directions: Use *commas, semicolons,* and *colons* where they are needed.

Like the "key to my heart" pin many pieces of Bakelite plastic jewelry were formed in   1

whimsical playful patterns. Some typical pieces include facsimiles of certain edibles   2

bananas cherries apples pickles and sections of oranges and watermelons. Bakelite   3

pieces tend to be big and chunky and they are usually realistic images of common items.   4

Bakelite which is heavier than ordinary plastic was molded and carved into the shapes   5

of dogs horses megaphones and cowboy boots. You might find earrings in the shape   6

of champagne glasses and pins in the shape of ladies' hats. If you happen to be in the 7
market for a ring that looks like a fire hydrant you might just find it in Bakelite. 8

You might find it but can you afford to buy it? That's another question. Like 9
depression-era tableware Bakelite jewelry has become so much in demand and so 10
expensive that it's hard to find an affordable piece. But a bargain can be had assuming 11
that you have the time and the inclination to visit enough flea markets and garage sales. 12
You can also find Bakelite pieces for sale at art deco galleries but you'll pay a pretty 13
penny for your own little bit of Americana. According to the experts the Northeast is 14
the best source for Bakelite but pieces can be found in the Midwest and the West too. 15

Let's assume that you find a piece and you can afford it. When you get it home 16
you can test it to see if you have the real thing or just plain old everyday plastic. 17
(Unfortunately most sellers will be reluctant to let you try this test before you make your 18
purchase.) You heat the tip of a pin until it's red-hot then you try to penetrate your 19
bracelet earring pin or whatever. (You of course will have chosen an inconspicuous spot 20
for the test.) If the tip of the pin does not penetrate your "find" you have Bakelite. If 21
it does let's hope you didn't pay too much. 22

Exercise Seven
Directions: Use *commas, semicolons,* and *colons* where they are needed.

After she had completed her first term in drama school in New York City she was told 1
that she had no talent and was asked to leave. When she won her first starring role in 2
a play and her performance was reviewed in the *New York Tribune* the critic said, 3
"Anyone who looks like that and acts like that must get off the stage." Nevertheless 4
she did have talent in fact she had great talent. And she never did get off the stage not 5
until her death at the age of 88. She was the sparkling the hilarious the indomitable Ruth 6
Gordon.

Ruth Gordon achieved her greatest fame through her role as Maude in the 1971 ·8

movie *Harold and Maude*. Her fame however did not come quickly. *Harold and Maude* 9

was a box office flop when it first opened. But the movie became something of a cult 10

film with college students and it finally showed a profit 12 years after its release. In the 11

film Ruth Gordon playing an old woman whose tattooed forearm recalls her years in 12

a Nazi concentration camp embodies the ultimate survivor. Filled with an exuberant 13

disdain for convention Maude has a love affair with 19-year-old Harold who easily could 14

have been her grandson. Harold whose unsuccessful attempts at self-destruction give 15

the movie its famous black humor learns from Maude how to live in the moment. 16

Living in the moment is something that came naturally to Ruth Gordon who often 17

said that the character of Maude was in reality more like her true self than any other 18

role she had played in the movies or on the stage. (She also won a certain amount of 19

fame and an Oscar for her portrayal of the devil-worshipping neighbor in *Rosemary's* 20

Baby.) Born Ruth Gordon Jones in Quincy Massachusetts on October 30 1896 she said 21

that her father who was a sea captain hoped that his daughter would grow up to 22

become a physical education teacher. But that's not what the captain's daughter had 23

in mind. After her first trip to Boston to see the play *The Pink Lady* she had no doubts 24

about her calling in life she was destined to become an actress. 25

Ruth Gordon also had another calling. In 1942 she married Garson Kanin who was 26

16 years her junior and together they became one of the classic American playwriting 27

teams. Both were capable of producing hits on their own. For example at the time of ·28

their wedding Gordon was writing a comedy called *Over 21* which turned out to be 29

a big success. Kanin created several comedies that made a star of Judy Holliday 30

including *Born Yesterday The Solid Gold Cadillac* and *Bells Are Ringing*. But they are 31

most famous for their collaborations especially *Adam's Rib* and *Pat and Mike*. Those 32

famous films were wonderful vehicles for Katharine Hepburn and Spencer Tracy an- 33
other great theatrical couple. 34

Ruth Gordon led a full active life inspiring others to hang in there for the long haul. 35
Accepting an award for one of her many performances she once got perhaps the most 36
appreciative heartfelt laugh of her long career. The ever-optimistic survivor well into her 37
eighties at the time marched to the podium looked out upon the faces of actors and 38
actresses who were decades younger than she held her award high and said, "I can't 39
tell you how encouraging this is for me." 40

Exercise Eight

Directions: Use *commas, semicolons,* and *colons* where they are needed.

Certain products however humble are considered "top of the line." So it is with the 1
often imitated but never duplicated Swiss army knife. Invented by Carl Elsener the first 2
Swiss army knife had a variety of built-in features two cutting blades a screwdriver a 3
can opener a reamer and a corkscrew. Originally called the *Offiziersmesser* ("officer's 4
knife") it was patented in 1897. 5

That was the very first Swiss army knife but the best of all is the Champion. The 6
Champion's design is so economical and so superb that it is included in a collection of 7
exceptionally well designed functional objects at the Museum of Modern Art in New 8
York. It weighs less than 160 grams and it fits neatly into the palm of the hand. The 9
Champion's excellence however is no accident. There are 348 separate steps in the 10
making of each Champion Swiss army knife. The most dramatic is the thorough testing 11
of each knife by one of the Swiss company's 800 employees he or she must open and 12
close every blade on every knife at a dizzying rate of speed without drawing blood. 13

Because there are so many cheap imitations the buyer must beware. If you can 14
afford a Swiss army knife and you want to be sure that you're getting the real thing 15

check your knife to see that it is stamped with the following words "VICTORINOX 16

SWITZERLAND" "STAINLESS" and "ROSTFREI." 17

Exercise Nine

Directions: Use *commas, semicolons,* and *colons* where they are needed.

We've all heard the expression *nuclear winter* but what exactly is meant by the term? 1

Although it is a very complex and controversial topic this much can be said. In the 2

aftermath of a nuclear war or a major nuclear exchange it is likely that the climate of 3

the earth would be dramatically affected. Particles of smoke resulting from fires burning 4

on the surface of the earth would rise and fill the upper atmosphere. In a short period 5

of time the smoke could be well distributed around the globe. If enough smoke is 6

produced it could block the sun this in turn would cause a cooling of the lower atmo- 7

sphere that could last for weeks or months. This desolate season would be a nuclear 8

winter. 9

Assuming that the sun would be severely obscured for a long enough period of time 10

some scientists predict that most living things on this planet would die. Nobody knows 11

how long a nuclear winter would last or exactly what its features would be everybody 12

knows that it must be avoided. Many scientists believe that the best hope for avoiding 13

this grim scenario lies in learning everything possible about what a nuclear winter would 14

entail. 15

Researchers at the University of Chicago think that we might be able to learn a lot 16

about what a nuclear winter would be like by studying how the dinosaurs met their 17

demise 65 million years ago. The possible connection was first discovered when a 18

graduate student Wendy Wolbach was examining sediments that are known to have 19

been laid down around the time of the dinosaurs' disappearance from the earth. Wol- 20

bach examining rocks with a scanning electron microscope that magnifies an image to 21

60,000 times its actual size realized that her rock samples were actually soot. The soot according to an article in a recent issue of *Science* magazine very likely resulted from a massive global fire. The global fire was in turn the result of a meteorite that crashed into the earth very possibly into suboceanic rock beneath the Bering Sea.

If this hypothesis is correct the fire that resulted was so enormous that it might have created an almost unimaginable amount of soot. The soot which would have absorbed sunlight more readily than dust could have caused the skies to darken. With the skies blackened the process of photosynthesis would have been stopped and the food chain that had supported the giant reptiles would have been broken. If a meteorite which is typically about six miles across did slam into the planet there would have been two other results toxic gases would have enveloped the earth and average temperatures would have dropped 20 to 60 degrees. This scenario which has been called a "natural nuclear winter" can serve as a preview of the likely effects of a nuclear war or massive nuclear accident in the twentieth century or beyond. Let's hope we can learn from the past.

Chapter 4
Revising Sentences

This chapter is about four different kinds of sentences that, from time to time, might need revision in your writing. Each unit is completely separate and independent of the other three units in the chapter. So if, for example, it's certain that you have no problems with dangling modifiers, you might be able to proceed directly to Unit 2. If you have any doubts about whether or not you need a particular unit, ask the advice of your teacher.

UNIT 1: Dangling Modifiers

In Chapter 3, Unit 3, you learned to punctuate sentences that have *introductory phrases*. In this unit, you'll learn to make sure that the introductory phrase that you set off with a comma really describes what it's supposed to describe—the subject of the main clause or the action of the subject. If the introductory phrase modifies some other word in the sentence (or a word that doesn't even appear in the sentence), then the introductory phrase is called a **dangling modifier.** A sentence that has a dangling modifier is a weak, awkward, illogical-sounding sentence.

Here's an example:

1. **Employed as a weekend weatherman on an Indianapolis TV station,** hailstones as big as canned hams were once predicted by David Letterman.

The subject of the sentence is the word *hailstones.* Whatever introductory phrase is attached to the sentence before the subject must describe the subject or the action of the subject. But the modifier in sentence 1 obviously is supposed to describe *David Letterman,* not hailstones or anything that hailstones could do. To see if an introductory phrase is well attached or if it's dangling, ask yourself a question like this: Can the word *hailstones* (your subject) be described as *employed as a weekend weatherman on an Indianapolis TV station* (your introductory phrase)? If it can, then you're okay. If it can't, then you have a dangling modifier.

149

Once you know you have a dangling modifier, there is usually more than one good way of revising it. Here are some correct rewrites for sentence 1:

(a)   Employed as a weekend weatherman on an Indianapolis TV station, David Letterman once predicted hailstones as big as canned hams.

(b)   David Letterman, who once worked as a weekend weatherman on an Indianapolis TV station, predicted hailstones as big as canned hams.

(c)   Hailstones as big as canned hams were once predicted by an Indianapolis TV station's weekend weatherman, who was none other than David Letterman.

Here is another sentence that has a dangling modifier. Please underline the dangling introductory phrase and write *S* over the subject of the sentence:

2.   Demonstrating his willingness to do practically anything for a laugh, viewers of his *Late Night* television show once had the pleasure of watching a potato chip–covered David Letterman lowered into an enormous vat of dip.

First, find the subject of the sentence as it is written above. Write the subject here:

_____ . Then ask yourself if that subject can be described by the introductory phrase. Complete this question: Can _____ be described as _____

_____

_____ ?

If you performed the test correctly, you asked, Can *viewers* (your subject) be described as *demonstrating his willingness to do practically anything for a laugh*? And the answer is *no*. It's *not* the viewers who demonstrated his willingness to do practically anything for a laugh. So the sentence has a dangling modifier. Please correct sentence 2 by rewriting it in three different ways:

(a)   _____

_____

_____

(b)   _____

_____

_____

(c)   _____

_____

_____

Exercise One

Directions: We'll start with an exercise that gives you introductory phrases. All you have to do is write short sentences so that the introductory modifiers are well attached, not dangling. Remember that each introductory phrase has to describe the subject or the action of the subject.

1. Leaving for the hospital in a hurry, _____

_____

2. Practicing four hours a day, _____

_____

3. Having been brought up by very strict parents, _____

_____

4. Promoted by a tasteless advertising campaign, _____

_____

5. Intended to reduce swelling, _____

_____

6. Describing her friend in glowing terms, _____

_____

7. Satisfied with the decision of the court, _____

_____

8. Caused by years of silence, _____

_____

9. Being a kindhearted, generous child, _____

_____

10. Topped off with whipped cream and a maraschino cherry, _____

_____

Remember to correct each exercise and discuss any problems before going on.

Exercise Two

Directions: Label each item *OK* or *DM* (dangling modifier). Then rewrite the sentences that contain dangling modifiers; try to use a variety of sentence-combining techniques as you do your rewrites in all the exercises. Use your own paper, please. This exercise and all similar exercises in the unit will be easier to do if you underline the introductory modifier and label the subject S before you make your decision. The information here is found in *Life-spans, Or, How Long Things Last,* by Frank Kendig and Richard Hutton.

1. _____ Refrigerated at the proper temperature, beer can be stored a maximum of three months; after that, it often has a buttery or papery taste.

2. _____ Wrapped individually in plastic or foil, hard candies and caramels can last anywhere from three to 12 months at room temperature.

3. _____ Cared for properly, the U.S. Army estimates that an M-1 rifle should last 10,000 rounds.

4. _____ Currently about four to five billion years old, scientists believe that the sun has a life span of ten billion years.

5. _____ Stored in a closed container in a cool place, loose tea and tea bags can be kept about 18 months before they begin to get stale.

6. _____ Performed upon average skin, plastic surgeons estimate that a successful face lift should last from six to ten years.

7. _____ Formed in the atmosphere within a period of ten minutes, experts estimate that a snowflake can last as little as ten minutes or as long as centuries.

8. _____ Describing the bra he created for Jane Russell, Howard Hughes claimed that it was made according to the same engineering principles as a suspension bridge and was designed to last just about as long.

9. _____ Used in practice only, an NFL (National Football League) football has a life span of two to three days.

10. _____ Used in an NFL game, a ball's life span is estimated to be six minutes of actual playing time. (How is this calculated? The authors of _Life-spans_ point out that the home team must provide 24 new balls for each game; of these, eight to 12 are normally used in a single game, then thrown out, given away, or reserved for practice.)

Exercise Three

Directions: As in Exercise One, write short sentences so that these introductory phrases are well attached.

1. Made from scratch, _____

_____

2. Restrained by handcuffs and manacles, _____

_____

3. Calculated to appeal to teenage moviegoers, _____

_____

4. Seasoned with loads of garlic and paprika, _____

_____

5. Having become first-time parents in their early forties, _____

_____

6. Being a curious little cat, _____

_____

7. Taking her final vows after many years of preparation, _____

_____

8. Reassuring all the new students in his class, _____

_____

9. Controlled entirely by computers, _____

_____

10. Appearing in the sky only once every 75 to 76 years, _____

_____

Exercise Four

Directions: Label each item *OK* or *DM*. Then rewrite the sentences that have dangling modifiers. Use your own paper, please.

These tidbits are from *Joan Embery's Collection of Amazing Animal Facts.*

1. _____ Weighing up to 32 ounces, Southeast Asia is the home of the world's largest bat, whose wingspan has been measured at five feet seven.

2. _____ Having no bark at all, the basenji dog of Africa makes the perfect hunting dog.

3. _____ Extremely long-lived, it is known that swans can survive up to 100 years. (Zoologists observed one swan who reached the age of 102.)

4. _____ Thought to be the heaviest insect in the world, the goliath beetle, which can weigh almost a quarter of a pound, has been observed peeling a banana while in captivity.

5. _____ Lacking the normal reddish orange coloring, some zoos have black and white Bengal tigers, all of whom are descendants of a single white male tiger named Bohan, who was found in a jungle in India around the middle of this century.

6. _____ Coated with a sticky mucus, a woodpecker's tongue is barbed for more efficient extraction of insects and grubs from the bark of trees.

7. _____ Commonly used in medicine before the twentieth century, doctors often placed maggots on wounds because the maggots would consume dead tissue and leave healthy tissue alone; that, of course, allowed for quicker healing and reduced the risk of infection.

8. _____ Being larger than the males in most cases, packs of hyenas are

led by the females.

9. _____ Having 900 different muscles in its body, a grasshopper's abil-

ity to jump 500 times its own height amazes scientists who have studied this tiny

creature.

10. _____ Expelling milk into the mouths of their baby calves through the

force of muscular contractions, mother whales use up the large reservoirs that are

stored in their mammary glands.

Exercise Five

Directions: Label each item *OK* or *DM*. Then rewrite the sentences that have dangling modifiers. Use your own paper, please. The facts, though not the dangling
modifiers, can be found in *This Day in Sports* by John G. Fetros.

1. _____ Concerned that the glow from lighted ballparks could endanger

shipping, New York Police Commissioner Lewis Valentine banned night baseball

games in New York in 1942. The ban lasted for the rest of World War II.

2. _____ Completing his trip in less than two months, George Wyman in

1903 became the first man to cross North America on a motorcycle.

3. _____ After starting out with the Harlem Globetrotters, the National

Basketball Association got its first black player in Nat "Sweetwater" Clifton in

1950.

4. _____ Swimming from France to England in 1950 and from England

to France in 1951, the record books show that Florence Chadwick was the first

woman to swim the English Channel in both directions.

5. _____ Hoping to create public awareness and turn it against Nazi

Germany, the Anti-Nazi League announced a boycott in 1937 against all U.S. fights

featuring former heavyweight champion Max Schmeling unless he agreed not to

take his cash prizes back to Germany.

6. _____ Executed by shortstop Neal Ball of the Cleveland Indians, the first unassisted triple play in a modern major league baseball game occurred in a game against Boston in 1909.

7. _____ Earning his place in history for something minuscule but mighty, the golf tee was registered under Patent no. 638,920 by George Grant in 1899.

8. _____ Playing for a $100,000 winner-take-all purse, Billie Jean King's defeat of the self-proclaimed male chauvinist Bobby Riggs was witnessed by 30,492 tennis fans at Houston's Astrodome in 1973.

9. _____ Having pitched one hitless inning, it was amazing to watch Cesar Tovar of the Minnesota Twins then go on to play all the other eight positions in a game against Oakland in 1968. Tovar was the second American League player to play all nine positions in a game.

10. _____ Using the rationale that sports should be a means to health rather than wealth, French professional athletes in the early 1940s were told by sports official Jean Borotra that they must also work at other occupations. He ruled that they could not participate in sports to the exclusion of all other income-producing work.

Exercise Six

Directions: Label each item *OK* or *DM*. Then rewrite the sentences that have dangling modifiers. Use your own paper, please. The information in this exercise is based on the value judgments of Peter Passell and Leonard Ross, who wrote a fascinating little best-seller called *The Best*. Our students tell us that this exercise is harder than most, so please take your time and remember that a challenge is good for the soul.

1. _____ Admitting their love for many of the hundreds of flavors of Baskin-Robbins ice cream, Peter Passell and Leonard Ross, the authors of *The Best*, confessed that mandarin chocolate was their ultimate favorite.

2. _____ Partially covered by glacial remnants of the Ice Age, Passell and Ross decided that Mount McKinley National Park in Alaska is America's best national park.

3. _____ Judged to be the best science fiction novel ever written, Alfred Bester, the author of *The Stars of My Destination* used a number of sci-fi staples in his book; for example, he included a technician trapped in a disabled spaceship and explosives that could be set off by brain waves.

4. _____ Speaking at the University of Kentucky's commencement exercises in 1956, former Vice-President Alben Barkley said, "I would rather sit at the feet of the Lord than dwell in the house of the mighty." Passell and Ross, noting that the esteemed gentleman "thereupon keeled over and died," gave Barkley the award for the best exit line.

5. _____ Displaying animals in their natural settings and completely barring old-fashioned cages, the authors chose the Milwaukee County Zoo as the best zoo in the world.

6. _____ Sniffing their disdain of all other brands, Jif was decreed the best peanut butter anywhere.

7. _____ Filled with high drama and first-rate poetry, the Book of Job deserves to be called the best book in the Bible, according to Passell and Ross.

8. _____ Writing to one of his detractors, Max Reger, a German composer, once explained, "I am sitting in the smallest room in my house. I have your review in front of me. Soon it will be behind me." Passell and Ross, quite understandably, chose Reger's quip as the best put-down of a critic.

9. _____ Set in a small town taken over by aliens, *Invasion of the Body Snatchers* rates as the best horror film ever made.

10. _____ Having created a duplicate of every citizen of the town, it was

the aliens' intention to have a convincing substitute for each member of the com-

munity.

Exercise Seven

Directions: Label each sentence *OK* or *DM.* Then rewrite the sentences that have
dangling modifiers. This also is a challenging exercise. Take your time, especially
in doing your rewrites. Use your own paper, please.

1. _____ Named in honor of a great American essayist, Ralph Waldo

Ellison once acknowledged the role his name played in influencing him to become

a writer.

2. _____ Being great admirers of Ralph Waldo Emerson, Ellison's par-

ents paid tribute to the man of letters by naming their baby boy Ralph Waldo.

3. _____ Unable to see into the future any more clearly than most of us,

Ellison's mother and father had no way of knowing that their tiny baby would

become another great American writer.

4. _____ Hailed as one of the best novels by a black writer and as one

of the best novels by an American writer of any color, Ellison traces an unnamed

protagonist through a series of harrowing adventures in *Invisible Man.*

5. _____ A critique of American culture, *Invisible Man* is a novel that

addresses many more issues than the issue of race.

6. _____ Combining a realistic and a surrealistic or dreamlike style, the

novel examines not only race but also trade unionism, the American Communist

party, and the relationships between men and women within political organiza-

tions.

7. _____ Having been expelled from an unnamed black college in the

South, a journey to New York City is undertaken by the book's central character.

8. _____ Exposed to much that he has never before experienced, it is fascinating to watch how the protagonist of *Invisible Man* becomes wise in the ways of the streets.

9. _____ Thrust into a position of prominence in a seemingly benevolent but truly sinister organization called the Brotherhood, his innocence and integrity are tested in a variety of ways that make for great reading.

10. _____ Being a long and sometimes difficult novel, some readers shy away from a book like *Invisible Man*, but in doing so, they're cheating themselves out of a great deal of excitement, humor, and insight.

UNIT 2: Faulty Parallelism

If you've been told that your writing is sometimes awkward in spots, one problem might be *faulty parallelism*. **Usually when you're writing about a series of things within one sentence, each item in the series should be in the same form as the other items.** If the items are in the same form, you have parallelism in your writing, and that's good. If they are not in the same form, you have faulty parallelism, and that's the problem we're going to work on in this unit.

When we talk about items being in the same form, we're talking about grammatical forms, such as **nouns, verbs, adjectives, adverbs, prepositional phrases**, and **clauses**. Here is an example of faulty parallelism in which it is easy to see that the writer is switching grammatical forms:

> (a) In order to be classified as great, a baseball player must hit with power, a high lifetime batting average is necessary, to field well, be a fast runner, and throwing with strength and precision.

After you read (a) aloud, do the same with (b), which is a good example of parallelism:

> (b) In order to be classified as great, a baseball player must hit with power, achieve a high lifetime batting average, field well, run fast, and throw with strength and precision.

Just by reading it aloud, you can tell that (b) has a nice sound, a flow, a repeated pattern that (a) lacks. By analyzing the structure of (b), you can see that the sentence has those good features because all the parts match in form and because all of them can be read with what we call a "**setup**." The setup in (b) is *a baseball player must.* Notice that each of the five items can be read fluently with *a baseball player must.* Read each item below aloud with the setup:

a baseball player must

> 1. hit with power
> 2. achieve a high lifetime batting average
> 3. field well
> 4. run fast
> 5. throw with strength and precision

In other words, each item in the series (1 through 5) can be read individually with the setup, which in this case is *a baseball player must.* In (b) the setup is the subject plus a helping verb, and the items all begin with base verbs (*hit, achieve, field, run,* and *throw*).

In your rewite of (a), what if you had repeated the word *must* five times? Then you'd have this: *In order to be classified as great, a baseball player must hit with power, must achieve a high lifetime batting average, must field well, must run fast, and must throw with strength and precision.* It sounds a little stiff and wordy, doesn't it? It shows one of the problems you might encounter in your rewrites. **Your revisions of sentences that contain faulty parallelism should cut down on wordiness, not add to it.** Therefore, use a word like *must* only once—in the setup—if you can, and that way you'll avoid awkward, pointless repetition. Repeat a word before each item in a series only if you have a special reason for doing so; one valid reason would be to give extra emphasis. But this will be the rare case, not the norm.

Before we move on, however, we want to point out that sentence (b) is not the only possible correction for the faulty parallelism in sentence (a). Here is another, quite different rewrite that is also good:

(c)   In order to be classified as great, a baseball player has to be more than a power hitter with a high lifetime batting average; he must also excel at running, fielding, and throwing.

Analyze how (c) shows parallel structure and discuss your analysis in class; also share any other good rewrites of (a) that you might have been able to create.

Important Notes on the Exercises

Our first note is really a note to teachers. Please take a look at Exercises Six and Seven before you assign any work. Some teachers prefer to have students do part of either one or both before doing Exercises One through Five.

Now here are some recommendations for students. When you try to correct faulty parallelism and to create good parallelism, you'll sometimes find that there's no way you can construct one setup that will work with all your items. That's no problem. In that situation, just create two setups. For instance, you might have written a list of qualities that a person should have to become a good doctor, but mixed in it are a number of observations about characteristics that probably do not predict success in medical practice. What are you going to do? You might unravel your items and create one setup for the "dos," or the *assets,* as you might call them, and another setup for the "don'ts," or the *liabilities.*

Sometimes it's not a matter of creating two setups but of simply removing one stubborn item and making a separate sentence with it. That's fine, too.

Quite a few of our students have found that they like to do this unit in pencil or try the exercises on their own paper first and wait until after class discussion before writing the revision of their choice on the lines that are provided in the book.

Also, in Exercises One through Five, you'll find that the problems become more challenging as you proceed, so don't skip the first few items, or you might find it rough going.

As usual, correct and discuss each exercise before going on.

Exercise One

Directions: In each item below, underline the part that is an example of faulty parallelism. Then rewrite that section, correcting the problem. (You don't have to rewrite the entire item, just the part that needs to be revised.) Try to use a good setup that you can read with all the parts that follow it. Read your revision aloud.

1. One key factor in the effort to revitalize our national system of education is to raise the minimum grade point average needed to gain entry into a college or university teacher-training program. In addition, if the teachers of the future are to come from the best class of students, they will need higher salaries, the issue of greater professional status being important, and if they have more opportunities for advancement.

   _____

   _____

   _____

   _____

2. Some transcontinental travelers have found ways of minimizing their great curse —jet lag. If you're flying from the United States to Europe, for instance, there is no way to avoid this phenomenon because traveling such a long distance in such a short time will inevitably disrupt the body's rhythms. But there are things you can do to adjust as quickly as possible. Seasoned travelers suggest that you take a daytime flight, should eat as little as possible on the plane, and napping as much as you can in the air. Then when you reach your destination, whatever you do, don't go to sleep until the sun sets.

   _____

   _____

_____

_____

_____

_____

3. Many parents find it difficult to know if a child is ready to start kindergarten. According to Louise Bates Ames and Frances L. Ilg of the Gesell Institute of Child Development, it's not just a matter of chronological age. Not all five-year-olds are ready to benefit from being in an organized school setting. Ames and Ilg suggest that before the child begins, parents should make sure he or she already has certain skills. The child who is ready for kindergarten should be able to name at least three or four colors, drawing or copying a square should be a simple matter, repeat a series of four numbers without practicing them, the ability to tell the right hand from the left, and if the child can identify what things like cars, chairs, and shoes are made of. The authors suggest, by the way, that most little ones are not ready for kindergarten until they're five and a half.

_____

_____

_____

_____

_____

_____

Exercise Two

Directions: In each item below, underline the part that is an example of faulty parallelism. Then rewrite that section, correcting the problem. Use a good setup that you can read with all the parts that follow it. Read your revision aloud.

1. *The Rule Book,* by Stephen M. Kirschner, Barry J. Pavelec, and Jeffrey Feinman, lists hundreds of factual, frivolous, and fascinating rules. It even includes "Rules to

Avoid Being Eaten by Sharks." If you happen to be stranded at sea with a group and you see sharks in the neighborhood, here's what you do. You bunch together and form a tight circle, should tie yourselves together if the seas are rough, advised to use shark repellent, keeping your clothes on is important, float to save energy, and to be ready to kick or punch the shark if your group is actually attacked.

_____

_____

_____

_____

2. Don Celender, an art historian at Macalester College in St. Paul, Minnesota, wrote to 165 people whose names seemed to describe their work. Celender wanted to find out if the people thought that they had been in any way influenced or predestined by their name to go into a certain line of work. He wrote to Hugh Law, an attorney in Missouri, a dentist in Ohio by the name of Lacy L. Toothman, in Michigan there was a barber named Jack Joe Barber, a Colorado geologist by the name of Donald Stone, and Texan Thomas Eagle, a veterinarian. Of the 57 people who responded, none thought that their names had played a role in their choice of a career.

_____

_____

_____

_____

3. Bird lovers are always looking for ways to attract more birds to their yards. Experts suggest that there are many things they can do. Bird lovers would be wise, for

instance, to provide shrubs and trees of various heights, the presence of a little

pond, also if it is possible to create a small clearing in a wooded area, and birds

love plants that produce seeds, berries, fruit, or nectar.

_____

_____

_____

_____

_____

Exercise Three

Directions: In each item below, underline the part that is an example of faulty parallelism. Then rewrite that section, correcting the problem. Use a good setup that you can read with all the parts that follow it. Read your revision aloud.

1. According to the authors of *The Best*, the best place to take a child in New York

   City is to the American Museum of Natural History. Why? They say that this

   particular museum has practically everything to appeal to the curious young mind.

   The institution has one of the most spectacular collections of dinosaur skeletons

   in the world, fabulous replicas of all kinds of animals being housed there, offers a

   re-creation of an entire African veld, and excellent models of every stage in the

   development of the human fetus.

   _____

   _____

   _____

   _____

   _____

2. Five states plus the District of Columbia claim variations of the rose as their official

   flower. The District of Columbia is represented by the American Beauty rose, there's the Cherokee rose of Georgia, Iowa's wild rose, the hawthorn rose is a

symbol of Missouri, North Dakota has the wild prairie rose, and New York simply

lists "the rose."

_____

_____

_____

_____

3. Believe it or not, there are about a dozen pet psychologists in the United States.

    According to one of them, animals can indeed experience psychological problems,

    and when they do, humans are often to blame. A psychological disorder in a dog,

    for instance, can supposedly have several causes: isolation from humans or other

    animals, the dog becomes confused about its place in the household hierarchy, to

    have had traumatic experiences early in life, and if its owners treat it like a human

    being.

    _____

    _____

    _____

    _____

    _____

Exercise Four

Directions: In each item below, underline the part that is an example of faulty
parallelism. Then rewrite that section, correcting the problem. Use a good setup
that you can read with all the parts that follow it. Read your revision aloud.

1. Many people are bothered by motion sickness, whether they're traveling by car, on

    a train, to take a bus, or flying. But there are things a person can do to prevent or

    at least minimize the problem. For example, it's best to eat only bland food before

    and during the trip, avoidance of cigar or cigarette smoke, reading is out, to focus your eyes on the horizon whenever possible, and getting a seat where there's the least motion, for instance, in the front seat of a car or over the wing in a plane, and no alcoholic beverages.

_____

_____

_____

_____

_____

2. Anorexia nervosa, which doctors have described as self-inflicted starvation, occurs in females more frequently than in males; in fact, for every 30 anorexic females, there is only one anorexic male. If this problem is going to affect a woman, it usually does so when she's between 16 and 18. An anorexic young woman typically weighs 25 percent or more less than her ideal weight, yet she insists that she's overweight. Some of the other symptoms of anorexia that often appear include a somewhat skeletal appearance, she might stop having her menstrual periods, blood pressure being lower than normal, for her skin to look yellow and feel like sandpaper, her face might be puffy, and if you observe downy hair on her face and body.

_____

_____

_____

_____

_____

3. According to the Lightning Protection Institute in Harvard, Illinois, there are certain things everybody should know in order to minimize the chances of getting hit by lightning. Most people are aware that they should not wait out a storm in a flat, open space if they can avoid it; it's simply best not to be the tallest thing around. But there are other things people should know. No one should ever seek protection under a tree, to try to avoid lying down on wet ground, and don't stay on a bike, horse, or golf cart. People who are inside should not talk on the phone, everyone should stay away from open windows, doors, and fireplaces, and finally, to keep your distance from large appliances, such as refrigerators, stoves, sinks, and television sets.

_____

_____

_____

_____

_____

_____

_____

Exercise Five

Directions: In each item below, underline the part that is an example of faulty parallelism. Then rewrite that section, correcting the problem. Use a good setup that you can read with all the parts that follow it. Read your revision aloud.

1. According to Philip G. Zimbardo and Shirley L. Radl of Stanford University, two of every five children are shy. But Zimbardo and Radl believe that shyness can be overcome. It's mostly a matter of increasing a child's self-esteem, which is largely in the control of the child's parents. Parents should never use the label "shy" in front of the child, don't put too much pressure on him or her, inviting other children

over for playtime, the child should learn enough personal and social skills to feel

confident, and exposure to people of all different ages, colors, and sizes.

_____

_____

_____

_____

_____

_____

2. According to *The Presidents, Tidbits & Trivia*, presidential salaries have increased

almost tenfold throughout our history. From the administration of George Washing-

ton through the first term of Ulysses S. Grant, the commander in chief earned

$25,000 a year. In his second term, President Grant doubled his luck, earning an

annual salary of $50,000. This level of compensation ($50,000 a year) lasted

through the presidency of Theodore Roosevelt. A salary of $100,000 was paid to

Lyndon Johnson, and that was the sum paid to each of Johnson's predecessors

from John F. Kennedy through Harry S. Truman. An income of $75,000 a year was

earned by all the presidents from William H. Taft, who followed Teddy Roosevelt,

through Franklin D. Roosevelt, who preceded Truman. Richard Nixon was the first

president to earn $200,000 a year, and that salary was also paid to Gerald Ford,

Jimmy Carter, and Ronald Reagan. Of course, the later presidents have also had

expense accounts and allowances for travel and entertainment.

_____

_____

_____

_____

_____

_____

_____

3. An article in *Psychology Today* describes a study that was conducted at the Center

for Creative Leadership in Greensboro, North Carolina. The purpose of the study

was to examine the careers of male executives who had shown great promise early

in their professional lives. Some of the men later fulfilled their potential while others

never lived up to it. The researchers found a number of so-called fatal flaws in the

men who did not achieve the great success for which they seemed to be heading.

Some of the most important fatal flaws were these:

(a) if the executive had a tendency to bully or intimidate others

(b) coldness or aloofness

(c) to be overly ambitious

(d) Was he unable to delegate authority or build a team?

(e) how much difficulty he had adapting to a boss who had a different style

(f) being too dependent upon his mentor

(g) betrayed another's trust

(h) problems in his ability to think strategically

_____

_____

_____

_____

_____

_____

Exercise Six

Directions: Choose three questions from this list. Write your answer to each question in a full sentence that demonstrates good parallel structure. Each answer should contain *three to five* items. Please use your own paper.

1. What do you like to do on a typical weekend?
2. What should a college education do for you?
3. What events or circumstances made a certain year in your life especially good or especially difficult?
4. What skills are required to play a specific position in a sport with which you are familiar?
5. What are some of the qualities that make you proud of a paper you've written?
6. What are three reasons why you like a particular holiday best?
7. What's so good about your favorite TV show?
8. What are some of the things toddlers are first taught not to play with or not to do?
9. For what would you wish if you were given three magical wishes?
10. Why do you dislike a certain day of the week (like Sunday or Monday, for example) or a particular month of the year (January, perhaps)?

Exercise Seven

Directions: Choose three items from this list. Then write a full sentence for each item, demonstrating the skills or qualities a person should have in order to succeed in that particular line of work. Make sure you have good parallel structure in your sentences. Please use your own paper.

clothing designer	free-lance writer
television anchorperson	union leader
actor or actress	engineer
parent	carnival worker or circus performer
member of the clergy	police officer
politician	movie reviewer
stand-up comedian	high school counselor
911 emergency operator	tax auditor
coach	astronaut
public defender	street performer (a mime, for example)
seventh-grade teacher	cabinet maker

UNIT 3: Passive Sentences

Like faulty parallelism, unnecessary passive sentences are a source of awkwardness in the writing of many students.

You know that the word *passive* ordinarily means weak, inactive. People are called passive if they wait for things to happen instead of making them happen. Passive sentences are somewhat similar. A passive sentence is not technically wrong like a run-on or a fragment, but it's weak, flat, dead. **The subject of a passive sentence does not act; it is acted upon.**

Here is an example:

1. (a)   All the continents except Antarctica were first set foot upon by James Cook, an English explorer.

Doesn't that sentence sound awkward? Why put *All the continents* in the subject position? Wouldn't *James Cook* be a more natural choice for a subject? After all, he's the one who *did* something. He acted; the continents were only acted upon. Here's an *active* rewrite of the sentence:

1. (b)   James Cook, an English explorer, was the first person to set foot upon all the continents except Antarctica.

Here's another example of a passive sentence:

2. (a)   In some of Sir Arthur Conan Doyle's stories, cocaine is occasionally indulged in by Sherlock Holmes.

Please answer these questions about sentence 2. (a):

(1)   What is the subject in the sentence as it is written? _____

_____

(2)   Is the subject doing something, or is it being acted upon? _____

_____

(3)   Who or what would be a more logical choice for the subject? _____

_____

[Answers: (1) *cocaine*; (2) *It's being acted upon*; and (3) *Sherlock Holmes.*]

Try rewriting sentence 2. (a), making it active:

2. (b)   _____

_____

_____

One active rewrite is this: *In some of Sir Arthur Conan Doyle's stories, Sherlock Holmes occasionally indulged in cocaine.* Some variations are acceptable; ask your teacher to check your answer if you're unsure.

Here's one more passive sentence to examine:

3. (a)   When the role of a man was played by Linda Hunt in the movie *The Year of Living Dangerously*, she became the first person to win an Oscar for an "opposite sex" performance.

Label the subject of 3. (a) and figure out who or what would make a more logical, active subject. Then do your active rewrite of the sentence here:

3. (b) _____

_____

_____

With all three pairs of sentences we've examined so far, notice how unnecessary wordiness is eliminated when you move from the passive to the active voice. Crispness and conciseness are important fringe benefits of being able to recognize and rewrite passive sentences.

Acceptable Passive Sentences

Sometimes passive sentences are all right. For instance, it's fine to use a passive sentence if you don't know who did a certain action. For example, it would be perfectly logical to write, "The music was written in the seventeenth century" if no one had ever been able to determine who composed the piece. The same goes for an anonymous poem, a purse stolen by an unidentified person, and so forth.

Another valid reason for using a passive sentence is the writer's desire to place emphasis on a certain area. For example, look at these sentences, each of which is passive for a good reason:

(a) The pterodactyl, a flying dinosaur, was discovered by O. C. Marsh in 1871.

(b) The ancient city of Troy, which for centuries was thought to be purely mythical, was discovered by Henry Schliemann.

In each example, the writer might have thought that the thing discovered—in one case, the pterodactyl and in the other, the city of Troy—was of greater historical importance than the person who discovered it. That value judgment then would have led the writer to put the discovery rather than the discoverer in the subject position. Certainly, another writer, perhaps with a different emphasis in mind, could have made *O. C. Marsh* and *Henry Schliemann* the subjects. The point is that it's all right to use a passive sentence if you have a valid reason for it.

Here is one more example of an acceptable passive sentence:

(c) The water in and around Minamata, Japan, had been completely contaminated, and many children from the area were born with severe birth defects as a result of the mercury their mothers had ingested.

The first clause—*The water in and around Minamata, Japan, had been completely contaminated*—is passive, but there may be a good reason for this construction. Perhaps the writer is not concerned at this point with the question of *who* contaminated the water. The writer might want the emphasis simply on the fact that the water was contaminated. He or she may be planning to bring up the name of the guilty party in the next paragraph or the next section of the paper or perhaps not at all.

Important Notes about the Exercises

Before you begin the exercises, you need to realize that the "by so and so" phrase does not always appear in a passive sentence; sometimes it is only implied. Such a sentence might still be in need of a good rewrite.

You'll also see that when you change some sentences from passive to active, you'll find other opportunities to make them crisper and less wordy.

Sometimes you'll find a sentence that is passive in more than one clause. Make sure you change each passive clause.

Finally, you'll notice that all passive sentences are not alike. Read them aloud, and you'll hear that some sound horrible, whereas others barely need to be rewritten or perhaps, in some cases, don't need to be rewritten at all. Your writing teacher will help you see these differences.

The important thing is to eliminate unnecessary passive sentences and to make your writing as active and lively as possible.

Exercise One

Directions: Rewrite these passive sentences, making them active. Please use your own paper.

1. Approximately 200 pounds are gained per day by the baby calf of a blue whale.
2. An age of over 80 years has been reached by goldfish in captivity.
3. The practice of monogamy is observed by storks.
4. Its tail is used effectively as a whip by an iguana when it is threatened.
5. One third of the total amount of canned fish in the United States is eaten by cats.

Exercise Two

Directions: Rewrite these passive sentences, making them active. Please use your own paper.

1. Their physical senses can be developed by human beings to a much higher degree than most people realize.
2. Enough examples from everyday life can be found by anyone to determine that this is true.
3. For example, the amount of alcohol or acid in a particular wine can be tasted by an experienced vintner to within one percent.
4. Differences between certain shades of red that are indistinguishable to the layman can be seen by expert color technicians.
5. Just by its feel, the moisture content of bread dough can be measured by some professional bakers to within two percent of accuracy when the dough is being kneaded by them.

Exercise Three

Directions: Rewrite these passive sentences, making them active. The information in Exercises Three through Five is from *The Book of Firsts* by Patrick Robertson. Please use your own paper.

1. The world's first known hotel was opened in January 1774 in Covent Garden, England, by David Low. The name given to the establishment by Low was Low's Grand Hotel.
2. The decision to admit students to a women's college on a full-time basis was first made by the administrators of Oberlin Collegiate Institute in Oberlin, Ohio.
3. The distinction of being the world's first full-time police detective was claimed by Frenchman Eugene François Vidocq, who was born in 1775.

4. The world's first jeep was designed in 1940 by Karl K. Fabst of the Bantam Car Co. in Butler, Pennsylvania, for the U.S. Army.
5. Fingerprints were first used systematically as a means of identification by William Herschel of the Indian Civil Service in the midnineteenth century. The ordeal of being fingerprinted—or more accurately, palmprinted—was first experienced by Rajyadhar Konai, a local contractor from the Indian village of Nista, on July 28, 1858.

Exercise Four

Directions: Rewrite these passive sentences, making them active. Please use your own paper. Consult *The Book of Firsts* if you want more information on early jazz.

1. The world's first jazz band was supposedly put together by black musician Buddy Bolden, a trumpet player, in New Orleans around 1900.
2. If historians want to validate Bolden's claim, the testimony of people who knew him or heard him play must be relied upon in large part.
3. However, one very convincing piece of evidence to support Bolden's claim has been found by music historians.
4. A demonstration of Bolden's style was made in a recording by Bunk Johnson, another musician, in the 1930s.
5. The fact that Bolden's "jazz" shows traces of ragtime and march music can be attested to by the experts who have listened to Bunk Johnson's rendition of Bolden's music.
6. Probably no one individual can be called the inventor of jazz, but an important stage in the evolution of earlier forms of traditional black music is marked by the playing of Buddy Bolden.
7. So, it is concluded by most historians of music that the first real jazz was played by Buddy Bolden's band in New Orleans until 1907 when a mental breakdown was experienced by the bandleader, and he was committed to an asylum.
8. Another claim to the title of the world's first jazz man was made by Ferdinand Joseph Morton, who is better known by his nickname "Jelly Roll."
9. Although his claim may be disputed by some, just as Buddy Bolden's claim is, Jelly Roll Morton's important role in the history of jazz must certainly be acknowledged by music lovers.
10. The first published jazz orchestration, "New Orleans Blues," was composed by Jelly Roll Morton in 1902, and that fact is not disputed by music historians anywhere.

Exercise Five

Directions: Underline all examples of weak or unnecessary uses of the passive voice. Then rewrite those sentences on your own paper, making them active. You might find a small number of passive sentences that don't need to be changed; in other words, you might see a logical reason why they can remain passive. The source of this information is *The Book of Firsts*.

Trousers were first worn as an item of feminine apparel by the famous French actress 1

Sarah Bernhardt. It is reported by Patrick Robertson in *The Book of Firsts* that Bernhardt 2

was photographed in pants in Paris by Melandri in 1876. Bloomers had been intro- 3 duced in 1848 by Amelia Bloomer, an American feminist, but they were really pan-taloons that were worn by a woman under her skirt. Skirts were not replaced by bloomers.

But pants were not really accepted by females in general until they were worn on the playing fields by "sporting women." Trousers were first worn for greater ease in playing sports by 25-year-old Eleonora Sears of Boston, Massachusetts. Permission to participate in a polo match against an English team was requested by Miss Sears at the Burlingame Country Club in 1909. A jacket and a pair of pants were worn by her at the time. According to Robertson, such shock was felt by the captain of the English team that he was rendered speechless, and Miss Sears was, without further ceremony, ordered to leave the playing field by the manager of the American team. But the belief continued to be held by Eleonora Sears and a few other pioneers that women could not successfully compete against men until they abandoned their skirts, which, by the way, were full-length—down to the ankles. The struggle was continued by Sears and others.

Progress was slowly made by sensible, practical women outside the world of sports, too. Trousers were first worn by women in uniform when an order was issued by the Prussian State Railways in 1916. The new regulation called for female guards and "conductresses" to wear the same wide gray trousers as the men.

Shortly after a tentative foothold was gained by women in sports and work, a role in this fashion revolution was played by the chic resorts along the Riviera in the late 1920s. There, pants were first worn by women as so-called beach pajamas. Slacks for regular daytime wear could finally be found in clothing stores by the casual female shopper in the early 1930s, but the appearance of a woman in pants was still something of a shocker for quite some time.

UNIT 4: Direct and Indirect Quotes

There are many times, especially in college-level writing, when you work with the words of others. There are two basic ways that you can present what others have said: (1) You can quote a person *directly*, using his or her exact words, or (2) you can quote *indirectly*, expressing the person's thoughts in your own words. An indirect quote is also called a *paraphrase*.

A direct quote is a presentation of the exact words that someone used. An indirect quote is a description of what was said.

Here is an example of a *direct quote*:

(a)   In a review of Woody Allen's *Hannah and Her Sisters*, critic David Ansen said, "Anyone bemoaning the disappearance of adult matter from the movies need look no farther."

In (a) the writer is choosing to use the exact words that Ansen used in his review, and to show that, the writer must enclose what Ansen said within a set of double quotation marks ("). Notice that the word *Anyone* is capitalized. The first word of a direct quote is usually capitalized. (We'll discuss an exception later.)

Below, the writer is choosing to quote Ansen *indirectly*:

(b)   In a review of a new Woody Allen movie, critic David Ansen said that anyone who's complaining that adult subject matter has disappeared from the movies doesn't have to look beyond *Hannah and Her Sisters*.

Sentence (b) contains an indirect quote, which is also called a paraphrase. In (b) the writer does not use Ansen's exact words but does communicate Ansen's point. When you quote someone indirectly, remember that you still must give the person credit. That's why Ansen's name is used in (b) just as in (a).

Stop now and write down something that your mother, your father, or a friend frequently says. First write it and punctuate it as a direct quote; then rewrite it as an indirect quote.

Direct quote: _____

_____

Indirect quote: _____

_____

Punctuating Direct Quotes

Now you know that you use double quotation marks before and after a person's exact words. That's almost all you need to know, but there is a little more to it. You also have to learn to use the correct punctuation to set off the attribution part of the sentence. By *attribution*, we mean the part that tells who said it; for instance, *he said* and *she remarked* are attributions. Often you use a comma to set off an attribution, sometimes a colon, and occasionally no punctuation at all.

1. Using a Comma

If the attribution is less than an S-V-C clause, use a comma after it. Study these correct examples, in which we have only S-V in each attribution.

She said, " _____ ."

He commented, " _____ ."

They insisted, " _____ ."

These can also come at the end of the sentence; in other words, the attribution can sometimes follow the direct quote. Then use a comma before it. Look at these correct examples:

" _____ ," said Barbara.

" _____ ," commented the captain.

" _____ ," they insisted.

When it's appropriate, an attribution can even interrupt a direct quote. For instance, a writer might choose to structure a sentence this way:

"Just once this week," James suggested, "let's try to get through an entire evening without turning on the television."

In such sentences the attribution is set off with two commas. Make sure to enclose each part of the quote within a set of double quotation marks. Use a period and a capital letter only if each of the two sections is a full sentence. This is a correct example:

"He doesn't know what to do," my mother said. "He's completely confused."

2. Using a Colon

If the attribution contains a complement or a complement-type word, use a colon after it. (If you need to review the idea of complements or complement-type words used with colons, turn to Chapter 3, Unit 7, page 123.) Study these correct examples and label each with *S, V,* and *C.*

The waiter gave us some advice: " _____ ."

She said only three words: " _____ ."

The lawyer issued one warning: " _____ ."

To test your understanding, insert a comma or a colon into each example:

(a) The teacher responded " _____ ."

(b) Max shouted " _____ ."

(c) " _____ " whispered the child.

(d) " _____ " said Kara.

(e) I asked " _____ ?"

(f) Her pain was revealed in her last question " _____ ?"

(g) " _____ " replied the interpreter.

(h) The pilot made an announcement " _____ ."

Discuss your answers with your writing teacher.

3. Using No Punctuation

Occasionally, no punctuation is used just before a direct quote or a part of one. Here are two correct examples:

(a) Jack Kroll, the well-known critic, called Henry Fonda, Gary Cooper, Spencer Tracy, and Jimmy Stewart a "celluloid Mount Rushmore of American icons."

(b) Helmut Schmidt once characterized the late Yuri Andropov as "a modern computer filled with Russian software."

Because of the way the quoted material is worked into the sentence, the first word of the direct quote is not capitalized, nor is the quote set off with punctuation.

One Last Note

Don't double your punctuation when the attribution comes after a direct quote. In other words, if a direct quote ends with a question mark or an exclamation point, omit the comma. These examples are correct:

"Who's watching the store?" she asked.

"Throw the ball!" they yelled.

Exercise One

Directions: **Make the necessary changes wherever you find direct quotes. Your changes will involve quotation marks, commas, colons, question marks, and capitalization. Some sentences might contain no direct quotes; those sentences should not be changed.**

1. Zsa Zsa Gabor once said I'm a wonderful housekeeper. Every time I get a divorce,

   I keep the house.

2. In 1787 the United States minted a copper coin with a simple motto mind your

   business.

3. *The Outer Limits,* a televised science fiction series, always opened with the same line there is nothing wrong with your set.

4. Assassination is the extreme form of censorship claimed George Bernard Shaw, the famous playwright.

5. George Gallup, the nationally known pollster, once said that he could prove the existence of God statistically.

6. How you gonna keep 'em down on the farm after they've seen Paris asked the lyrics of a popular post–World War I song.

7. Joe Nuxhall, a longtime Cincinnati Reds' radio announcer, invariably ends each broadcast the same way. This is the old left-hander he says rounding third and heading for home.

8. In 1960 this short statement of faith was added to all U.S. banknotes in God we trust.

9. In *The Mother's Almanac,* authors Marguerite Kelly and Elia Parsons say that they've observed that a happy family operates within a framework of safety, discipline, and good manners, and they point out that this framework must be created by both parties—parents and children.

10. *Omni,* the science magazine, once sponsored a contest to find the best unanswerable question. The first prize went to a person who wrote in and asked why is it possible to tickle someone else but not to tickle yourself.

As usual, please correct each exercise and discuss any problems before continuing.

Exercise Two

Directions: Make the necessary changes wherever you find direct quotes. Your changes will involve quotation marks, commas, colons, question marks, and capitalization. Some sentences might contain no direct quotes; those sentences should not be changed.

1. Beware of all enterprises that require new clothes warned Henry David Thoreau.

2. Most people say cross my heart and hope to die, but Beaver Cleaver used to say cross my heart and hope to spit.

3. The late actor Richard Burton was known for his interesting observations and unusual quips. Once he said that he believed Jesus Christ was of Welsh extraction.

4. The slogan of the Russian revolution was bread, land, peace.

5. Yogi Berra once made this classic response to what he probably regarded as a stupid question from a reporter slump? I ain't in no slump. I just ain't hitting.

6. For lovers wrote John Cheever touch is metamorphosis.

7. Mauve is just pink trying to be purple noted the painter James A. McNeill Whistler.

8. When he was asked about the difficulty of writing, Red Smith, the famous sports columnist, answered there's nothing to it. All you do is sit down at a typewriter and open a vein.

9. This is Carl Reiner's definition of comedy comedy is truth—just before people notice it.

10. Boasting of the power of his music, Little Richard once said it regenerates the heart, makes the liver quiver, the bladder splatter, and the knees freeze.

Important Notes about Exercises Three and Four

Some of the items in the next two exercises are actually dialogues; in other words, they contain direct quotes from more than one person. Now normally when you write dialogues in your own papers, you'll start a new paragraph to indicate each change of speaker. But if we did that here, the indentations would make it too easy for you to locate direct quotes. If the exercises were that easy, they wouldn't be of much value to you.

Just for practice, your writing teacher might ask you to take a couple of the items that involve more than one speaker and write them out with the appropriate indentations.

Exercise Three

Directions: Read the following passages. Then, as you have been doing in the earlier exercises, make the necessary changes wherever you find direct quotes. You can read more about these anecdotes in the *Speaker's Treasury of Anecdotes about the Famous.*

1. After he had attended an opening night performance, the writer George S. Kaufman was asked for his opinion of a certain play. It's not quite fair for me to say Kaufman remarked. I saw it under peculiarly unfortunate circumstances. The curtain was up.

2. When Hank Aaron was up to bat for the first time in his major league career, the catcher for the opposing team tried to rattle him by saying hey, kid, you're holding your bat all wrong. You should hold it with the label up so you can read it. The young rookie for the Milwaukee Braves, who later went on to become the greatest home-run hitter of all time, was not at a loss for words. He simply replied I didn't come up here to read.

3. Once when Samuel Clemens, also known as Mark Twain, was traveling around the country on the speakers' circuit, he stopped to get a haircut before his evening appearance in a small town in Pennsylvania. The barber asked him if he was a stranger in town, and when Mr. Twain replied that he was, the barber said we're having a good lecture tonight sir. The barber continued to explain that it was going to be a lecture by the famous Mark Twain, and he asked his customer if he was, by any chance, planning to attend. When Mr. Twain replied that he thought he would attend, the barber asked have you got your ticket yet. Mr. Twain answered no, not yet. The barber shook his head and said then, sir, you'll have to stand. Dear me! Samuel Clemens complained. It seems as if I always have to stand when that fellow Twain talks.

4. William Lyon Phelps, who taught English literature at Yale University, once received an interesting exam from a student just before the Christmas break. On the exam the student had written God only knows the answer to this question. Merry

Christmas. Professor Phelps returned the student's test with this comment written across the bottom God gets an A you get an F. Happy New Year.

5. Another figure who minced no words with his students was Dr. Samuel Johnson. To one of his protégés, he once said I found your speech to be good and original. However, the part that was original was not good. And the part that was good was not original.

6. The famous writer Somerset Maugham was in London, recovering from the flu. His phone rang, and it was a female admirer who inquired could I send you fruit, or would you rather have flowers. The 88-year-old Maugham's response was a classic it's too late for fruit—too early for flowers.

7. The comic sparring between Jack Benny and Fred Allen is legendary. Once, just after Jack Benny had told a joke at Fred Allen's expense, Allen retorted that was a very funny remark, Jack. Your writers did very well—but the fact is you couldn't ad-lib a belch after a Hungarian dinner.

8. The Polish pianist Ignace Paderewski had just finished performing a private concert when he learned that the hostess for the evening was especially fond of one particular selection he had played. What a beautiful piece she said. Who composed it. The pianist replied Beethoven, madam. The woman then responded ah, yes, and is he composing now. No said Paderewski he is decomposing.

9. Someone once asked Johnny Unitas, the famous quarterback, why he decided to retire from professional football when he did. He answered I could have played two or three more years. All I needed was a leg transplant.

10. Oscar Wilde, who was not known for his humility, had just attended the opening night performance of a play he had written. Oscar, how did your play go tonight asked a friend. Oh, the play was a great success Wilde claimed but the audience was a failure.

Exercise Four

Directions: Continue to make the necessary changes wherever you find direct quotes. You can read more about the information in this exercise in the *Speaker's Treasury of Anecdotes about the Famous* and in *The Quintessential Quiz Book.*

1. In 1946 Winston Churchill traveled to Fulton, Missouri, to deliver a speech, which turned out to be his famous Iron Curtain address, and to be present at the dedication of a bust in his honor. After his speech a rather attractive and ample woman approached the wartime prime minister of England and said Mr. Churchill, I traveled over a hundred miles this morning for the unveiling of your bust. Churchill, who was known far and wide for his quick wit, replied madam, I assure you, in that regard I would gladly return the favor.

2. Once G. K. Chesterton and several other famous writers were asked what one book they would take with them if they were stranded on a deserted island. The complete works of Shakespeare answered one writer. I'd choose the Bible insisted another. Then Chesterton was asked what book he would select. I would choose replied the English man of letters *Thomas's Guide to Practical Shipbuilding.*

3. In the late 1900s the man who was shot out of the cannon every day at the Barnum and Bailey circus decided to quit. His wife had asked him to find a less risky way of making a living. P. T. Barnum hated to lose a good man, so he sent him a message I beg you to reconsider—men of your caliber are hard to find.

4. The famous actress Lynn Fontanne and actor Alfred Lunt were perhaps even more devoted to their marriage than they were to their profession. In a play called *At Mrs. Beans's,* Fontanne was required to hit her husband in the face, but in rehearsal she found that she simply could not do it. For a half hour Fontanne repeatedly tried to hit him, but each time she pulled back her hand at the last minute. Finally Lunt yelled for God's sake, Lynn, you're the lousiest actress I've ever played opposite! Fontanne's difficulty disappeared instantly, and she smacked him. Her husband

howled in pain, but from that time on, each night at that moment in the perform-ance, before his wife could bring herself to let him have it, Alfred Lunt had to whisper you know you're lousy, dear.

5. Novelist John O'Hara's wife of several years divorced him allegedly because she discovered that writers were simply too difficult to live with. She came to see them as moody, quirky, and unpredictable. But later, the same woman fell in love with another famous writer. When O'Hara read the announcement of his former wife's upcoming wedding, he sent her a cable that read heartiest congratulations and best wishes. Then he signed it Frying Pan.

6. Fiorello La Guardia, who served from 1934 to 1945, was one of New York City's most colorful and best-loved mayors. A very active public servant, he was con-stantly popping up in unexpected places and doing unexpected things. On one terribly cold day he decided to preside over night court, and a case was brought before him involving an elderly woman who had stolen a loaf of bread. She ex-plained that her family was starving, but the mayor said that he had no choice but to punish her. The law makes no exceptions declared La Guardia. I must fine you ten dollars. He then reached into his own pocket, took out a ten-dollar bill, and threw it into the sombrero that he was famous for wearing. Then he added further-more, I'm going to fine everybody in this courtroom fifty cents for living in a town where a person has to steal bread in order to eat. He instructed the bailiff to collect the fines and give them to the defendant. The woman left the courtroom with $47.50.

7. The comedian Fred Allen was famous for insults such as this one what's on your mind—if you'll forgive the overstatement.

8. If you were my husband, I'd poison your coffee Lady Astor once told Winston Churchill. And if I were your husband he replied I should drink it.

9. On her deathbed, Gertrude Stein, the famous writer and patron of the arts, asked well, what *is* the answer. After a long pause, she added but what then is the question.

10. Probably the most famous quote from an Arthur Conan Doyle mystery is this one elementary, my dear Watson. But nowhere in Doyle's stories does Sherlock Holmes actually say those exact words. The common misquote probably comes from a passage in "The Crooked Man" where Watson cries excellent! to which Holmes replies elementary.

Exercise Five

Directions: Select a total of five direct quotes from Exercises One through Four and rewrite them on your own paper as indirect quotes. In class, discuss the frequent use of the word *that* in indirect quotes. Also notice how present tense often becomes past tense as you shift from direct to indirect.

Exercise Six

Directions: Write your own anecdote or dialogue, using some direct and some indirect quotes. For example, you might describe a typical family conversation around the dinner table or a recent night out with friends. Please do this exercise on your own paper.

Chapter 5
Free Exercises in Sentence Combining

This is an important chapter for everyone. It doesn't matter what your strengths and weaknesses are; the exercises in Chapter 5 will help you reinforce the skills you've learned to this point and assist you in gaining greater flexibility and variety in your sentence structure.

The chapter contains a series of sentence-combining exercises to do on your own paper. In terms of sentence structure, sentence combining is a great finishing touch. You've learned a lot of *dos* and *don'ts*, and this is an excellent way of reviewing and exercising them. If you've had a hard time with run-ons, for example, this chapter will serve as another opportunity to work on them. The same goes for fragments, dangling modifiers, and faulty parallelism. After all, these errors are nothing more than missteps in the process of sentence combining. If you've had any difficulty making compound, complex, or embedded sentences, or remembering the rules for punctuating them correctly, the exercises in this chapter will also help you. If you need more work on semicolons and colons, try to use them whenever they're appropriate.

Now let's examine how free sentence-combining exercises work. Please read the sentences in Group 1 carefully.

GROUP 1
Agatha Christie disappeared in 1924.

She was a famous English mystery writer.

She was missing for ten days.

Her disappearance made headlines in the British newspapers.

It made the front page.

If these five sentences appeared consecutively in a college student's paper, they would certainly be judged to have a choppy, overly simple sound. On the other hand, if they appeared in the writing of a ten-year-old, they would probably be regarded quite **187** favorably. Adult writers generally use short, unconnected sentences for dramatic effect, and they use them infrequently. Normally, adult writers are interested in showing relationships between facts, and that's why they automatically combine clauses most of the time. Here are some of the ways that the sentences in Group 1 can be combined:

(a) Agatha Christie, a famous English mystery writer, was missing for ten days in 1924, and her disappearance made front-page headlines in the British newspapers.

(b) The ten-day disappearance of Agatha Christie, a famous English mystery writer, made front-page headlines in the British newspapers in 1924.

(c) When Agatha Christie dropped out of sight in 1924, British newspapers featured the disappearance of the great English mystery writer in front-page headlines until she resurfaced after ten days.

(d) In 1924, banner headlines in British newspapers announced the ten-day disappearance of the famous English mystery writer, Agatha Christie.

(e) Missing for ten days in 1924, Agatha Christie, an Englishwoman who was already famous for her "whodunits," found herself front-page news in the British press.

(f) The ten-day disappearance of Agatha Christie, a famous English mystery writer, was well covered by the British press in 1924; in fact, the story made front-page headlines.

Notice that the meaning of each sentence in Group 1 is preserved in every variation, (a) through (f). **In sentence combining, the wording and the order of information can change, but the meaning has to stay basically the same.**

Try your hand at combining the sentences in Groups 2 through 5. Your combinations and those of your classmates and teacher should be discussed in class before you begin the exercises. Try two or three combinations for each group. Remember that the whole idea is to change the wording and the order of information; just be sure to keep the same basic meaning intact.

GROUP 2
Christie was finally found at a resort spa.

She was suffering from a form of temporary amnesia.

(a) _____

_____

_____

(b) _____

_____

_____

(c) _____

_____

_____

GROUP 3

Her amnesia had resulted from an emotional breakdown.

The emotional breakdown was caused by the death of her mother.

It was also caused by her husband's request for a divorce.

(a) _____

_____

_____

(b) _____

_____

_____

(c) _____

_____

_____

GROUP 4

Christie had checked into the spa under an assumed name.

She used the name of the woman her husband wanted to marry.

She was recognized by people who had seen her picture in the newspapers.

They reported her whereabouts to the authorities.

(a) _____

_____

_____

(b) _____

_____

_____

(c) _____

_____

_____

GROUP 5

Agatha Christie later underwent psychiatric care.

She divorced her first husband.

She married an archeologist.

She continued her phenomenal literary career.

(a) _____

_____

_____

(b) _____

_____

_____

(c) _____

_____

_____

When you discuss the combinations that work, you'll notice that some of them were made using techniques that you didn't learn in this book, and yet they're completely acceptable and probably very effective. That's why these are called "free" sentence-combining exercises. You are free to use your common sense—your intuitive language skill—in addition to the structures, patterns, and rules we've taught.

Reversing the Process

There's a very important skill you can develop as a result of your work in this chapter. It's the ability to break your own sentences down and recombine the clauses. After you've done a few exercises in the book, try to find an awkward or weak sentence in one of your own papers and break it down into a list of simple or at least short sentences. Then recombine them in a number of ways, just as you would if they were presented in *Easy Writer II*.

Final Notes

Some students love sentence combining; others find it monotonous. For most people, the trick is to work on the exercises in chunks of not more than 30 to 45 minutes. If you try to do two or three hours' worth of sentence combining in one sitting, you're probably going to get very little out of the experience. If it starts to seem like busywork, take a break and come back fresh. It's *not* busywork.

Most teachers ask students to come up with two or three combinations for each group. You and your teacher will develop your own guidelines.

Once in a great while, you might find a group for which you can make only one satisfactory combination.

If a numbered "group" actually consists of only one sentence, it's a transitional sentence or a sentence that is short for some other intended effect. (For example, see the first numbered item of Exercise One, Selection C.) This kind of sentence should not be combined with anything else or rephrased. Just go on to the next group.

Sometimes you'll see items that should be put into parallel form; it's up to you to do so. We've altered the natural parallelism of some listed items (in other words, we made them somewhat awkward) in order to give you a little challenge here and there.

All students should begin their work in this chapter by doing a few selections from Exercise One. After you discuss Exercise One in class, your teacher may assign the remaining exercises in any order, depending upon students' time, need, and interests. Exercises Two through Six are not arranged in order of difficulty. Each contains some easy groups and other challenging ones.

Guide to the Exercises in Chapter 5

Exercise Four: *Control and Well-being*

Exercise Five: *Good Kids*

Exercise Six: *Mabel K. Staupers and Black Nurses in the Military*

Exercise One:

Odd Moments in the World of Sports

This exercise consists of ten short items (A-J) based on sports oddities described in *The Great American Sports Book* by George Gipe.

SELECTION A

1. Two Eskimo football teams were practicing before a game.

   The teams were from King's Island, Alaska.

   They were getting ready for the 1938 New Year's Day Ice Bowl game.

2. They had been practicing on an ice floe.

   The ice floe was huge.

   It was flat.

   It was near their village.

3. They went out to practice.

   The date was December 18, 1937.

   They couldn't find their practice field.

   Gale-force winds had blown it away.

SELECTION B

1. The French Boxing Federation made a decision.

   It made the decision in 1924.

   The federation issued an official ban.

   It was a ban against fighters kissing each other.

   Fighters had traditionally kissed each other at the end of each bout.

SELECTION C

1. How slow can you go and still win?

2. The slowest time for a winning racehorse was set in 1945.

   It was set during a steeplechase.

3. The horse was named Never Mind II.

   Never Mind II refused a jump.

   His jockey gave up.

   He returned the horse to the paddock.

4. When the jockey arrived at the paddock, he learned that all the other horses had

   met one of two fates.

   Some of the horses had fallen.

   The rest had been disqualified.

5. So he jumped back onto Never Mind II.

   He rode him onto the track.

6. Never Mind II won the race.

   The race was two miles.

   His winning time was 11 minutes and 28 seconds.

   The race is normally finished in four minutes.

SELECTION D

1. Here's another odd bit of trivia.

   It is from the world of horseracing.

2. A jockey had just won the first race of his career.

   His name was Hayes.

   The date was June 4, 1923.

   After his victory, he immediately dropped dead.

SELECTION E

1. The first official baseball game played in the United States took place on June 19, 1846.

   It was between the "New York nine" and the Knickerbockers.

2. During the game, a New York player swore at the umpire.

   He started a baseball tradition by doing so.

   The tradition is long.

   The tradition is rich.

3. The New York player was named Davis.

   He was fined for his outburst.

   The fine was six cents.

SELECTION F

1. Hockey is known for its violence.

   Most of it seems to be intentional.

2. But one hockey game was marked by a very unusual incident.

   It was an incident of unintentional violence.

   It happened in 1930.

   The game was in Quebec.

   It was a junior amateur game.

3. A puck was lined at the goalie.

   The goalie was Abie Goldberry.

   The puck struck a pack of matches.

   The matches were in Goldberry's pocket.

   His uniform caught on fire.

4. The fire was put out.

   It was put out by players and spectators.

   Abie Goldberry was badly burned in the bizarre incident.

SELECTION G

1. During a basketball game at St. Peter's High School, all of the players on one team,

   with one exception, fouled out.

   The game was between sophomores and seniors.

   The game was played on March 16, 1937.

   The high school was in Fairmount, Virginia.

   The exception was Pat McGee.

2. When all the others fouled out, the game was tied.

   The score was 32–32.

   There were four minutes left to play.

3. It didn't look good for McGee's team.

4. But McGee faced the five players on the opposing team.

   He scored a goal.

   He made a foul shot.

   He defended his team's basket.

   He prevented his opponents from scoring.

5. McGee won the game for his team.

He did it single-handedly.

The final score was 35–32.

SELECTION H

1. In 1958 Robert F. Legge swam the Panama Canal.

Legge was a U.S. Navy doctor.

He was 53 years old.

The canal was 28.5 miles long.

His time was 21 hours and 54 minutes.

2. During the swim, he encountered only two live creatures.

One was a boa constrictor.

The other was an iguana.

3. At times, progress was difficult.

He had to contend with occasional swells.

The swells were a result of the heavy traffic of ships.

4. When he arrived at Balboa, he was met by a greeting party.

It consisted of several hundred well-wishers.

It also included a toll collector.

The toll collector charged Legge 72 cents.

That was the minimum fee for a one-ton vessel in ballast.

SELECTION I

1. In 1890 a postseason baseball series was played.

It was a best-of-seven series.

It was between New York of the National League and St. Louis of the American

Association.

2. New York had won three games.

    St. Louis had won two.

    Then the St. Louis Browns won their third game.

    The series was all tied up.

    It was three games apiece.

3. After they evened up the series, the Browns stayed out all night.

    They were celebrating.

    The next day, they claimed to be "too tuckered out" to take the field.

    As a consequence, the final game was canceled.

    The best-of-seven series still stands as "tied 3-3" in the record books today.

SELECTION J

1. In 1865 Louis Fox was playing John Deery in Rochester, New York.

    They were playing pool.

    They were playing for a $1000 purse.

2. Louis Fox was a billiard champion.

    He was enjoying a very comfortable lead.

    Suddenly, a fly landed on the cue ball.

3. The problem was how to get the fly to move without moving the cue ball.

4. Those who were present tried everything.

    The fly would not budge.

    It didn't matter what anyone did.

5. Fox was more than bugged by the presence of the fly.

    He became completely rattled.

6. He miscued.

    He lost the match with Deery.

He rushed out of the pool hall.

He was angry.

7. Several days later his body was found.

    It was floating in the river.

    The river was near the pool hall.

    Many people assumed that Fox committed suicide after his strange loss.

Exercise Two:

Sweet Dreams

PART A

1. Recently, the editors of *Psychology Today* asked their readers a question.

    They asked readers if they remembered their dreams.

2. More than 1000 of the magazine's readers responded.

    Approximately 95 percent of the readers reported that they do remember at least

    some of their dreams.

    About 68 percent claimed to have a recurring dream.

3. Two different themes were represented most frequently in the recurring dreams.

    One was the experience of being chased.

    The other was the sensation of falling.

4. They reported other recurring themes.

    Those themes included flying.

    They included appearing naked or almost naked in a public place.

    Another one was being unprepared to take a test.

    One was the act of returning to the dreamer's childhood home.

5. About 45 percent of the readers said that they sometimes dream about celebrities.

    The celebrities that were noted most frequently were so-called sex symbols and

    rock stars.

6. After sex symbols and rock stars, people most often reported dreaming about politicians and historical figures.

   One such historical figure was Abraham Lincoln.

7. Lincoln himself put a lot of stock in dreams.

   He believed that one dream forewarned him of his own assassination.

8. Of those who responded to the *Psychology Today* survey, 28 percent had seen themselves die in a dream.

   That sounds very ominous.

   Some experts say a dream of one's own death should not be at all frightening.

PART B

1. Ann Faraday is a psychologist.

   She is the author of *The Dream Game.*

   She says that a dream about one's death often indicates something far different from what you might expect.

2. She says it usually symbolizes the death of a self-image.

   The self-image is obsolete.

   She says it signals an opportunity to move to a higher state of self-definition.

3. The interpretation of dreams in general is a highly controversial area.

4. There are those who follow Sigmund Freud.

   They believe that dreams are the key to the unconscious.

5. Then there are those who follow the thinking of Francis Crick.

   He is a Nobel laureate.

   He believes that dreams are a garbage disposal for the mind.

6. Their function is to clear out a certain type of information.

   That information is useless.

   It interferes with rational thought.

It interferes with memory.

This is what Crick believes.

7. Then there is a third school of thought.

It consists of psychologists who believe that dreams are not important in themselves.

They believe that dreams become important because people think they are important.

8. These psychologists believe that people give dreams meaning.

People give them influence.

They give them power.

Exercise Three:

A Giant of a Man

PART A

1. *The People's Almanac #3* includes a cautionary tale.

   The almanac is the work of David Wallechinsky and Irving Wallace.

   The tale is for anyone who has ever daydreamed about what it would be like to be a giant.

2. It is not a tall tale.

   It is a true story.

   It is the story of Robert Wadlow.

   He was probably the tallest person who has ever lived.

3. Wadlow was born in Alton, Illinois.

   He was born on February 22, 1918.

   His weight at birth was nothing unusual.

   He was eight-and-a-half pounds.

4. His family history was normal.

   There were no unusually tall members in his family.

5. But he grew rapidly.

   He grew steadily.

   This was true from birth.

   It didn't stop until his death.

6. He was weighed at six months.

   He was 30 pounds.

   The average six-month-old baby weighs from 15 to 17 pounds.

7. He was weighed again at 18 months.

   His weight was 62 pounds.

   The average toddler at that age weighs 24 or 25 pounds.

8. He underwent his first thorough examination at the age of five.

   He was five feet four inches tall.

   He weighed 105 pounds.

9. He started school when he was five and a half.

   He was wearing clothes made for 17-year-olds.

10. He was measured again at the age of eight.

    He had reached a height of six feet.

    His father was Robert Wadlow, Sr.

    His father started wearing hand-me-downs.

    The hand-me-downs came from his son.

PART B

1. When Robert Wadlow was 12, his rapid growth was finally diagnosed.

   The diagnosis was excessive pituitary gland secretion.

After that, careful records of his growth were kept.

They were kept at Washington University.

Washington University is in St. Louis, Missouri.

2. He grew an average of three inches a year.

This rate of growth continued throughout his entire life.

At his death he was eight feet eleven.

He died on July 15, 1940.

3. His early death was not surprising.

4. Pituitary giants usually die before middle age.

Their organs outgrow their own ability to function correctly.

5. Physical coordination becomes difficult for a giant.

As a result, a giant usually has many more accidents than a normal-sized person

has.

6. A giant's accidents also tend to result in more serious injuries.

This problem is compounded by the fact that a giant's body heals more slowly.

7. Wadlow in particular had more than his share of physical problems.

They began with an operation for a double hernia.

The operation took place when he was two.

8. Everything he encountered in this world was on the wrong scale.

School desks were too small.

Doorways were too low.

Beds were too short.

Chairs were too tiny.

9. He had terrible problems with his feet.

10. Doctors advised Wadlow to walk as much as possible.

Walking was supposed to build up the strength in his feet.

It did not.

It damaged his arches even more severely.

11. For a while he attended Shurtleff College.

He wanted to become a lawyer.

He had to drop out.

The reason was that it was too difficult for him to walk from classroom to class-

room.

PART C

1. Robert Wadlow's life was marked by tragedy.

His life was not completely tragic.

2. He was intelligent.

He was charming.

He had good parents.

They tried to make his life as normal as possible.

They tried to make it as full as possible.

3. His boyhood days were filled with typical things.

They were filled with hobbies.

They were filled with sports.

He belonged to the Boy Scouts.

He loved to read.

4. But his life was also filled with things that were not so typical.

5. The more unusual aspects of Wadlow's story started when he was discovered by

the media.

That discovery happened when he was nine.

6. It happened when the Associated Press came across a photograph.

The Associated Press circulated it in newspapers all across the nation.

7. That's when Robert Wadlow became a public person.

8. From that time on, he had to deal with a steady stream of people.

   Some were reporters.

   Some were medical researchers.

   Some were curiosity seekers.

   Some were entrepreneurs.

9. Theatrical agents pressured him to perform.

   They made very attractive offers.

   They wanted his services.

10. His parents rejected all opportunities to make money from his misfortune.

11. He did, however, make appearances for the Peters Shoe Company.

    They were paid appearances.

    The Peters Shoe Company was in St. Louis.

12. This endorsement arrangement was appropriate.

    Wadlow had to have specially made shoes.

    He often outgrew new shoes even before they were delivered.

13. Robert Wadlow also worked for the Ringling Brothers Circus.

    He worked for Ringling Brothers in New York and Boston.

    He did so for a short time.

    This was in 1937.

    There were strict conditions in his contract with the circus.

14. These were the conditions of the contract.

    He would make only three-minute appearances.

    He would make them in the center ring.

He would not make them in the sideshow.

He would wear ordinary street clothes for his appearances.

15. Wadlow occasionally made appearances for churches.

    He also helped to raise funds for charities.

    He accepted no pay for these activities.

PART D

1. In 1936 Robert Wadlow had a visit from a doctor.

    He was a doctor from a small town in Missouri.

    The doctor was interested in studying giantism.

2. He happened to catch Wadlow on a bad day.

    Bad days were relatively rare for Wadlow.

3. The doctor later wrote an article about Wadlow.

    The article was published in the *Journal of the American Medical Association.*

    The article described Wadlow as dull.

    It described him as surly.

4. According to information cited in *The People's Almanac #3,* this characterization

    is generally true of most pathological giants.

    It was not true of Robert Wadlow.

    He was truly an exceptional human being.

5. The unflattering description in the medical journal hurt Wadlow deeply.

    It disillusioned him.

    It did so for two reasons.

6. For one thing, all his life he had put up with medical researchers.

    The medical researchers invaded his privacy.

    They took up his time.

He had always done so voluntarily.

He had usually done so graciously.

7. For another thing, the article was based on the doctor's impressions.

   Those impressions were made very quickly.

   The doctor's only visit with Wadlow had lasted less than an hour.

8. Wadlow wanted his character vindicated.

   His family did, too.

   They took legal action against the doctor.

   They also took legal action against the American Medical Association (AMA).

9. The AMA strongly defended the doctor.

   The litigation dragged on and on.

   The matter was not resolved when Wadlow died.

   He died at the age of 22.

10. Robert Wadlow stipulated that after his death he wanted his body to be kept out of the hands of medical researchers.

    His stipulation was partly the result of this episode.

11. In accordance with his wishes, there was no examination of his body after his death.

12. He was buried in a custom-built casket.

    The casket was ten feet long.

    The casket was placed inside a tomb.

    The tomb was almost impregnable.

    The tomb was in his hometown.

13. More than 46,000 people came to the funeral home in Alton, Illinois.

    They paid their last respects to Robert Wadlow.

Exercise Four:

Control and Well-being

PART A

1. Judith Rodin is a psychology professor.

    She teaches at Yale University.

    She has been involved in some of the most important studies on a number of topics.

    One topic is bystander intervention.

    One is learned helplessness.

    One is obesity.

    One is aging.

2. She is interested in relationships.

    One that especially interests her is the relationship between the mind and the body.

    Another one is the relationship between biology and environment.

3. Older people, in particular, have benefitted from Rodin's research.

4. In fact, it's been said that it's not easy for her to find places in Connecticut where

    she can continue to study the problems of older people in nursing homes.

    This is because so many positive changes have already been made in the state's

    nursing homes as a result of her work.

5. Rodin conducted a study of the issue of perceived choice among residents of

    nursing homes.

    She did this at one point in her career.

    She did this with psychologist Ellen Langer.

    The study was fascinating.

    It was described in a recent issue of *Psychology Today*.

6. Perceived choice is the amount of control that a person believes he or she has over

    events.

7. Rodin already knew that the degree to which people feel they can exert control in important areas of their lives influences three things.

    It influences their happiness.

    It influences their ability to perform.

    It influences their sense of well-being.

    She knew this on the basis of laboratory studies.

PART B

1. But Judith Rodin and Ellen Langer wanted to investigate perceived choice or control in a real-life setting.

    The real-life setting they chose was a nursing home.

2. They were especially interested in one relationship.

    It was the relationship between the degree of control that the nursing home residents thought they had and the residents' health and happiness.

3. Rodin and Langer believed that a nursing home might be a place where the effects of increased control could show up dramatically.

    Improvements in well-being could be quite obvious.

    They would show up in people who were already sick or frail.

4. It would be more difficult to show the positive benefits of an increased sense of control in people who were younger and healthier.

    In those people, any benefits would more likely be in the form of prevention rather than improvement.

5. The results of the study were indeed dramatic.

6. Nursing home residents in the study were given new choices.

    These were in areas in which they had previously had no choice.

    Many of the new choices seemed quite trivial.

7. For example, residents were allowed to choose when to see a movie.

   They were allowed to arrange their rooms as they wished.

PART C

1. The choices may have been trivial.

   The results were not.

2. The researchers used a variety of methods to measure the effects of the residents'

   new sense of control.

   The researchers discovered that the residents' new sense of control had a number

   of effects.

   One effect was an improvement in their health.

   One effect was an improvement in their overall mental state.

   One effect was a drop in the death rate at the nursing home.

3. Why would new choices in trivial areas of life have such profound effects?

4. Rodin explains that the choices seem trivial only to people who have a broad range

   of choices in their lives.

   To those who have little or no choice, any choice at all has great impact.

5. A sense of control or perceived choice created a profound psychological state.

   It is a state in which the residents felt better about themselves.

6. They felt a sense of power.

   That sense of power caused them to respond more positively to family members.

   It caused them to respond more positively to other residents.

   It caused them to respond more positively to nurses and doctors.

   In turn, it caused everyone in their lives to respond more positively toward them.

7. Choosing when to see a movie or where to put a picture on a wall might seem

   trivial.

But Rodin says that small bit of control can have an energizing effect.

It can have that effect in every aspect of an older person's life.

Exercise Five:

Good Kids

PART A

(This exercise is based on material in *More FYI: For Your Information.*)

1. Dr. Marian Radke Yarrow is chief of the Laboratory of Developmental Psychology.

    The laboratory is part of the National Institute of Mental Health.

    Dr. Carolyn Zahn-Waxler is a psychologist.

    Yarrow and Zahn-Waxler conducted a study.

    The study was to find out if kindness and selfless behavior are possible in very

    young children.

2. Many child development experts doubt that they are.

    Those experts insist that children are not really capable of kindness until around

    age five.

3. That is when the superego begins to emerge.

    The *superego* is a term from Sigmund Freud.

4. The superego is part of a person's psyche.

    It is the part that incorporates the moral standards of society.

    It is mostly unconscious.

5. But Yarrow and Zahn-Waxler found that young children are capable of both empa-

    thy and altruism.

    These young children include infants and toddlers.

6. The researchers set up a group.

    It included 24 families.

    It was a representative group.

7. Some of the babies in the study were as young as ten months

8. The researchers trained the mothers.

   The mothers were taught how to record their babies' responses to a variety of displays of human emotion.

   They were to record how their babies reacted to displays of affection, happiness, and kindness.

   They were also to record how their babies reacted to displays of pain, sadness, anger, and fatigue.

PART B

1. The study was over in nine months.

   Then the mothers reported their findings.

   Some mothers were very surprised at what they had found.

   There was much more empathetic and altruistic behavior than they would have predicted.

2. There were many examples.

   One example was a one-year-old who comforted another child with hugs and pats.

   She also offered her blanket on occasion.

3. Another toddler tried to protect his mother.

   This happened on a visit to the doctor.

   The toddler tried to hit a throat swab out of the doctor's hand.

   The doctor was trying to examine the mother.

   The mother had a sore throat.

4. There was also a lot of sympathetic mimicry.

   This is when a child sees someone else get hurt.

   The child says "Ouch!" or winces even though the physical pain is being experienced by someone else.

5. There is a great deal of debate about what causes some babies, toddlers, and young preschoolers to be this way.

   Some experts say these qualities may be inborn in certain human beings.

   Others say these qualities are not inborn at all.

   These experts insist qualities such as kindness and selflessness are taught or developed.

6. This is an example of the famous "nature or nurture" argument.

7. In Yarrow and Zahn-Waxler's study, there were major differences among the children.

   The differences were in the degree of kindness and selflessness.

   None of the differences related to the sex of the children.

   None of the differences related to family size.

8. The only factor that seemed to make a difference was the behavior of the parents.

9. Children were much more likely to be altruistic and empathetic if their parents did certain things.

   These included offering lots of hugs and kisses.

   They included offering tissues and Band-Aids.

   They included offering words of praise and encouragement.

   They included explaining to the little ones why the feelings of others matter.

Exercise Six:

Mabel K. Staupers and Black Nurses in the Military

PART A

1. Mabel Keaton Staupers was one of the outstanding women of the twentieth century.

   She was a black woman.

She was fast-talking.

She was energetic.

2. She broke a link in a chain.

She did it almost single-handedly.

It was a chain that had kept many black women from using their talents and skills.

It was a chain that had denied them their full rights as American citizens.

3. Her story is fascinating.

It is inspiring.

It is a classic David and Goliath tale.

It is told in *Black Leaders of the Twentieth Century.*

4. It is the story of a battle between one woman and two branches of the American military.

The woman was the executive secretary of the National Association of Colored Graduate Nurses (NACGN).

The branches of the military were the U.S. Army and the Navy.

5. Mabel K. Staupers' accomplishment must be viewed within the context of a certain period in American history if it is to be fully appreciated.

6. It was around the time that the United States entered into World War II.

American blacks had recently become much less accepting of the racial status quo.

There were many reasons for this.

One was the anti-Nazi mood of the nation.

7. For some blacks, their unequal treatment in their own country was highlighted in an ironic way by America's opposition to Nazi Germany.

8. In opposing the philosophy and actions of Germany's Nazis, the U.S. government did a lot of talking.

So did many members of the press.

So did much of the general public.

They all talked a lot about the ideals upon which America had been founded.

9. They contrasted Germany to an America that was pure in the realization of its democratic ideals.

They spoke of an America that was just in its treatment of people of different backgrounds.

Those backgrounds might include religion, ethnic origin, or race.

10. Such statements about this country struck some Americans as hypocritical.

They struck some Americans as ironic.

Some of those Americans were black.

Some were white.

11. One person summed this up well at the time.

He was Walter White.

He wrote, "World War II has immeasurably magnified the Negro's awareness of the disparity between the American profession and practice of democracy."

PART B

1. It was during this time and in this context that Mabel K. Staupers began her long fight.

Her fight was for the rights of black nurses.

She used patience.

She used persistence.

She used a great deal of political savvy.

2. Staupers was born in Barbados, West Indies.

She was born in 1890.

She came to New York with her parents.

They came to New York in 1903.

3. She graduated from Freedmen's Hospital School of Nursing.

   It was in Washington, D.C.

   She graduated in 1917.

   Then she began her career.

   Her first position was as a private nurse in New York City.

4. She played an important role in establishing the Booker T. Washington Sanatorium.

   The Booker T. Washington Sanatorium was in Harlem.

   It was the first facility in the area where black doctors could treat patients.

5. Then she worked as the executive secretary for the Harlem Committee of the New

   York Tuberculosis and Health Association.

   She did that for 12 years.

6. Finally, Staupers was appointed executive secretary of the NACGN.

   That was in 1934.

   In her new position, she focused on one main goal.

   That goal was to help black nurses become fully integrated into the mainstream of

   American health care.

7. Then the United States entered World War II.

   It was 1941.

8. Mabel K. Staupers had a perfect opportunity to realize her goal.

   The war created a great demand for nurses to care for the wounded.

9. That demand could result in the acceptance of black nurses into the Army and Navy

   Nurse Corps.

   That acceptance could be a vehicle.

It could be a vehicle for the integration of blacks into the profession of nursing in America.

1. Staupers knew that black nurses had suffered great discrimination in World War I.

   She vowed that would not happen again if she could help it.

2. So Staupers fought her own battle.

   She fought it throughout the years of the American war effort.

   She fought it on various fronts.

3. First, she fought the exclusion of black women from the Army and Navy Nurse Corps.

4. Then later, the Army established a quota system for black nurses.

   She fought the quota system.

   She fought it because it implied that black nurses were inferior to other nurses.

5. At one point, she fought another policy of the military.

   It was the policy of having black nurses care for black soldiers and no others.

6. Later she discovered the Army was finally assigning black nurses to care for white soldiers.

   But those white soldiers included no Americans.

   The white soldiers were German prisoners of war.

   She fought that practice, too.

1. These were tough battles.

   Staupers eventually found a powerful ally.

   That ally was First Lady Eleanor Roosevelt.

2. Eleanor Roosevelt began lobbying for black nurses.

3. She talked to Norman T. Kirk.

   He was the surgeon general of the U.S. Army.

   She talked to W. J. C. Agnew.

   He was a rear admiral in the U.S. Navy.

   Most of all, she talked to her husband.

   Her husband was Franklin D. Roosevelt.

4. Meanwhile, Staupers staged a public confrontation with Norman T. Kirk.

   It was a confrontation that received a good deal of coverage in the press.

5. Kirk described the dire shortage of nurses in the Army.

   He predicted that a draft for nurses might be necessary.

   He made his prediction in a speech at the Hotel Pierre.

   The Hotel Pierre is in New York.

6. Staupers was in Kirk's audience.

   The audience was made up of about 300 people.

   The audience included nurses.

   It included politicians.

   It included private citizens.

7. She rose to her feet.

   She asked the surgeon general, "If nurses are needed so desperately, why isn't the Army using colored nurses?"

8. She explained to the entire audience that there were 9000 registered black nurses in the United States.

   The Army had taken 247.

   The Navy had taken none.

9. Kirk was visibly uncomfortable, according to newspaper reports.

   He did not have much of an answer for Staupers.

PART E

1. At about the same time, President Roosevelt announced his desire to amend the

   Selective Service Act of 1940.

   He wanted it amended so that nurses could be drafted.

   He made his desire known in a radio address.

   The address was broadcast on January 6, 1945.

2. The public reaction was tremendous.

   The injustice of calling for a general draft while at the same time discriminating

   against black nurses was obvious to almost everyone.

3. Staupers showed a lot of political savvy in the way she handled the public's dissatis-

   faction with the plans of the top brass.

4. She gave speeches.

   She issued press releases.

   She urged people to send telegrams to President Roosevelt.

5. The groups that sent messages of protest to the White House included the National

   Association for the Advancement of Colored People (NAACP).

   They included the Congress of Industrial Organizations.

   They included the American Federation of Labor.

   They included the United Council of Church Women.

   They included the Catholic Interracial Council.

   They included the Alpha Kappa Alpha Sorority.

   They included the New York Citizens' Committee of the Upper West Side.

6. The great wave of public protest had an effect.

   The policies of exclusion, segregation, and quota systems for black nurses were

   ended.

   They were dropped by the Army.

   They were dropped by the Navy.

   They were dropped by the War Department.

7. A few weeks later a black woman was the first to break the color barrier in the U.S.

   Navy Nurse Corps.

   She was Phyllis Dailey.

8. The Army also began to accept black nurses with no restrictions.

9. Most of the credit goes to one woman.

   It goes to one woman alone.

   It goes to Mabel K. Staupers.

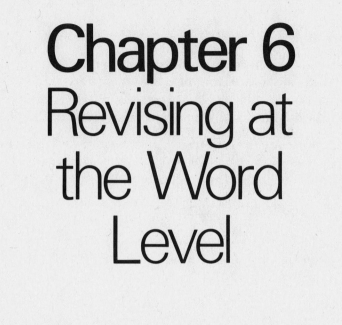

Chapter 6
Revising at the Word Level

One student might need to do all the units in this chapter, and another might need to do only one or two. If you're unsure about your needs, please rely on the advice of your writing teacher.

These units are all independent of one another; therefore, they can be done in any order.

UNIT 1: Subject-Verb Agreement

We all follow a system of subject-verb agreement, even those of us who might not be able to define what subject-verb agreement is. If you listen to your speech and the speech of your family and friends, you'll find that most people follow a fairly consistent pattern. For instance, you probably say *She smiles* and *He laughs,* or you say *She smile* and *He laugh.* In other words, you have your own unconscious rules about adding or dropping the *-s* or *-es* on a verb when it's in the present tense. You usually don't stop and think about this, but you do have rules that you follow with great consistency.

The problem is that your rules for subject-verb agreement might be different from those that have been established as "standard." To learn new rules for verb forms now —as an adult—you need to stop and think about subject-verb agreement. You need to become conscious and deliberate about language.

If you're an adult who's learning a new system of subject-verb agreement, this unit will be only a starting point for you. You will need to work very carefully finding and revising examples of disagreement in your own writing, and you might even need to make up additional exercises for yourself. We'll show you how to do that later.

If you use the standard forms in your speech most of the time, then you don't need to work on the basic system of subject-verb agreement, and your teacher will probably tell you to skip ahead to the section entitled "Three Important Points" on page 227 and begin your subject-verb agreement work there. What you will be doing in this unit is focusing on the trouble spots. Those are the areas where most writers do occasionally vary from the standard rules. Some of the things that create errors in **221** subject-verb agreement are prepositional phrases within the complete subject, the word *or* between singular key words in the subject, and delayed subjects (those that follow the verb).

The Standard Rules

Subject-verb agreement is basically a problem only in the present tense. Here are the standard rules that you should learn to follow:

If your subject is singular, add *-s* or *-es* to your verb.

For example:

S   V

1. (a)   One teenage <u>suicide</u> <u>occurs</u> every 90 minutes in the United States.

The subject *suicide* is singular (one), so we added an *-s* to the verb *occur* and produced *occurs*. Now we'll make the subject plural (more than one) and see how the verb changes to agree with it:

S   V

(b)   Teenage <u>suicides</u> <u>occur</u> at the rate of one every 90 minutes in the United States.

The rule shown in 1. (b) is this:

If your subject is plural, use the base verb.

The word *suicides* is plural, so we used the base verb *occur* to agree with it. By *base verb* we mean a verb with no ending—no *-s* or *-es*, no *-d* or *-ed*, no *-ing* or any other ending.

Label the subject in each example below and fill in the standard form of the verb, choosing from *live* and *lives*:

2. (a)   The pint-sized sand cat _____ on the extremely hot sand

dunes of African, Asian, and Arabian deserts.

(b)   Pint-sized sand cats _____ on the extremely hot sand dunes of

African, Asian, and Arabian deserts.

[*Answers:* If you used an *-s* in (a) and the base verb in (b), you're on the right track.]

Study these correct examples and read them aloud several times before you do the first exercise, please:

(a)   A steak sizzles.
Steaks sizzle.

(b) The horse prances.
     Horses prance.

(c) One light flickers.
     Five lights flicker.

(d) The roof leaks.
     Roofs often leak.

(e) The girl stretches.
     The girls stretch.

(f) A balloon pops.
     Balloons pop.

(g) The group decides.
     The groups decide.

Exercise One

Directions: Fill in each blank with the verb that agrees with the subject. Use the base verb or add *-s* or *-es*. For example:

The plan succeeds.
The plans succeed.

1. A carpenter _____ . *(build)*

   Carpenters _____ .

2. One star _____ . *(shine)*

   All the stars _____ .

3. The golfer _____ . *(putt)*

   Golfers _____ .

4. Roses _____ . *(grow)*

   A rose _____ .

5. The chimneys _____ . *(smoke)*

   The chimney _____ .

6. A pitcher _____ . *(pitch)*

   Pitchers _____ .

7. One loaf _____ . *(rise)*

   The loaves _____ .

8. Bombs _____ . *(explode)*

   A bomb _____ .

9. The popsicle _____ . *(melt)*

   Popsicles _____ .

10. Last-minute shoppers _____ . *(rush)*

    A last-minute shopper _____ .

A Note on Spelling

In the next exercise, you'll notice that sometimes a small spelling change is necessary before you add an *-s* or *-es* to a base verb. For example, with a word that ends in *-y*, such as *fry*, you change the *-y* to *-i* before you add *-es*. So *fry* becomes *fries*.

Exercise Two

Directions: Fill in each blank with the verb that agrees with the subject. Use the base verb or add *s* or *-es*. Make other spelling changes where necessary.

1. The article _____ . *(explain)*

   The articles _____ .

2. One baby _____ . *(cry)*

   All the babies _____ .

3. One player _____ . *(win)*

   Four players _____ .

4. The team _____ . *(perform)*

   The teams _____ .

5. The ink spots _____ . *(dry)*

   An ink spot _____ .

6. The soldiers _____ . *(march)*

   A soldier _____ .

7. The telephone _____ . *(ring)*

   Telephones _____ .

8. Ideas _____ . *(form)*

   An idea _____ .

9. Chickens _____ . *(hatch)*

   A chicken _____ .

10. A peacemaker _____ . *(pacify)*

    Peacemakers _____ .

NOTE: If you need more of this kind of basic practice in subject-verb agreement, it's easy to make up your own exercises, using the preceding two as models. Make up a couple every week during the time you're taking your writing course. Ask your teacher or a tutor to check your answers and, of course, pay close attention to the subjects and verbs in your own writing.

Two Important Exceptions

There are two important exceptions to the standard rules that we have described. One involves the word *I,* and the other involves the word *you.* When *I* and *you* are used as subjects, they always appear with the base verb. These are correct examples: *I want, I sing,* and *I give; You want, You sing,* and *You give.* Even though *I* is singular and *you* can be singular or plural in its meaning, each pronoun—*I* and *you*—agrees with a base verb.

The Verbs *To Be* and *To Have*

Here's an easy way to approach subject-verb agreement when the verb is a form of *to be* or *to have.* Just as with regular verbs, the correct form to match a singular subject will end in *-s.* The correct form to match a plural subject will not end in *-s.* Study these correct examples:

SINGULAR SUBJECT	PLURAL SUBJECT
The dessert *is* delicious.	The desserts *are* delicious.
The dessert *was* delicious.	The desserts *were* delicious.
The dessert *has* pizzazz.	The desserts *have* pizzazz.

Notice that all the words that agree with the singular subject *dessert* end in *-s: is, was,* and *has.*

Also notice that the verbs that agree with the plural subject *desserts* do not end in *-s.* They are *are, were,* and *have.*

Fill in the blanks:

1. (a) A typical food allergy _____ *(are/is)* most likely to be caused

   by eggs, milk, fish, nuts, wheat, peas, and soybeans.

(b)   Typical food allergies _____ *(are/is)* most likely to be caused

by eggs, milk, fish, nuts, wheat, peas, and soybeans.

2. (a)   Allergy victims _____ *(has/have)* ten times as much immuno-

globulin E in their blood as normal people.

(b)   An allergy victim _____ *(has/have)* ten times as much im-

munoglobulin E as a normal person.

[*Answers.* 1. (a) is; 1. (b) are; 2. (a) have; 2. (b) has.]

Now try this simple exercise.

Exercise Three

Directions: Fill in each blank with the verb that agrees with the subject. Remember: A singular subject agrees with a verb that ends in *-s*—with the exceptions of *I* and *you,* which are treated as plural subjects.

1. A Steven Spielberg movie _____ *(has/have)* certain characteristics.

   Steven Spielberg movies _____ *(has/have)* certain characteristics.

2. Her attitude _____ *(is/are)* wonderful.

   Their attitudes _____ *(is/are)* wonderful.

3. The mail carriers _____ *(was/were)* late.

   The mail carrier _____ *(was/were)* late.

4. Soft pretzels _____ *(is/are)* one of life's little necessities.

   A soft pretzel _____ *(is/are)* one of life's little necessities.

5. One fingernail _____ *(was/were)* polished with jade green lacquer.

   Her fingernails _____ *(was/were)* polished with jade green lacquer.

6. That policy _____ *(is/are)* very effective.

   Those policies _____ *(is/are)* very effective.

7. The average student _____ *(has/have)* always had to work hard to

   achieve success.

Most students _____ *(has/have)* always had to work hard to achieve

success.

8. The rings _____ *(has/have)* great sentimental value.

   The ring _____ *(has/have)* great sentimental value.

9. A glass bottle _____ *(is/are)* on the window ledge.

   Two glass bottles _____ *(is/are)* on the window ledge.

10. The puzzle _____ *(was/were)* impossible.

    The puzzles _____ *(was/were)* impossible.

Three Important Points

There are three important points about subject-verb agreement that everyone should know. We'll look at each one before you begin the more difficult exercises.

1. Using *And* and *Or* Between Key Words in the Subject

You probably already know that two singular words joined with *and* form a plural subject. But you should also know that two singular words joined with *or* form a singular subject. Study these correct examples:

                              S   S

1. (a) A magazine subscription **and** a book club membership make good gifts for the person who has everything.

                              S   S

   (b) A magazine subscription **or** a book club membership makes a good gift for the person who has everything.

Fill in the blanks:

  2. (a) Red and blue _____ *(is/are)* most people's favorite colors.

    (b) Red or blue _____ *(is/are)* the average person's favorite color.

[*Answers.* 2. (a) are; 2. (b) is.]

2. Using Prepositional Phrases in the Subject

Remember when you worked with prepositional phrases in Chapter 1, Unit 4? The reason for introducing them at all was to warn you that the key word in the subject is never within a prepositional phrase, and the key word in the subject is, of course, the word with which the verb must agree. So you have to be careful to set off any prepositional phrases that appear within the complete subject of a sentence.

Study these correct examples:

$$\overset{\text{S}}{} \quad \overset{\text{V}}{}$$

1. (a)   Rock and roll <u>festivals</u> <u>are</u> a common feature of summertime entertainment in the United States.

$$\overset{\text{S}}{} \qquad\qquad\qquad \overset{\text{V}}{}$$

   (b)   Any <u>history</u> (of rock and roll festivals) <u>is</u> sure to begin with Woodstock.

In 1. (a), the word *festivals* is the key word in the subject, and because it is plural, it agrees with *are.* But in 1. (b), the word *festivals* is not the key word in the subject. Why not? It's not the key word because it's in a prepositional phrase—*of rock and roll festivals.* (The preposition is *of.*) A prepositional phrase modifies the subject, but it never contains the subject.

In 1. (b), the key word in the subject is *history,* and because *history* is a singular word, it agrees with the verb *is.*

Fill in the blanks:

2. (a)   Easter Island _____ *(has/have)* baffled historians and anthropologists for many years.

   (b)   The gigantic stone statues on Easter Island _____ *(has/have)* baffled historians and anthropologists for many years.

[*Answers.* In 2. (a), the subject is *Easter Island,* and the verb is *has.* In (b), the subject is *statues,* and the verb is *have.* In (b), the prepositional phrase *on Easter Island* should be enclosed within parentheses.]

3.   **Using Delayed Subjects**

There are two kinds of sentences that have delayed subjects. A subject is called "delayed" when it follows the verb.

One kind of sentence with a delayed subject is one that begins with the word *there* or *here.* If a sentence begins with either word, you have to look beyond the verb to find the real subject—the word with which the verb must agree. Study these correct examples:

$$\qquad\qquad \overset{\text{V}}{} \qquad\quad \overset{\text{S}}{}$$

1. (a)   There <u>was</u> one bad <u>joke</u> in the middle of the script.

$$\qquad\qquad \overset{\text{V}}{} \qquad\qquad \overset{\text{S}}{}$$

   (b)   There <u>were</u> several bad <u>jokes</u> in the middle of the script.

$$\qquad\quad \overset{\text{V}}{} \qquad \overset{\text{S}}{}$$

2. (a)   Here <u>is</u> the best <u>play</u> of the day.

$$\qquad\quad \overset{\text{V}}{} \qquad\qquad \overset{\text{S}}{}$$

   (b)   Here <u>are</u> the two best <u>plays</u> of the day.

Think of the words *there* and *here* as empty sentence starters. They're not the subjects in any of the four sentences above. They're just sort of placeholders that indicate where the subject word would normally be.

The other kind of sentence with a delayed subject is a question. In these sentences the question word acts in the same way as *there* or *here.* Study these correct examples:

$$\overset{V}{}\qquad\overset{S}{}$$

3. (a)   What <u>is</u> your <u>plan</u>?

$$\overset{V}{}\qquad\overset{S}{}$$

   (b)   What <u>are</u> your <u>plans</u>?

$$\overset{V}{}\qquad\qquad\overset{S}{}$$

4. (a)   Where <u>was</u> his new <u>shirt</u>?

$$\overset{V}{}\qquad\qquad\overset{S}{}$$

   (b)   Where <u>were</u> his new <u>shirts</u>?

Write *S* over the real subject and fill in each blank with the correct verb:

5. (a)   There _____ *(is/are)* at least one good solution to this

      problem.

   (b)   There _____ *(is/are)* at least two good solutions to this

      problem.

6. (a)   Here _____ *(is/are)* the most important factors to consider.

   (b)   Here _____ *(is/are)* the most important factor to consider.

7. (a)   How _____ *(do/does)* your garden grow?

   (b)   How _____ *(do/does)* your flowers grow?

8. (a)   When _____ *(is/are)* the parties supposed to begin?

   (b)   When _____ *(is/are)* the party supposed to begin?

[*Answers.* 5. (a) is, solution; 5. (b) are, solutions; 6. (a) are, factors; 6. (b) is, factor; 7. (a) does, garden; 7. (b) do, flowers; 8. (a) are, parties; 8. (b) is, party.]

Important Note on the Exercises

The remaining exercises in the unit demand a good grounding in all the points we've covered. If you need to review, please do so before you proceed.

In the exercises, when the directions ask you to label the subject, please understand that you're really being asked to mark the *key word or words* within the complete subject.

Exercise Four

Directions: Write *S* over the subject of each clause. Then fill in the blank with the form of the verb that agrees with the subject.

1. According to the latest records kept by the U.S. Agriculture Department, 1431 pounds of food _____ (are/is) consumed by the average American in one year. Twenty years ago the average intake of food per person _____ (was/were) 1381 pounds. Forecasters in the department's Economic Research Service _____ (say/says) that increases in the consumption of chicken, fish, vegetables, and vegetable oil _____ (are/is) expected. Meat and fruit _____ (appear/appears) to be on the decline.

2. The correct term for American buffaloes _____ (are/is) American bison.

3. Only the true fan among fans _____ (care/cares) enough about sports trivia to know that the real names of "the Georgia Peach" and "the Galloping Ghost" _____ (was/were) Ty Cobb and Red Grange.

4. According to chiropractors, poor posture habits in a child usually _____ (begin/begins) around age eight.

5. *Final Payments* and *The Company of Women* _____ (are/is) excellent novels by Mary Gordon. *Men and Angels* _____ (are/is) her most recent book.

6. Traditionally, there _____ (are/is) three gold balls on a sign that _____ (hang/hangs) over a pawnshop. The balls on the sign _____ (go/goes) back to the coat of arms of the Medicis, who _____ (was/were) a famous Italian family of bankers.

7. The numbers on opposite sides of a die always _____ (add/adds) up to seven.

8. A problem with a parent or the breakup of a relationship with a girlfriend or boyfriend _____ (are/is) perceived by teenagers as ranking very high

on a scale of stressful events, according to a recent study at Vanderbilt University in Nashville, Tennessee. However, the study found that the most stressful life event for teens _____ *(was/were)* receiving a failing grade on a report card.

9. There _____ *(are/is)* 729 vehicles for every 1000 people in Casper, Wyoming, and that fact _____ *(mean/means)* that Casper _____ *(rank/ranks)* first among America's cities in cars and trucks per capita. In vehicles per household (rather than per person), Simi Valley, California, _____ *(top/tops)* the list. Approximately 2.2 vehicles per household _____ *(are/is)* to be found there.

10. The price tag on the Mad Hatter's hat in Lewis Carroll's *Alice in Wonderland* _____ *(say/says)* "10/6," which _____ *(mean/means)* ten shillings and sixpence.

Exercise Five

Directions: Write *S* over the subject of each clause. Then fill in the blank with the form of the verb that agrees with the subject. This collection of strange facts _____ *(are/is)* based on information in *Life-spans, Or, How Long Things Last.*

1. One of every seven pennies in circulation eventually _____ *(end/ ends)* up out of circulation. This _____ *(happen/happens)* because the penny's owner _____ *(plunk/plunks)* it into a piggy bank or _____ *(force/forces)* it into early retirement in the bottom of a dresser drawer or in an inner compartment of an old purse. One of every 14 nickels _____ *(share/shares)* a similar fate.

2. Most nuts _____ *(stay/stays)* fresh for one year if they _____ *(remain/remains)* in the shell. However, pecans and Brazil nuts _____ *(keep/keeps)* for only six months unless you _____ *(store/stores)* them in the refrigerator.

3. Moonbeams, which _____ (are/is) rays of light from the sun reflected

 off the moon, _____ (take/takes) 1.3 seconds to travel from the moon

 to the earth.

4. The life span of a deck of cards _____ (depend/depends) upon a

 number of factors. The moisture in the hands of the card players

 _____ (are/is) one important factor because the moisture and oil in

 human skin definitely _____ (affect/affects) the cards' longevity. The

 condition of any and all playing surfaces on which the cards _____

 (are/is) used _____ (are/is) also significant. For some people a deck of

 cards _____ (last/lasts) a lifetime. For professional gamblers the aver-

 age pack _____ (has/have) outgrown its usefulness after two to five

 hours of playing time. After that, the cards usually _____ (show/

 shows) enough wear and tear that they _____ (slow/slows) down the

 dealer if they _____ (are/is) not replaced with a fresh pack.

5. A series of elastic waves, most often caused by the earth's rupture along a fault,

 _____ (are/is) better known as an earthquake. The length of most

 earthquakes _____ (are/is) not more than a few seconds, but major

 earthquakes, such as the one in Lisbon, Portugal, in 1975, _____

 (has/have) been clocked at over five minutes. Certainly one of the most devastating

 earthquakes in recent times _____ (was/were) the one to hit Mexico

 City in September 1985.

Exercise Six

Directions: Write *S* over the subject of each clause. Then fill in the blank with the form of the verb that agrees with the subject. These items are also based on information in *Life-spans, Or, How Long Things Last.*

1. The U.S. Code, Title 23, Section 109, _____ *(say/says)* that a road should be built to last a minimum of 20 years before it _____ *(need/ needs)* a major overhaul. A road or a highway _____ *(are/is)* going to fare well or not so well, depending upon a number of factors. Here _____ *(are/is)* some of them. Where _____ *(are/is)* the road or highway located? How much heavy traffic _____ *(do/does)* it carry? What materials _____ *(was/were)* used in the construction of the road?

2. As we all _____ *(know/knows)*, there _____ *(are/is)* some pilots who make a living by skywriting or skytyping commercial messages. You _____ *(has/have)* probably never asked yourself how long these messages _____ *(are/is)* visible in the air, but here _____ *(are/is)* the answer anyway. The average skywritten message _____ *(last/lasts)* five to seven minutes before it _____ *(evaporate/evaporates)*. But some _____ *(has/have)* much more staying power. In fact, one skywriter _____ *(report/reports)* that the word *PEPSI*, written in mile-high letters, _____ *(was/were)* still visible after 54 minutes.

3. How long _____ *(do/does)* a woman's reproductive capacity last? The answer in some cases _____ *(are/is)* well into her midfifties. In fact, in some parts of the world, it _____ *(are/is)* not terribly uncommon to find women who _____ *(are/is)* still having babies in their late 40s and beyond. Albania's rate of births for mothers over 50 years of age _____ *(are/is)* higher than that of any other country in the world.

4. The two separate parts of a pacemaker _____ (are/is) a pulse generator and an implantable lead. The pulse generator _____ (contain/con-
tains) the battery and circuitry. The wire and the electrode attached to the heart
_____ (form/forms) the implantable lead. Pacemakers
_____ (has/have) varying life spans, and the difference in life spans
basically _____ (reflect/reflects) variations in the quality and cost of
the pulse generator.

5. If you _____ (ask/asks) the average consumer, you'll probably find out
that a bottle of hand lotion or a can of shaving cream _____ (are/is)
expected to last indefinitely. But most cosmetics and toiletries
_____ (has/have) life spans of only two to two-and-a-half years. Some
_____ (are/is) especially delicate and short-lived. The active ingredients in a bottle of hair coloring, for example, _____ (are/is) easily
oxidized, and therefore, the potency of an opened bottle of dye often
_____ (change/changes) rather quickly. The oil in hand lotion and face
creams also _____ (present/presents) problems for the consumer
who _____ (stock/stocks) up ahead because the oil sometimes
_____ (become/becomes) rancid, and that, in turn,
_____ (cause/causes) the product to give off an odor or take on a
different color. Products for use around the eye _____ (are/is) especially tricky. A woman who uses eyeshadow, for example, _____
(introduce/introduces) germs into the pot of eyeshadow every time she
_____ (dip/dips) her finger into it. Consumers should be advised to
throw out eyeshadow, eyeliner, and mascara after three months, even if a particular
product _____ (are/is) not entirely used up. Most such products

_____ *(do/does)* contain antibacterial agents, but they

_____ *(don't/doesn't)* completely ensure against contamination, and

they _____ *(don't/doesn't)* last forever.

Exercise Seven

PART A

Directions: Write *S* over the subject of each clause. Then fill in the blank with the form of the verb that agrees with the subject. Here you'll work with some of the imaginary features of imaginary creatures that are found in myth and literature. Consult *Life-spans, Or, How Long Things Last* if you want more information about what you read here.

1. One of the most famous mythological creatures _____ *(are/is)* the centaur, an immortal being who _____ *(are/is)* pictured as half man and half horse. The habits of the typical centaur _____ *(are/is)* rather alarming: they _____ *(feast/feasts)* on raw flesh, _____ *(consume/consumes)* unbelievable amounts of liquor, and _____ *(spend/spends)* a great deal of time chasing the ladies. But there _____ *(are/is)* centaurs who march—or trot—to the beat of a different drummer. There _____ *(are/is)* the noble Chiron of Greek mythology, for instance. Hercules and Achilles _____ *(was/were)* educated by him.

2. Then you _____ *(has/have)* your dryads, although the proper name for dryads, of course, _____ *(are/is)* hamadryads. They _____ *(live/lives)* in trees, and the longevity of their dwellings _____ *(determine/determines)* their own life span. When a tree _____ *(go/goes)* down, its little occupant _____ *(go/goes)* with it. A dryad's death wail, which _____ *(are/is)* too high-pitched for a human being to hear, supposedly _____ *(cause/causes)*

every tree in the forest to shiver and shake. The next time you
_____ (are/is) out in the woods, don't be too sure it
_____ (are/is) just a breeze that's shaking those leaves.

3. The race of fairies _____ (has/have) a good chance of living until
Doomsday, according to legend. Fairies, by the way, _____ (are/is) not
always as tiny as Tinkerbell. Some _____ (measure/measures) up to
the approximate size of humans, and a few _____ (grow/grows) even
larger. The Western fairy, you'll be glad to know, _____ (live/lives) nine
ages and nine ages more. The Chinese fairy, which _____ (transform/
transforms) itself into any shape it _____ (desire/desires),
_____ (live/lives) 1000 years. The barriers between space and time
_____ (are/is) easily crossed by these creatures.

4. Elves _____ (are/is) a little different. There _____ (are/
is) elves who _____ (are/is) immortal, but they _____
(are/is) the ones who _____ (choose/chooses) not to live among people. The effect of being around human beings _____ (are/is) apparently not terribly beneficial.

5. A gnome or an earth spirit _____ (live/lives) 400 years, and during
that time, it _____ (guard/guards) hidden treasures that
_____ (are/is) buried in the earth. The exact location of a diamond
mine or a lode of gold _____ (are/is) safe with a gnome. There
_____ (are/is) many things that we _____ (know/knows)
about gnomes, including the fact that they _____ (are/is) made of
earth, and the fact that the writers of myth usually _____ (describe/
describes) them as red-eyed, hunchbacked, and runty-legged.

PART B

Directions: Write *S* over the subject of each clause. Then fill in the blank with the form of the verb that agrees with the subject. The discussion of mythological creatures _____ *(continue/continues).*

1. Hobbits _____ *(grow/grows)* to a height of about three feet and

   _____ *(live/lives)* a century or more. On their 111th birthday, if they

   _____ *(are/is)* lucky enough to live so long, they _____

   (celebrate/celebrates) it as a very special occasion.

2. Any story about dragons _____ *(are/is)* sure to please a little girl or

   boy. Dragons _____ *(appear/appears)* in literature and myth in a vari-

   ety of ways. For example, the giant red dragon in the Book of the Apocalypse

   _____ *(symbolize/symbolizes)* Satan, but in Chinese mythology the

   role that the dragon _____ *(play/plays)* _____ *(are/is)*

   exactly the opposite. The dragon, for example, _____ *(has/have)* en-

   joyed honors as a national deity and _____ *(was/were)* often consid-

   ered a model for the ideal man rather than a force that man must overcome. Still

   today, every 12 years the dragon _____ *(blow/blows)* the fire of new

   life into the Chinese New Year.

3. Sirens _____ *(are/is)* singing bird-women who _____

   (live/lives) in the high cliffs near the sea. Some _____ *(come/comes)*

   with the tails of mermaids; some _____ *(do/does)* not. There

   _____ *(are/is)* sirens whose songs _____ *(are/is)* ignored,

   and they _____ *(die/dies).* Then there _____ *(are/is)* si-

   rens who, with their beautiful, mysterious music, _____ *(lure/lures)*

   sailors, _____ *(lull/lulls)* them to sleep, and _____ *(tear/*

   tears) them limb from limb. In other words, a siren _____ *(are/is)* no-

   body to fool around with.

4. The legends about the unicorn _____ *(are/is)* many. Chinese myths _____ *(hold/holds)* that a unicorn _____ *(appear/appears)* only when a righteous leader _____ *(are/is)* born. (The last one _____ *[was/were]* on the scene around the time of Confucius, who lived from 551 to 479 B.C., so that should tell you something about the state of the world.) Another theory or myth _____ *(suggest/suggests)* that unicorns became extinct because the other passengers on Noah's Ark _____ *(was/were)* not too eager to have these strange, one-horned creatures along, and they denied the unicorns a berth.

5. One of the most beautiful symbols of rebirth in all of literature _____ *(are/is)* the phoenix. According to legend, there _____ *(are/is)* only one of these gorgeous red and gold birds alive at any one time. At the end of its long life, the large bird, which _____ *(has/have)* a wonderful voice, _____ *(prepare/prepares)* a woody nest and _____ *(sit/sits)* in it. There the phoenix _____ *(are/is)* consumed by flames. But after the phoenix _____ *(burn/burns)*, a small white grub _____ *(appear/appears)* and _____ *(make/makes)* its way out of the ashes. Before long, the white grub _____ *(become/becomes)* the new phoenix.

UNIT 2: *-Ed* Endings

The primary purpose of this unit is to help students who often drop the *-d* or *-ed* endings on regular verbs. Some students also have trouble with certain irregular verbs, so we have included a list of the most frequently used irregular verbs at the end of the unit.

The first thing you need is the ability to distinguish between *regular* and *irregular* verbs. **If a verb is regular, its past tense and past participle are formed by adding *-d* or *-ed* to the base verb.** For example:

	BASE VERB	PAST TENSE	PAST PARTICIPLE
I	ask	asked	have asked

If a verb is irregular (in other words, not regular), it does not follow this nice, easy pattern of adding -*d* or -*ed.* For example, *give* is an irregular verb. Here are its three main forms:

	BASE VERB	PAST TENSE	PAST PARTICIPLE
I	give	gave	have given

You're already familiar with base verbs and past tenses, but the term *past participle* might be new to you. What does it mean? The *past participle* is the form of a verb that is used with helping verbs such as *have, has,* or a form of the verb *to be* when it is used to make the passive voice. (See Chapter 4, Unit 3, if you need to review the definition of *passive voice.*) These examples show how the presence of a helping verb signals the need for a -*d* to be added to the regular verb *purchase*:

(a) I *have purchased* the suit.

(b) She *has purchased* the apartment building.

(c) He *had purchased* the license only 30 minutes before the wedding.

(d) The tainted medicine *was purchased* in a drug store two miles from the victim's home.

(e) Fourteen square acres in the middle of the city *were purchased* by an international corporation.

Now that you've read through the list, go back and underline the helping verb and circle the -*d* on *purchased* in each example.

The Three Trouble Spots

When writers drop -*d* and -*ed* endings, they drop them on *past tense verbs, past participles,* and *adjectives that are derived from verbs.* Of these three trouble spots, the first—past tense—is the easiest. The other two are more challenging for most students who need this unit. Study these correct examples:

1. (a) Yesterday the doctor *prescribed* a basic blood pressure medicine for Carl. (past tense)

 (b) Another specialist *has prescribed* treatment for him on several occasions. (past participle)

 (c) The *prescribed* pills were very effective. (adjective derived from a verb)

You can probably see why most students would have the least difficulty with 1. (a). The word *Yesterday* is a context clue for the past tense, and that helps you remember to add the *d* to *prescribe.*

In 1. (b) and (c), there are no obvious context clues for the past tense, but there are other clues for the student who's wondering whether to use a -*d.* The clue in 1. (b) is the helping verb *has.* And sometimes, as you'll see in the exercises, a sentence contains more than one helping verb. For example, you'll see sentences with longer verb phrases such as this one:

A third doctor *would have prescribed* something else.

In 1. (c) the clue is the noun *pills*. Someone did the act of prescribing the pills, and now they can be described as *prescribed*. Adjectives that are made from regular verbs end in *-d* or *-ed*.

In this set of three examples, add *-d* where it belongs and, each time, make a note of why you added it:

2. (a) Sharon had change tremendously since high school.
   (b) After the birth of his first child, Gregory was a change man.
   (c) We change our phone number after a few crank calls.

Two Notes on Spelling

There are two spelling rules that you need to remember.

1. **With a verb that ends in *-y*, you usually change the *-y* to *-i* before you add *-ed*. Examples: fry → fried; satisfy → satisfied**
2. **With a verb that ends in a consonant preceded by a short vowel, you usually double the consonant before you add *-ed*. Examples: trip → tripped; wrap → wrapped**

If you don't remember how short vowels sound, please consult a dictionary or ask your teacher for help.

Some Common Errors

There are a few common errors that many students make. They involve *used to, supposed to, old-fashioned*, and *prejudiced*. Add *-d* or *-ed* where they are needed in these sentences and discuss any questions with your teacher before you begin the exercises:

(a) I use to be afraid of the dark.

(b) Jane is really an old-fashion girl.

(c) We are suppose to be home by midnight.

(d) That was a prejudice remark if I ever heard one.

(e) Do you suppose we can get some ice cream?

(f) Prejudice is the act of prejudging.

(g) The thing that use to drive me crazy was his gum-chewing.

(h) They were suppose to preregister to vote.

(i) I do not believe that this is a prejudice community.

[*Answers.* (a) used; (b) old-fashioned; (c) supposed; (d) prejudiced; (e) *no change*; (f) *no change*; (g) used; (h) supposed; (i) prejudiced.]

Exercise One

Directions: Add *-d* or *-ed* endings where they are needed. Underline the word that you change and label your reason for the change in the space provided after the sentence. Use the labels *V* for past tense verb, *VP* for verb phrase, and *ADJ* for an adjective derived from a verb.

Sometimes spelling changes might also be required when you change the ending of a word. Please make the necessary changes in this exercise and in all the other exercises in this unit.

1. Charlotte Corday murder Jean Paul Marat, a famous eighteenth-century French

   revolutionary, while he was taking a bath. _____

2. Shredded wheat, the world's first ready-to-eat dry cereal, was introduce in 1893.

   _____

3. In 1956 a trailer truck that was hauling 400 crates of eggs slammed into the Rhyne

   Bridge in Charlotte, North Carolina. The bill for the damage truck and bridge came

   to $6000. But guess what? Not one egg was broken. _____

4. *The Fire Next Time* by James Baldwin is a distinguish collection of essays on the

   hearts and minds of American blacks. _____

5. In his paintings Monet capture the colors of the water lilies and other flowers in

   his famous ponds and gardens at Giverny, France. _____

6. The much admire *Huckleberry Finn* by Mark Twain is often called the greatest novel

   of American boyhood. _____

7. The first zoo in the history of the world was establish in Egypt around 1500 B.C.

   _____

8. According to a recent study of hundreds of couples, morning sickness and other

   pregnancy-related symptoms are experience by one in ten expectant fathers.

   _____

9. Yes, the last word in sentence 8 is suppose to be *fathers*, not *mothers*.

   _____

10. The same study show that one in ten new fathers also suffered from postpartum

    blues. _____

Exercise Two

Directions: Add *-d* or *-ed* endings where they are needed. Make other spelling changes as the need arises. You can read more about the information in these items by consulting *The Book of Lists #3.*

(a) Jean-Baptiste Moliere, who live from 1622 to 1673, was not only a famous   1

dramatist and actor but also a classical scholar. For years and years, he had slave away   2

on a translation of a work entitle *On the Nature of Things* by Lucretius, a much-admire   3

Latin poet. Moliere, like many of his contemporaries, wore a wig, and one day it   4

happened that a servant who was employ in the home of the great playwright need   5

material to make curl papers for setting Moliere's wig. As you may have already guess,   6

the servant rip out a few pages from Moliere's belove translation of Lucretius. Moliere   7

subsequently flip his wig, shall we say, and toss the rest of the manuscript into the fire.   8

It's anybody's guess what happen to the servant.   9

(b) It is often note that it takes all kinds, and that may be largely true, but sometimes   10

it is next to impossible to fathom another person's great passions in life. The authors   11

of *The Book of Lists #3* decide to include an inventory of 25 "curious histories and   12

esoteric studies." The books they chose are certainly curious and esoteric. Believe it   13

or not, a book has been written and publish that is entitle *Cluck!: The True Story of*   14

Chickens in the Cinema. The 1981 book by Jon-Stephen Fink, which is fully illustrate,   15

lists every film in which a chicken has appear on the screen, and that includes chickens   16

that are alive and well, recently expire, and roast, bake, or broil. Movies in which no   17

fowl appear on camera but in which a word such as *hen* or *rooster* was utter are also   18

list.   19

(c) *The Book of Lists #3* also includes a perhaps somewhat morbid but nonetheless   20

fascinating list of people who perish while performing in public. One example is that   21

of Dieter Schepp and Richard Faughan. Schepp was the nephew of the great acrobat   22

Karl Wallenda, and Faughan was Wallenda's son-in-law. Both were kill when the   23 troupe's almost legendary "human pyramid" collapse in Detroit, Michigan, in a perform- 24

ance in the winter of 1962. By grasping the balance wire with his legs and literally 25

holding on for life, Karl Wallenda, the patriarch of the famous family, save himself and 26

his niece Christiana. Mario Wallenda, who was the adopt son of Karl, was permanently 27

paralyze from the waist down as a result of the tragic fall. Karl Wallenda met his own 28

death in the spring of 1978 while he was performing on the high wire in Puerto Rico 29

to promote interest in the Pan American Circus. While he was making his way across 30

a 750-foot wire that connect two hotels in San Juan, he lost his balance. Although he 31

struggle for a time, he never regain it, in spite of the horrify cries of the rest of his troupe, 32

who yell, "Sit, Poppy, sit!" The great Wallenda could not recover and crash onto a taxi 33

on the city street 100 feet below. But his family took comfort in knowing that he die 34

doing what he love to do. 35

Exercise Three

Directions: Add *-d* or *-ed* endings where they are needed. Make other spelling changes as the need arises.

Believe it or not, as recently as 80 years ago you could have order a house from the 1

Sears, Roebuck catalog. That's right—a house. And what's really amazing is that the 2

complete package was price at a tidy little sum of $645. The house that the fame 3

mail-order company offer was not at all skimpy, either. It contain six rooms and a pantry, 4

a porch, and a reception hall. Also include in the $645 package were built-in china 5

cabinets, bookcases with leaded-glass doors, wood paneling for the bathroom, and 6

solid wooden doors throughout the house. Sears promise to provide all the materials 7

that would be require to finish the job, including ceiling, siding, piping, gutters, sash 8

weights, hardware, cypress siding, cedar shingles for the roof, and enough paint and 9

varnish for two coats. The wood that was use in Sears houses was highly value oak and 10

yellow pine. In fact, the design and the quality of all the materials were so good that 11 the National Trust for Historic Preservation in Washington, D.C., has publish a book for   12

people who want to see their Sears homes restore.   13

Sears, Roebuck charge only $1 if a customer was interest in seeing the house plans   14

before ordering them, and if the customer later decide to purchase the house itself, that   15

$1 was return to him or her in the billing for the total project. Sears use to offer   16

financing with no money down, and the company help the customer by providing   17

advances for labor costs. The labor costs, which had to be pick up by the customer,   18

plus other expenses not include in the catalog deal, finally push the average cost per   19

home to a grand total of $2218. There were almost 100 different homes from which   20

to choose, and by the time Sears stop offering the house in 1937, more than 100,000   21

had been built. Now the average cost of a home in the United States is suppose to be   22

over $70,000, and most modern homes don't include many of the elegant extras of   23

the Sears home.   24

Exercise Four

Directions: Add *-d* or *-ed* endings where they are needed. Make other spelling
changes as the need arises.

It use to be that most people confine their choices for indoor pets to a couple of   1

animals; people almost seem a little prejudice toward anything except a dog or a cat.   2

But this isn't really true anymore. Now a lot of offbeat animals are finding their way into   3

the hearts and homes of all sorts of creature-loving Americans. It may well be that the   4

trendiest new pet of them all is the ferret.   5

It is believe that ferrets, which are a domesticate variety of the polecat, were first   6

tame by the Egyptians about 1500 B.C. when the little creatures were charge with the   7

task of making Egyptian homes mouse-free. They are relate to otters, minks, weasels,   8

and skunks, and like some of their kin, they have a musky smell, which is derive from   9 scent glands that are located near the base of their tails. Although some people don't 10

mind the smell, it can be unpleasant in full-grown male ferrets, and it is advise that, for 11

their own health and for the sake of their owners, ferrets be spay or castrate unless they 12

are going to be bred. 13

What are the attractions of the ferret? For one thing, they rarely make a peep, so 14

they are a perfect solution for a pet-loving person who lives in an apartment building 15

where dogs and cats are ban. They are also easily litter-train, and although some owners 16

let their ferrets have free run of the house, many of the animals are satisfy to spend most 17

of their time in a roomy cage. But they are most love and cherish by their owners 18

because they're full of life and load with personality. Ferrets are amuse for hours and 19

hours on end by crawling in and out of paper bags, laundry baskets, shoes, and boots, 20

and by chewing on bottle caps, ping pong balls, and rubber toys. In fact, ferrets play 21

so hard and use up so much energy that some have been observe suddenly dropping 22

off into a dead sleep in the middle of a game. 23

What are the disadvantages of ferret ownership? For one thing, these animals are 24

aptly name, the word *ferret* being derive from the Latin *furittus,* which means "little 25

thief." Ferrets are known to dig for, chew up, and make off with just about anything 26

found in one's home. Even ferret owners who think they have completely ferret-proof 27

their house might come home to find a little tunnel being hollow out of their new couch. 28

Also, ferrets are generally good-nature but not always a wise choice in homes with small 29

children; they sometimes bite if they're handle too roughly or if they're play with too 30

long. 31

There are a lot of pros and cons and plenty of factors to be consider, but if you're 32

an animal lover and a free spirit who's in the market for a pet, ferrets probably deserve 33

to be check out. 34

The Irregular Verbs

The irregular verbs are not as easy as those that end in -d or -ed. To learn these, you have to memorize them. Here is a list of the most frequently used irregular verbs. Underline the verb forms that sound unfamiliar to you; then practice them in your writing as often as you can. We're using *have* as the helping verb, but you know that other helping verbs are used as well.

	PRESENT	PAST	PAST PARTICIPLE
I	become	became	have become
I	begin	began	have begun
I	break	broke	have broken
I	bring	brought	have brought
I	buy	bought	have bought
I	build	built	have built
I	choose	chose	have chosen
I	come	came	have come
I	do	did	have done
I	drive	drove	have driven
I	eat	ate	have eaten
I	fall	fell	have fallen
I	feel	felt	have felt
I	fight	fought	have fought
I	find	found	have found
I	forget	forgot	have forgotten
I	forgive	forgave	have forgiven
I	get	got	have gotten
I	give	gave	have given
I	go	went	have gone
I	grow	grew	have grown
I	keep	kept	have kept
I	know	knew	have known
I	lead	led	have led
I	leave	left	have left
I	lose	lost	have lost
I	make	made	have made
I	meet	met	have met
I	pay	paid	have paid
I	read	read	have read
I	ride	rode	have ridden
I	rise	rose	have risen
I	run	ran	have run
I	say	said	have said
I	see	saw	have seen
I	sell	sold	have sold
I	sing	sang	have sung
I	sleep	slept	have slept
I	speak	spoke	have spoken
I	spend	spent	have spent
I	stand	stood	have stood

I	take	took	have taken
I	teach	taught	have taught
I	tell	told	have told
I	think	thought	have thought
I	throw	threw	have thrown
I	wear	wore	have worn
I	win	won	have won
I	write	wrote	have written

UNIT 3: Consistency of Verb Tense

What's wrong with this sentence?

I was driving to work, and my car runs out of gas.

The problem is that the writer started the sentence in the past tense (with *was driving*) and ended it in the present tense (with *runs*). If there is a logical reason for switching into another verb tense, it's fine to do so. But what logical reason could this writer have? The sentence has two possible corrections:

Past tense: I <u>was driving</u> to work, and my car <u>ran</u> out of gas.

Present tense: I <u>am driving</u> to work, and my car <u>runs</u> out of gas.

Correct illogical changes in verb tense in these examples:

(a)   Archduke Franz Ferdinand of Austria was killed in Sarajevo in June 1914, and his assassination sets off World War I.

(b)   Marcus Garvey, who was the most influential black leader in the United States in the 1920s, advocates black separatism and leads a "back to Africa" movement.

(c)   Mars is the fourth planet in order of distance from the sun, and to the naked eye, it appeared to have a reddish tint.

[*Answers.* In (a) *sets off* should be *set off*; in (b) *advocates* should be *advocated,* and *leads* should be *led*; and in (c) *appeared* should be *appears.*]

Logical Changes in Verb Tense

What's a good reason for switching verb tenses? Maybe you want to write about something that used to be true and no longer is. For example, you might write, "When I *was* a child, I *wanted* to watch cartoons bright and early every Saturday morning, but now, I *like* to sleep until noon." The first clause describes something that was true in the past, so it's natural to use the past tense; the second clause describes something that is true in the present, so it's natural to use the present tense. This is not an example of illogical tense switching. The sentence would lack logic if the writer *didn't* switch tenses.

But switching verb tenses without a good reason causes a lot of trouble for many students. In fact, if tenses are switched back and forth just a few times, a student's paper can look much less organized than it really is. A paper that has illogical or inconsistent verb tenses seems incoherent; the writer appears to lack control of his or her material.

Writing about Literature

Sometimes it's natural to write a paper predominantly in the past tense, and sometimes it's natural to write mostly in the present tense. Occasionally, you have a choice. For example, a writer can often talk about literature in either the past or the present tense. The reason for this is that a piece of literature was written in the past, but we also tend to think of it as something that lives in the present.

Therefore, in writing about *The Great Gatsby* by F. Scott Fitzgerald, we can choose to say, "Jay Gatsby *represented* the American dream" or "Jay Gatsby *represents* the American dream." The important thing is to be consistent. If you choose to write about a work of literature in the present tense, stay with the present tense; if you choose to use the past, stay with the past.

The Helping Verb *Had*

The helping verb *had* is used when you are writing in the past tense and you wish to indicate something that happened even earlier. For instance, these are correct examples:

(a) Samantha *started* breakfast at seven o'clock this morning; by that time, she *had read* the morning paper and *washed* two loads of clothes.

(b) Frank *had visited* France three times in the 1960s and 1970s before he *made* his first trip with Catherine last year.

A Special Note about *Will/Would* and *Can/Could*

Before beginning the exercises, it's important for you to realize that the verb *would* is the past tense of *will*, and the verb *could* is the past tense of *can*. For example:

1. (a) He *will* bake a chocolate pecan pie today.
   (b) He *would* have baked a chocolate pecan pie yesterday if he had found the ingredients he needed.

2. (a) Right now I *can* hardly wait for my children to get home.
   (b) Yesterday I *could* hardly wait for my children to get home.

Many students have a special problem with the helping verb *would*. It's a mistake to use it when you really mean the simple past tense. For example, it's an error to write, "When I lived in New York, I *would see* at least two plays a week." Why is this wrong? It's wrong because the writer simply means that he or she *saw* at least two plays a week.

The word *would* should be used only when the writer means that something would happen only if a certain condition were fulfilled. The condition is usually found in a clause that begins with the word *if*, but the condition can also be implied rather than stated. Notice in 1. (b) that the writer *would* have baked the pie only *if he had found the ingredients he needed*. First he had to have the ingredients—that's the condition that had to be fulfilled before he would bake the cake.

If you're writing about something that happened often in the past but there's no condition to be fulfilled, no notion of "if" involved, simply use the past tense. Don't add *would*. To check your understanding, mark each sentence below *correct* or *incorrect*:

1. Marty would have been on time if he had been given the right directions.

   _____

2. Aunt Dana would kiss you if you stood still for a minute. _____

3. During our teens, we would always watch *American Bandstand* after school.

4. When Louise and Kim were studying last night, Louise would crack her gum

   and drive Kim crazy. _____

5. Matthew would have finished college on time, but his mother contracted a

   serious illness, which created the need for him to work full-time in the family

   business for a year. _____

[*Answers.* Items 1, 2, and 5 are correct because each has a condition to be fulfilled. Items 3 and 4 are incorrect because neither one involves any notion of a condition to be fulfilled. Try to correct the problems in verb tense in 3 and 4. If any items are unclear, please discuss them with your writing teacher before you begin the exercises.]

Exercise One

Directions: Underline all verbs and verb phrases. Then correct any examples of inconsistent or illogical verb tense. (In these exercises, you can cross out the wrong tenses and write in the corrections; you don't need to rewrite the sentences on your own paper.) Our source is the *Pictorial History of American Sports* by John Durant and Otto Bettmann.

If you're a typical American, you've probably used the expression "the real McCoy" 1

more than once. But have you ever wondered where it would have come from? The 2

phrase, meaning the genuine article, seemed to go back to an American boxer, Norman 3

Selby, who lived from 1873 to 1940 and who is known in the ring as Kid McCoy. 4

According to the story, around the turn of the century, an impostor was bumming free 5

drinks at bars along Broadway in New York by claiming to be Kid McCoy, who has once 6

held both the welterweight and middleweight boxing titles. One night in walks Norman 7

Selby, that is, Kid McCoy. He overheard the impostor bragging about his great feats 8

in the ring and decided to straighten him out. "You're not McCoy. I am," says Selby, 9 and knocks the faker to the floor. Without missing a beat, the bartender looked at the ₁₀

assembled crowd of patrons, pointed at the still-standing Selby, and announces, "That ₁₁

guy must be the real McCoy." ₁₂

If you're an aficionado of the fights, you might prefer this story, but there would ₁₃

be another possible explanation of the term. One authority on colloquial expressions ₁₄

—or slang—maintains that the history of the phrase is not sports-related but drug- ₁₅

related. According to this theory, the expression "the real McCoy" is a corruption of ₁₆

Macao, a port city on an island by the same name in the South China Sea, about 40 ₁₇

miles west of Hong Kong. For many years, uncut heroin of very high quality was ₁₈

supposed to be readily available in Macao. Therefore, to a dope dealer or addict, "the ₁₉

real Macao" was the real stuff, the purest heroin money could buy. ₂₀

Which explanation would be the real McCoy? We'll probably never know. ₂₁

Exercise Two

Directions: **Underline all verbs and verb phrases. Then correct any examples of inconsistent or illogical verb tense.**

Recently, experts in preventive medicine announced new reasons why fish is such an ₁

important element in a healthy diet. It's common knowledge that fish is high in protein ₂

and low in fat, and for that reason, fish would always be a favorite with the diet- ₃

conscious. But now it turns out that fish has other benefits, too. ₄

Perhaps surprisingly, the varieties of fish that could have been considered relatively ₅

high in calories when compared with other fish are the ones most enthusiastically ₆

recommended by nutritionists. The so-called fatty fish varieties contained a very benefi- ₇

cial oil, which is made up of something called omega-3 fatty acids. What can these fatty ₈

fish oils do for you? According to scientists, they had the power to lower your risk of ₉

heart disease, and they offered a certain amount of protection against the agonies of ₁₀

arthritis and asthma. They would also quite possibly reduce the risk of breast cancer, ₁₁ but that is a benefit that scientists would need to research in more depth and over a   12

longer period of time.   13

The fish that have enough oil to be recommended highly are tuna, herring, salmon,   14

whitefish, and large bluefish. Shad, mackerel, and pompano would also be included.   15

People who are concerned about calories should not avoid these varieties of fish; they   16

are "fatty" only when compared with other types of fish. A serving of Chinook salmon,   17

for instance, at 180 calories per three-and-a-half-ounce portion, had more than twice   18

the calories of a similar serving of sole, but it would have only about half the calories   19

that were in three-and-a-half ounces of beefsteak. Fortunately, shrimp and lobster are   20

also high in omega-3 fatty acids, and they are not nearly as high in cholesterol as   21

nutrition experts previously thought.   22

So fish might not be brain food, but it's a pretty smart thing to eat.   23

Exercise Three

PART A

Directions: Underline all verbs and verb phrases. Then correct any examples of inconsistent or illogical verb tense. The information comes from Gerald E. Finley's *Van Gogh* and other sources.

The next time you're feeling unappreciated, underestimated, or just plain unlucky, stop   1

and consider the life of Vincent van Gogh, perhaps the most famous archetype of the   2

genius who is unrecognized in his own lifetime.   3

Van Gogh, who is today hailed as one of the most important artists of all time, was   4

born in Groot Zundert in Holland on March 30, 1853. He was the oldest of six children,   5

and although he was from a warm and loving home, he was a very sensitive child who   6

was often depressed even in his early years.   7

When he was 16, he began working as a clerk in an art gallery in The Hague. The   8

gallery was operated by the firm of Goupil and Company, which transferred him to its   9

branch in London. There he falls desperately in love with his landlady's daughter, but   10 she is already engaged to someone else, and he is devastated. After being transferred 11

to Paris, van Gogh would argue terribly with his colleagues in the office, and the 12

atmosphere becomes so tense that he is eventually asked to leave in 1876. In the 13

meantime, he developed a very strong interest in religion and engages in nightly Bible 14

study. 15

Next van Gogh found a position teaching French and German. But he was not 16

happy in the position, and after a time, he took another in a school run by a clergyman. 17

Then he begins to think that perhaps his real destiny is to enter the ministry. (Another 18

factor in this decision may have been the fact that his father and several other ancestors 19

are Protestant clergymen.) 20

After returning home and receiving encouragement from his father, van Gogh 21

decided to begin studying for the entrance exam for divinity school in Amsterdam. He 22

studies for 14 months straight and is finding the philosophy of Calvinism and the Greek 23

and Latin languages very difficult. Finally, he reached the conclusion that he was not 24

meant to preach the Gospel but to apply it in a practical way. 25

PART B

Directions: Underline all verbs and verb phrases. Then correct any examples of inconsistent or illogical verb tense.

Months later, he decided to try again, but this time he goes to a lay ministry school in 1

Brussels. There he studied, and later he found a place for himself with a poverty-stricken 2

congregation of miners. But in his extreme empathy and his desire to serve his poor 3

community, he begins to live in a way that does exactly the opposite: it alienates the 4

village people from him. He neglected to wash, he would sleep on bare planks in a little 5

hut, and he rushes wildly about in the villages in his congregation, reading the Bible and 6

tending the sick and in general scaring the simple folk half to death with his strange 7

ways. The Reverend van Gogh simply did not act in the ways that the villagers were 8 accustomed to seeing ministers act. He was dismissed, and because he is caught ₉ completely unprepared for his dismissal, he is once again devastated. ₁₀

Depressed, he withdrew from almost everyone except his beloved younger brother ₁₁ Theo, and he began to sketch the land and its people. After about a year of traveling ₁₂ and sketching, in 1880 he finally makes a momentous decision: he decides to be what ₁₃ he must have been all along—an artist. ₁₄

But that choice, tragically, did not solve the many problems that plagued Vincent ₁₅ van Gogh's life. He again falls in love, this time with his cousin, a young widow, who ₁₆ did not return his passion. From his cousin, he moves right along in his profoundly ₁₇ unlucky quest for love, this time to a prostitute named Christien. Pregnant and sick, ₁₈ Christien moves in with van Gogh, who was now living and working in The Hague; she ₁₉ was to be both his mistress and his model. He was delighted; this was his chance to ₂₀ have love and a family to call his own. But Christien, who appears in his famous painting ₂₁ entitled *Sorrow*, was not all that van Gogh might have hoped for. She was difficult to ₂₂ live with, and she squandered all the money that Theo would send to help support van ₂₃ Gogh as an artist. ₂₄

PART C

Directions: Underline all verbs and verb phrases. Then correct any examples of inconsistent or illogical verb tense.

At Theo's urging, Vincent van Gogh leaves Christien and returned, heartbroken and ₁ confused, to the home of his parents, as he did so many times before. Finally, he began ₂ to paint steadily, his favorite subjects being the peasants and the earth they work. His ₃ famous painting *Potato Eaters* is from this period (1883–1885). During this period, he ₄ has yet another disastrous encounter with a woman; this young woman even attempted ₅ suicide as a result of their love affair and of her father's disapproval. Van Gogh was also ₆ greatly hurt by his own father's sudden death.

However, during this period, which includes the last five years of his life, he begins 8 to develop an intense interest in color theory—in what color expresses in and of itself. 9 Through his brother Theo, he became acquainted with Toulouse-Lautrec, Cézanne, 10 Gauguin, Seurat, and others. He began to experiment with small dots and threads of 11 color as a result of his exposure to the Impressionists and Neo-Impressionists. 12

By 1888, van Gogh is sick, and he is distraught over his inability to sell his paintings. 13 (In his entire lifetime, he sold only one.) At that time, he went to the south of France, 14 where, according to critic Gerald E. Finley, he "found true emotional release through 15 brilliant color." He would be especially taken with the color yellow and very excited 16 about the symbolic value of the sun in his work. He often uses stars, sunflowers, and 17 lanterns as the sun's equivalent or substitute. Typical of this period in van Gogh's work 18 are *The Night Café* and *The Sower*. 19

PART D

Directions: Underline all verbs and verb phrases and correct examples of inconsistent or illogical verb tense.

Soon van Gogh became interested in establishing an artists' colony. He persuades Paul 1 Gauguin to move into his little yellow house with him in 1888, but they have trouble 2 living together harmoniously. After a number of violent quarrels, including one at a café 3 on Christmas Eve, Gauguin decided to move out. It was Christmas night, and Gauguin 4 was out for a stroll when van Gogh tries to attack him with a razor. Van Gogh was 5 dissuaded from violence by Gauguin, but he was soon overcome with remorse and turn 6 his violence upon himself. He returned to his room in the house he shared with Gauguin, 7 sliced off one earlobe, and sends it to a brothel he has visited on occasion. 8

Hospitalized, van Gogh painted the very famous *Self-Portrait with Bandaged Ear*, 9 and he wrote to Theo, "Well, well, there are moments when I am twisted by enthusiasm 10 or madness or prophecy." He attempts to continue his painting after his release from 11 the hospital, but after fearful townspeople have him committed, he realizes the extent 12

of his illness and requested to be transferred to an insane asylum at Saint-Remy in 13

1889. 14

Because of doctors, especially a Dr. Rey, who did recognize his genius, van Gogh 15

was given special privileges so that he can paint while at the asylum at Saint-Remy. 16

There he painted the sun, the stars in the night sky, fields, cypress trees, mountains, and 17

olive orchards. Landscapes became distorted, and forms seem to writhe. According to 18

some critics, the act of painting became a substitute for healthy relationships with other 19

human beings. 20

Van Gogh moved again, at the suggestion of Theo, and became the patient of a 21

Dr. Gachet, who is himself a painter and a friend of many painters. For a time, van Gogh 22

seemed to flourish under Dr. Gachet's care; he would spend his time painting and 23

talking about his ideas on color and light and the function of art. 24

But then before too long, he wrote to his dearly beloved Theo, "I see no happy 25

future at all." He obtained a revolver, and on July 27, 1890, he went out into a field, 26

a field such as the ones he painted so many times in more bearable days, and shot 27

himself in the chest. He survived two days. 28

UNIT 4: Apostrophes

Apostrophes (') are used in two ways: to show possession and to make contractions. We'll spend most of this unit working on possession.

Possession

An apostrophe is added to a noun to show that the noun owns something. For example, if a girl has her own room, you might refer to it as *the girl's room.* Notice that two nouns are involved: *girl* and *room.* The apostrophe is added to the noun that possesses (owns) the other.

In the phrase *the girl's room,* the letter *-s* is also added to the word *girl.* But if we were referring to a room shared by *two* girls, the correct form would be *the girls' room.* The apostrophe would be placed *after* the *-s.* In the latter example, the *-s* is already part of the word because we're talking about two girls, not one girl. And when a word already ends in *-s* before it becomes possessive, you add only the apostrophe.

In other words, ask yourself, "Who owns the room?" If the answer is *the girl,* then you have a word that ends in the letter *-l,* so you add an apostrophe plus *-s.* But if the answer to the question is *the two girls,* a word that already ends in *-s,* then you add only the apostrophe.

Make these into possessive phrases:

(a)   the voice of the singer = _____

(b)   the voices of the four singers = _____

(c)   the fleas belonging to one dog = _____

(d)   the fleas belonging to 12 dogs = _____

[*Answers.* (a) the singer's voice; (b) the four singers' voices; (c) one dog's fleas; (d) 12 dogs' fleas.]

Now try these:

(e)   the crop of one farmer = _____

(f)   the crops of many farmers = _____

(g)   the actions of a lawyer = _____

(h)   the actions of the lawyers = _____

[*Answers.* (e) one farmer's crop; (f) many farmers' crops; (g) a lawyer's actions; (h) the lawyers' actions.]

Plural Words That Do Not End in *-S*

Sometimes the plural words that end in letters other than *-s* give students trouble, but they really shouldn't. These words follow the same rule we've described. In other words, whether something belongs to one *man* or to two *men,* you'll show possession in the same way—by adding *'s.* Why? Because neither *man* nor *men* already ends in *-s* before you make it possessive. They both end in *-n.* These are correct examples: *the man's motive, the men's motive, the woman's car, the women's cars.* This rule holds true for all the plural nouns that end in *-men* and for nouns such as *people, children, mice,* and *geese.*

Exercise One

Directions: Write sentences in which you make possessive phrases from those below. Add an apostrophe or an apostrophe plus *-s* as needed. Use your own paper, please.

1. the duties of one librarian

   the duties of two librarians

2. the excitement of the child

   the excitement of the children .

3. the shoes of the dancer

   the shoes of both dancers

4. the pet chameleon of one boy

   the pet chameleons of three boys

5. the history of the family

   the histories of the two families

6. the schedule of the woman

   the schedules of the women

7. the images of the poet

   the images of many poets

8. the carrots belonging to one rabbit

   the carrots belonging to all the rabbits

9. the performance of one drummer

   the performance of the drummers

10. the trips of the businessman

    the trips of the businessmen

Exercise Two

Directions: After checking your sentences for Exercise One, follow the same directions for this exercise.

1. the assignments of one soldier

   the assignments of four soldiers

2. the secrets of my mother

   the secrets of both mothers

3. the cigars of the man

   the cigars of the men

4. the clay belonging to the sculptor

   the clay belonging to the sculptors

5. the mood of the freshman

   the mood of the freshmen

6. the tools of the carpenter

   the tools of the carpenters

7. the improvement of one student

   the improvement of all the students

8. the instruments of one musician

   the instruments of the musicians

9. the support of one congresswoman

   the support of both congresswomen

10. the decision of the police officer

    the decision of the police officers

Exercise Three

Directions: Change these phrases into ones that require an apostrophe or an apostrophe plus *-s.* Then make the necessary additions. For example, *the personality of my brother* = my brother's personality.

1. the priorities of the mayor = _____

2. the training of the pilots = _____

3. the TV family of Bill Cosby = _____

4. the game plan of the coaches = _____

5. the ice cream sandwiches of the vendor = _____

6. the toys belonging to the babies = _____

7. the agreement of the friends = _____

8. the voice of Whitney Houston = _____

9. the role of Bruce Willis in *Moonlighting* = _____

10. the role of Cybil Shepherd in *Moonlighting* = _____

_____

Exercise Four

Directions: After Exercise Three is corrected, follow the same directions for Exercise Four.

1. the imagination of the children = _____

2. the suits belonging to the women = _____

3. the preferences of the viewers = _____

4. the dress rehearsal of the actors = _____

5. the guarantee of the manufacturer = _____

6. the responses of the people = _____

7. the condition of the animals = _____

8. the small-town roots of John Cougar Mellancamp = _____

_____

9. the color forecasts of most designers = _____

10. the advice of two mechanics = _____

Exercise Five

Directions: Write ten sentences, each one having a possessive phrase that requires an apostrophe or an apostrophe plus *-s.* Use your own paper, please. This is an important exercise because often, after working with possession for a while, students begin to add *'s* to words that simply are plural or end in *-s* but are not possessive. Be careful.

Two Important Notes about Exercises Six through Eleven

Some sentences in the exercises may contain no words that call for an apostrophe; other sentences may have more than one.

Make sure that you correct each exercise and discuss any errors before you proceed to the next one.

Exercise Six

Directions: Add apostrophes where they are needed. If you underline the words to which you add the apostrophes, they'll be easier to find and correct.

1. What do people like to order when they go out to eat? That was the National Restaurant Associations question, and it recently asked researchers from NPD Research Inc. to find the answer by surveying the members of 12,800 households.

2. The research organizations national survey reached all parts of the United States, and the pollsters discovered that Americans top five restaurant food choices are French fries, hamburgers, salads, breads, and pizza.

3. But all the various regions of the country have their own special favorites when it comes to ordering in the nations cafés and restaurants.

4. In New England, for instance, restaurant diners top menu choices include heroes and subs, doughnuts and sweet rolls, and sandwiches made of egg salad, tuna salad, and chicken salad.

5. A typical New Yorkers order is likely to include—in addition to heroes, subs, and salad-type sandwiches—frozen yogurt, sherbet, and types of pasta other than spaghetti.

6. In the mountain states of Arizona, Colorado, Idaho, Montana, Nevada, New Mexico, Utah, and Wyoming, peoples favorites range from tacos, burritos, and enchiladas to chicken nuggets and ham and cheese sandwiches.

7. It is anyones guess as to why, but North Dakotans restaurant preferences are mostly on the soft side; mashed potatoes, ice cream, doughnuts, sweet rolls, pancakes, and waffles rated the highest.

8. In Alaska, California, Hawaii, Oregon, and Washington, residents first loves are burritos, enchiladas, tacos, taco salads, and Oriental foods.

9. When food lovers in the South Atlantic states eat out, they are most likely to order the following items from a restaurants menu: breakfast sandwiches, shellfish, potato skins, and chicken.

10. In Illinois, Indiana, Michigan, Ohio, and Wisconsin, restaurant customers tastes are likely to run to chili, French toast, cheese, roast beef, and barbecued ribs.

Exercise Seven

Directions: Add apostrophes where they are needed.

1. A parents greatest fear is that some harm will come to his or her child.

2. Grace Hechinger addresses this fear in a book called *How to Raise a Street-Smart Child*.

3. Hechinger, the mother of two boys, is a journalist and an educator who has written extensively on womens concerns and issues of family life. She has collaborated with her husband on a number of projects; the couples list of coauthored books includes *Teenage Tyranny*, *The New York Times Guide to New York City Private Schools*, and *Growing Up in America*.

4. Hechingers how-to book on keeping children from becoming victims makes some interesting observations and offers a few unusual bits of advice for parents.

5. One problem that concerns the author is that many childrens training at home puts them at risk when they are outside the home.

6. Most parents are concerned about kids manners, and they generally teach their children to be polite and respectful of adults.

7. Yet children are bound to encounter many different types of people when they are outside their parents influence and control, and some adults motives for wanting to speak to or interact with children may be far from benign.

8. One of Hechingers suggestions is that mothers and fathers make it clear that some rules are to be routinely followed only in the home, not outside it.

9. For example, she maintains that some parents insistence that their children answer every question that they're asked by an adult is misguided and dangerous.

10. Another problem is some youngsters belief that it is best to be seen and not heard; if a child is being forced into a strangers car or is being harassed in any way by an adult, screaming and screaming loudly may be that childs only chance.

Exercise Eight

Directions: **Add apostrophes where they are needed.**

1. Louis Harris, one of the countrys most famous pollsters, recently surveyed the American public on the topics of pain and stress.

2. His surveys funding came from companies and corporations within the drug industry.

3. The reason for the drug industrys interest in peoples pain is, of course, obvious.

4. Over 1200 people were polled, and peoples responses to the nationwide survey are fascinating.

5. According to Louis Harris poll, pain and the problems it causes have an enormous impact on life in the United States.

6. For example, Americas loss in work time due to pain-related causes is an average of 550 million workdays a year.

7. And there are tremendous differences in the amount of pain reported by males and females and by people of different races, regions, incomes, and educational levels.

8. Womens experience of pain is apparently quite different from mens; for instance, 78 percent of the women who were polled had suffered headaches in the previous year, but only 68 percent of the men had experienced headaches in the same period.

9. The poll also showed that, on the average, a college graduates life is filled with more pain and stress than the life of a person who did not graduate from an institution of higher learning.

10. Whites complaints of pain were more frequent in the survey than the reports made by blacks or Hispanics.

11. Easterners of all races said that they experience more pain than Americans who live in other regions of the country.

12. If a survey respondents annual salary was between $15,000 and $50,000, that respondent reported having more headaches than respondents who earned more or less money.

13. One of the most surprising findings of the survey is that teenagers headaches occur more frequently than the headaches of senior citizens.

14. It is also true that young people from 18 to 24 years of age experience more stomachaches and dental problems than people who are over 65.

15. A senior citizens most typical problem, as far as pain is concerned, is felt in the joints. According to the surveys findings, joint pain is the only type of physical pain that is more frequent in older people than in younger people.

Exercise Nine

Directions: Write a paragraph or short essay on the relationship between stress and pain in your own life or in the life of someone you know well. Use as many possessive words as you can—both singular possessives and plural possessives. Underline them and insert the apostrophes in all the right places.

Exercise Ten

PART A

Directions: Add apostrophes where they are needed.

1. In the early days of rock and roll, black musicians had a hard time getting their records played on many radio stations.

2. In fact, it was a common practice for a black artists recording of a song to be "covered" by a white artist.

3. The term *cover* or *cover record* was used in the recording industry in the 1950s to mean a white artists version of a song that had originally been recorded by a black singer or a black group. Frequently, the songs that were covered had not only been recorded but also written by a black musician or black musicians.

4. Often when a black artists record was just beginning to climb the charts, along came a white singers version of the same song; back in those days, most disc jockeys at white-oriented radio stations lost little time in making the switch.

5. In case after case, disc jockeys gave most or all of the airplay to the white cover version and stopped playing the original black recording of the song.

6. Many critics who have written about the history of popular music have called this a racist practice; however, some disc jockeys who were working at the time insist that the critics accusation is unfair.

7. The disc jockeys explanation is that the motivation behind the practice was purely economic: white audiences were not yet buying black artists records, and the purpose of playing songs on the air was to call peoples attention to them and to get people to buy them. If the audience wouldn't buy a recording by a black singer, the disc jockeys at the time supposedly reasoned, why not try the same song recorded by a white singer?

8. Another factor often cited is that the record companies responsible for cover versions of black songs had substantial financial resources to promote their products.

9. One thing is certain: whether it was motivated by racism or economics, the practice of covering black recordings took a lot of money out of a lot of black musicians pockets.

10. It also prevented some black singers careers from ever really getting off the ground.

PART B

Directions: Add apostrophes where they are needed.

1. One good example of a black musician whose songs were frequently "covered" was Antoine Domino, better known as "Fats" Domino.

2. Fats Domino made many great recordings in the 1950s and 1960s, but he never had a number-one song on the charts.

3. Dominos "Ain't That a Shame" came close in 1955, but the songs success was short-circuited by a cover version sung by Pat Boone.

4. Two years later Rick Nelsons cover version of Fats Dominos "I'm Walkin'" had a similar effect.

5. Another example involves Lavern Baker, who is probably most famous for "See See Rider." Bakers release of a song called "Tweedlee Dee" was doing phenomenally well on all the charts until a version of the same song was released, featuring a white artist named Georgia Gibbs.

6. Gibbs cover version of "Tweedlee Dee" became a much bigger hit and knocked Bakers right off the charts.

7. "Little Richard" Penniman wrote his classic "Tutti Frutti" in 1955 while he was washing dishes at the Greyhound bus station in Macon, Georgia. Little Richards original did well, but Pat Boones cover version did even better.

8. Later, Little Richard came out with "Long Tall Sally," and he wanted to make sure that his recording would stand up well against any white singers copy. Pat Boone recorded "Long Tall Sally," but this time Little Richards version outsold Boones.

9. It was a crazy time, a time when societys difficulties in matters of race were reflected in the music industry in peculiar ways. It was a time when one record companys goal was to make Chuck Berry sound "a little whiter" while another

studio was signing up Elvis Presley because he was "a white boy who sounded black."

10. However, things did change, and many of the changes were brought about because of a great musical genius, Ray Charles. Charles first national hit, "I've Got a Woman," went to the top of both the so-called race charts and the pop charts. The black audiences enthusiasm for Ray Charles and his music was eventually almost mirrored by the white audiences acceptance. In fact, Ray Charles was probably the first musician to reverse the cover process. In 1962 he made his own version of a country and western song that had been recorded by Don Gibson four years earlier. In a way, Ray Charles "I Can't Stop Loving You," which became a number-one national hit, might be called the first black cover.

Exercise Eleven

PART A

Directions: Add apostrophes where they are needed. To read more on this topic, see *The Westerners* by Dee Brown.

The time the Pony Express ran was a short but colorful period in Americas history. The ₁

express mail service was the creation of Alexander Majors, William Waddell, and ₂

William Russell, three men who made and lost a lot of money in the development of ₃

the Old West. The mens backgrounds were very similar: each had come to Missouri in ₄

his youth at a time when the Missouri frontiers future looked unlimited because of the ₅

prosperous fur trade. All three had worked as clerks in banks and stores and had saved ₆

their money so that they could later venture into the areas of wagon freighting and ₇

stagecoach operations. ₈

But it was William Russells scheming and lobbying in Washington, D.C., that got ₉

the Pony Express off to a galloping start. Alexander Majors and William Waddell, ₁₀

Russells partners, were at first reluctant to become involved in the venture because they ₁₁ had just lost a great deal of money on a stagecoach line to Colorado, where gold had 12

been discovered in 1858, and in their view, the Pony Express prospects for financial 13

success looked slim. But Russell had independently traveled to the nations capital and 14

had secured a promise of help from a Senator William Gwin of California. The senators 15

interest in the idea stemmed from the fact that his constituents biggest complaint was 16

the lack of a speedy mail or passenger service from the West to the East and back. After 17

Senator Gwin promised to help get a subsidy from the U.S. Congress, Russell told 18

Majors and Waddell that if he had to travel back to Washington and report that he 19

couldn't proceed with the plans because of his partners lack of confidence in him, the 20

humiliation would be more than he could bear. So he pleaded and pleaded for support 21

from the two. Majors eventual answer was yes, and after a time, Waddells response 22

was also affirmative. 23

With Majors and Waddells support, Russell went about setting up the overland mail 24

service. Within 60 days, he had acquired the top-quality horses that were needed to 25

do the job, he had bought all the grain and other equipment necessary, and he had set 26

up stations and trained station masters. One of the most important steps in the process 27

of establishing the Pony Express was finding the right kind of riders. Russell had very 28

specific ideas about his riders qualifications, as one can see from looking at the adver- 29

tisement that he placed in newspapers all up and down the frontier. The ad read: 30

"WANTED—Young, skinny, wiry fellows not over 18. Must be expert riders willing to 31

risk death daily. Orphans preferred." From those who answered the ad, Russell chose 32

80 riders, one of whom was William Frederick Cody, later to become famous as Buffalo 33

Bill Cody. (Cody, by the way, was 15 at the time.) James Butler Hickok, Codys friend 34

who was also to become a legend in the Old West, was not accepted as a rider. Wild 35

Bill Hickoks age and weight disqualified him; he was 25 years old and somewhat over 36 the 125-pound limit. Hickok did, however, end up working in a clerical capacity at a   37

Pony Express station.   38

PART B

Directions: Add apostrophes where they are needed.

Each rider who signed on with the Pony Express had to take a solemn oath, promising   1

not to get drunk, gamble, use profanity, treat his horses poorly, or abuse Indians rights   2

or, for that matter, the rights of anyone he might encounter on his cross-country trips.   3

He was then equipped with a copy of the Bible, two Colt revolvers, and a rifle. (The   4

riders rifles turned out to be a little cumbersome, so they were later recalled.)   5

Then it began, at five o'clock on the afternoon of April 3, 1860. A rider dressed   6

in a red shirt and blue trousers jumped onto a black horse and sped west from St.   7

Joseph, Missouri, while at the same time, a rider in Sacramento, California, mounted   8

a pure white horse and headed east. It is recorded that both cities streets were decked   9

out in red, white, and blue for the historic occasion.   10

On the first run of the Pony Express, 25 letters were delivered, and correspondents   11

paid $5 for each half ounce of mail they sent. People were soon amazed at the reliability   12

of the Pony Express, not to mention its speed, and as enthusiasm grew, people learned   13

how to use it as cheaply as possible. Letter writers tricks included inscribing their   14

messages on tissue paper that was so thin and light it was almost transparent. Similarly,   15

editors in several cities began printing special editions of their newspapers on extra-thin   16

paper.   17

Altogether William Russell spent about $700,000 on the Pony Express even   18

though he knew, from rather early on, that even his ponies most gallant efforts could   19

never compete with the telegraph when it was finally stretched from coast to coast. (It   20

already reached from the East Coast to St. Joseph, Missouri, when the express began.)   21

Telegraph lines were completed before long, and when that day came, newspapers on   22 both the East and West coasts carried brief announcements of the discontinuation of ²³

the Pony Express on October 26, 1861. ²⁴

One farewell, published in the pages of the Sacramento *Bee*, expressed thousands ²⁵

and thousands of nineteenth-century Americans affection for the short-lived Pony Ex- ²⁶

press and, in doing so, both applauded and lamented the supremacy of the telegraph ²⁷

over the horse-and-man-powered express. "Farewell and forever, thou staunch, wilder- ²⁸

ness-overcoming, swift-footed messenger," wrote the *Bee*s editor. "Rest upon your ²⁹

honors . . . your destiny has been fulfilled." The conclusion of the editorials bittersweet ³⁰

salute serves as an early example of the American peoples ambivalence about advanc- ³¹

ing technology: "Nothing that has blood and sinews was able to overcome your energy ³²

and ardor; but a senseless, soulless thing that eats not, sleeps not, tires not . . . has ³³

encompassed, overthrown, and routed you." ³⁴

A Final Note on Possession

What you've learned in this unit is the simplest system for showing possession. But there are variations on the rules. For example, you have the option of adding an *-s* to a one-syllable name that already ends in *-s*, such as *James*. (In other words, you could write about *James' future* or *James's future*.) If you added the extra *-s*, you'd be doing so as a guide to pronunciation. However, you don't have to add that extra *-s*. Your teacher may discuss this variation or other ones, but the basic rules you've learned in this unit are sufficient to meet the standards of most college teachers.

Contractions

Using apostrophes to make possessives is challenging for many students, but using them for their other purpose—making contractions—is easy.

A *contraction* is a shortened form of two words, and contractions are usually acceptable in informal speech and writing. (We use them freely in this book.) The only thing you have to remember is that the apostrophe is placed at the spot where one or more letters have been omitted. For example, *I am* becomes *I'm*, and *you have* becomes *you've*.

Make contractions of the following pairs of words:

you are = _____   are not = _____

could have = _____   he is = _____

were not = _____   I am = _____

you had = _____

did not = _____

she will = _____

it is = _____

they have = _____

are not = _____

had not = _____

should not = _____

I would = _____

was not = _____

who is = _____

would not = _____

were not = _____

there is = _____

have not = _____

can not = _____

Correct your answers by consulting a dictionary or your teacher or tutor.

UNIT 5: Pronoun Problems

There are a number of problems that pronouns can present for writers, but two are especially common: *agreement* and *case*. We'll take agreement first.

Pronoun-Antecedent Agreement

You know that subjects have to agree with verbs. Well, pronouns have to agree, too. They have to agree with the nouns that they replace or to which they refer. Those nouns are called *antecedents*; they are the words that appear first and are then replaced by pronouns. For example, if you're talking about Patrick, and after a while you start referring to Patrick as *he,* then *Patrick* is the antecedent, and *he* is the pronoun that takes the place of it or refers to it. *Patrick* and *he* agree because they are both singular. You also have agreement when both the noun antecedent and the pronoun that replaces it are plural. You have disagreement only when one is plural and the other singular. **Here are examples of the error of pronoun-antecedent disagreement:**

(a) The mailman came late, but *they* always do on Mondays.

(b) A student is very fortunate if *they* have a job waiting for *them* after graduation.

(c) All the votes were in, but *it* didn't add up to a clear picture.

Rewrite (a) through (c) to make the antecedents and the pronouns agree in number.

It's really very simple. Singular pronouns agree with singular nouns. Plural pronouns agree with plural nouns.

Avoiding *His or Her* When You Can

Sometimes it's better to change a noun than a pronoun. This is especially true if not changing the noun antecedent forces you to use an expression such as *he or she* or *his or her.* Sometimes it's unavoidable, and you have to use *he or she* (unless you prefer *he* or *she* alone). But most of the time, this awkward option can be avoided by making the antecedent noun plural. For example, it's acceptable to write, "A *student* should think seriously about *his or her* real interests," but it's preferable to write, "*Students* should think seriously about *their* real interests."

Singular Collective Nouns

When you're working on pronoun-antecedent agreement, it's important to remember that words such as *group, family, team,* and *association* are normally considered singular. Each collective noun refers to one entity even though it may bring to mind a number of people. Therefore, a team, for example, is considered an *it,* not a *they.*

Prepositional Phrases

Here, as elsewhere, you have to be careful about prepositional phrases. Writers sometimes produce mistakes in pronoun-antecedent agreement by making a pronoun agree with a word inside a prepositional phrase when it really agrees with the noun before the prepositional phrase. Look at this correct example:

> ante
>
> The *number* (of people) who are sick with the flu is almost incredible, and medical authorities tell us that *it* is still rising.

We say *it is still rising,* not *they are still rising,* because the antecedent is the singular word *number.* In other words, the people are not rising; the number is rising.

This does not mean that an antecedent never agrees with a noun inside a prepositional phrase. For example, what is the antecedent of *their* in this correct example?

> The location of the boys was not released until their parents had been notified.

You simply have to use your powers of logic to make sure that your pronouns and antecedents agree.

Exercise One

Directions: Fill in the blank with the correct pronoun. Also write *ante.* (for antecedent) over the noun or noun phrase that agrees with the pronoun you choose.

1. Everyone has heard of the Medal of Honor; _____ *(it was/they were)*

   first awarded during the Civil War.

2. Every man, woman, and child in America should say "Thanks!" to the Hurley

   Machine Company because in 1907 _____ *(it/they)* came out with

   the very first electric washing machine.

3. Nikon cameras are the cameras that news photographers use most often. _____ *(It was/They were)* also immortalized in Paul Simon's song "Kodachrome."

4. The Salvation Army is ever hopeful. _____ *(It has/They have)* as _____ *(its/their)* slogan, "A man may be down, but he's never out."

5. The Neanderthal man was discovered in 1856; _____ *(he was/they were)* found in Germany.

6. Apparently, neither Gary Player nor his son had any major objection to entering into serious competition with a member of _____ *(his/their)* own family. The Players were the first father and son to compete in the same U.S. Open golf tournament.

7. Ostrich eggs are not known for _____ *(its/their)* daintiness; in fact, if you happened to have one, it would take you four hours just to hardboil _____ *(it/them)*.

8. As the ill-fated *Andrea Doria* sank, the orchestra continued to perform; in fact, the last song _____ *(it/they)* played was "Arrivederci Roma."

9. Paper straws were invented in 1886 by Marvin Stone. He made _____ *(it/them)* by rolling paraffin-coated paper by hand.

10. (a) The McDonald's fast-food empire is constantly coming up with something new to promote business and keep customers happy, but one of the smartest things _____ *(it/they)* ever did was to build indoor and outdoor playgrounds at many of _____ *(its/their)* restaurants.

    (b) The people at McDonald's are constantly coming up with something new to promote business and keep customers happy, but one of the smartest things

_____ *(it/they)* ever did was to build indoor and outdoor playgrounds

at many of _____ *(its/their)* restaurants.

Correct Exercise One and discuss problems before continuing.

Exercise Two

Directions: Fill in the blank with the correct pronoun. Also write *ante.* over the noun or noun phrase that agrees with the pronoun you choose.

1. The John F. Kennedy memorial stamp was issued on May 29, 1964;

   _____ *(it was/they were)* worth five cents.

2. The rulers of Great Britain hold a lease on Hong Kong, but _____

   (it will/they will) lose control there when _____ *(it expires/they expire)*

   in 1997.

3. Herschel Walker led the U.S. Football League in rushing yardage in 1983, which

   was _____ *(its/their)* first season.

4. The Fairy Investigation Society has _____ *(its/their)* headquarters in

   Dublin, Ireland.

5. If kept as pets, tarantulas are supposedly intelligent enough to recognize

   _____ *(its/their)* masters.

6. In 1729 the French National Assembly adopted the guillotine as

   _____ *(its/their)* official form of execution.

7. Perhaps neither Orville nor Wilbur Wright could have made such an amazing contri-

   bution to the development of transportation without the benefit of working so

   closely with _____ *(his/their)* brother.

8. No matter who *Time* magazine chooses as _____ *(its/their)* "Man of

   the Year," it's obvious from the letters to the editor in the next few issues that

   plenty of people invariably feel free to express _____ *(its/their)* ap-

   proval or disapproval vigorously.

9. The Buffalo Bill Historical Center makes _____ *(its/their)* home in Wyoming.

10. For a short period of time, the convertible was not being produced by auto manufacturers in the United States; however, _____ *(it was/they were)* reintroduced in 1982 with the Chrysler Le Baron.

Exercise Three

Directions: Label each sentence *OK* or *pro.-ante. dis.* (pronoun-antecedent disagreement). Then in the sentences where you find pronoun-antecedent disagreement, write *ante.* over the antecedent, cross out the wrong pronoun, and write in the correct one. (Sometimes when you change a pronoun, you may also have to make an adjustment in subject-verb agreement.)

1. _____ If the typical American is doing their part, they're eating a little over 20 quarts of ice cream every year.

2. _____ The Illinois Wildlife Federation offers a $500 reward to anyone who provides information that leads to the arrest and conviction of a person who has killed a bald eagle within the state, but so far, they have recognized no valid claims.

3. _____ Throughout the decades, millions of Americans have bought U.S. war bonds; it was first issued during the War of 1812.

4. _____ The Catholic church has not published their *Index of Forbidden Books* since 1966.

5. _____ You might call the little thing that you put above your lowercase *i* a "dot," but you can also call it a "tittle."

6. _____ Perhaps one of the strangest offers ever made was put forth by Cutty Sark, the famous whiskey manufacturer. They have pledged one million pounds to any person who can convince the Science Museum of London that they have captured a spaceship or other vehicle from outer space.

7. _____ A visitor to the home of the shy, reclusive Emily Dickinson was sometimes in for quite a surprise. The poet often spoke to them from an adjoining room, never showing her face at all.

8. _____ Even though Walt Disney himself wore a mustache, not one of all the males who are employed by the Disney empire is allowed to have hair above their upper lip.

9. _____ Charles Schultz's cartoon strip "Peanuts" first appeared in 1950, and it has been delighting both children and adults ever since.

10. _____ The number of teeth in a baby's mouth at ten months is highly variable, but generally it ranges from six to eight, with four on the top and two to four on the bottom.

11. _____ Don and Phil Everly, important figures in the history of rock and roll, went through more than a decade without speaking to each other before they patched things up and, shortly thereafter, performed a reunion concert at London's Royal Albert Hall.

12. _____ If you are planning to set up a birdbath next summer, experts say that they should contain a depth of two-and-a-half inches of water.

13. _____ The only modern language that capitalizes their first-person singular pronoun is English.

14. _____ For a runner to achieve a four-minute mile, they have to maintain an average speed of 15 miles per hour.

15. _____ According to news accounts, the number of AIDS (acquired immune deficiency syndrome) cases among the people of several nations in Africa is rising rapidly, and they are expected to continue to rise until further research yields more information on techniques of prevention and cure.

Pronoun Case

The words *I* and *me* are two different cases of the same pronoun—the first-person singular pronoun. *He* and *him* are two cases of the same pronoun, and so are *she* and *her*. When pronouns are used alone, native speakers of English rarely make mistakes with them, but when they are used in combination with a noun, mistakes are common. These are called mistakes in pronoun case. Here's an illustration of this:

(a)   *She* is a frisky little child. (correct)

(b)   Christopher and *her* are frisky little children. (incorrect)

In (a) the word *she* is obviously correct; *she* is the right pronoun to use in the subject position. But in (b) the word *her* is used as a subject, along with the word *Christopher.* The point is that no native speaker would write, "*Her* is a frisky little child," but many native speakers would make the error that is represented in sentence (b).

It's the act of pairing a pronoun with a noun that seems to make writers occasionally lose their bearings. To avoid errors in pronoun case, all you have to do is watch for the pairings and mentally omit the noun. Then see what pronoun sounds right if used alone. That's the case of the pronoun that is correct when used alone or when used in combination with a noun.

Sometimes when you perform this test of omitting the noun, you also have to make a slight adjustment in subject-verb agreement or in the general phrasing of the sentence. For example, in (b) when you mentally omit the words *Christopher and*, you move from a plural subject to a singular subject, so you also have to change *are* to *is*. Then you ask yourself if it sounds right to say "Her is" or "She is."

Exercise Four

Directions: **Fill in each blank with the correct case of the pronoun.**

1. When did you last write a letter to _____ *(he/him)* and Annie?

2. Cody and _____ *(her/she)* are coming to Milwaukee for a visit in the spring.

3. Why don't you allow the Joneses and _____ *(them/they)* to go ahead and file the suit?

4. My dad and _____ *(I/me)* really should write a book together.

5. The Blue Devils and _____ *(us/we)* battled throughout the entire tournament.

6. I'd like to take a trip to Yugoslavia with Grandma Rosie and _____ *(her/she)*.

7. We can't wait until the Sethneys and _____ (they/them) finally get

here.

8. Is the box that just arrived for Robin and _____ (I/me)?

9. Jackie and _____ (he/him) met about a year ago at the bank where

she worked.

10. The man was rather rude to my brother and _____ (I/me).

Exercise Five

Directions: **Fill in each blank with the correct case of the pronoun.**

1. Harry and _____ (them/they) moved to Columbus, Ohio.

2. That teacher and _____ (I/me) finally developed a good working rela-

tionship.

3. Caitlin Anne and _____ (he/him) love to go to the museum on Satur-

days.

4. The partnership was a great success for the Szczurs and _____

(us/we).

5. _____ (Her/She) and her brother walk three or four miles a day.

6. The insult was aimed directly at the principal and _____ (I/me).

7. I want to see John and _____ (he/him) in my office as soon as

possible.

8. Scott and _____ (I/me) challenged Kristi and _____

(her/she) to a rematch to be held in Owatonna, Minnesota.

9. The train left without Grandma Evie and _____ (us/we).

10. If you want to see something amazing, just take a look at who's standing behind

Dick and _____ (them/they).

UNIT 6: Easily Confused Words

This unit is a brief review of some of the common word pairs that often cause trouble for writers. We've selected our own "top 20" for the exercises, and you might know of others that cause you uncertainty. It would not be difficult for you to make up your own exercises on pairs that are not found here; if you do so, ask your teacher to check your work.

Below are the pairs that we'll consider in this unit. You can see that some are homonyms (words that sound alike but have different meanings), and some are not.

1. a / an	11. it's / its
2. accept / except	12. passed / past
3. affect / effect	13. principal / principle
4. amount / number	14. than / then
5. bare / bear	15. their / there / they're
6. coarse / course	16. threw / through
7. conscience / conscious	17. to / too / two
8. finally / finely	18. weather / whether
9. have / of	19. who's / whose
10. hear / here	20. you're / your

Read and complete the explanations before you do the exercises. Consult your dictionary if you need more information on a particular pair.

On pages 287–288 you'll find an answer key for the blanks within the explanations.

Troublesome Pairs

1. A / An

A and *An* are both noun markers. *A* is used before words that begin with consonant sounds, and *an* is used before words that begin with vowel sounds. You probably remember that the vowels are *a, e, i, o,* and *u.*

There are two more things you should know. One is that the letter *h* is sometimes silent, and when it is, you use *an.* For example, you write, "It is *an* honor to speak before the assembly." On the other hand, when *h* is sounded, you use *a.* For example, you might say, "I wonder if there is *a* heaven."

The other special concern is the letter *u.* Words that begin with a long *u* are preceded by *a*; words that begin with a short *u* are preceded by *an.* Study these correct examples: *a* united student body; *an* unsung hero.

Complete:

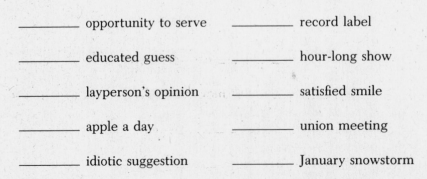

_____ opportunity to serve	_____ record label
_____ educated guess	_____ hour-long show
_____ layperson's opinion	_____ satisfied smile
_____ apple a day	_____ union meeting
_____ idiotic suggestion	_____ January snowstorm

_____ Haitian custom	_____ upper-middle-class neighborhood
_____ heavy load	_____ terrific smile
_____ quirky light switch	_____ honest day's work
_____ nectarine	_____ April shower
_____ unfriendly gesture	_____ hot potato
_____ edible plant	_____ obstetrician's schedule
_____ album cover	_____ Italian import

2. Accept / Except

Accept is the verb form of the noun *acceptance,* and it means to receive something, not to reject it. The word *except* is a preposition that is related to the noun *exception.* Examples: You *accept* praise from your teacher. You might enjoy all dances *except* the polka.

Complete:

(a) Many people find it hard to _____ criticism.

(b) Inez likes everything about this country _____ the pace of American

life.

(c) Everyone came to the bon voyage party _____ the guest of honor.

(d) You have to _____ yourself before anyone else can

_____ you.

3. Affect / Effect

If you look in a good dictionary, you'll find a complete explanation of the difference between these two words. For our purposes, it's enough to say that *affect* is a verb, and *effect* is usually a noun. Examples: Your moods *affect* your performance. The *effect* of too little sleep is obvious.

Complete:

(a) Changes in the weather _____ her tremendously.

(b) The immediate _____ of the move to a new school was dramatic.

(c) Each of your decisions could _____ all of us.

(d) The compliment had a wonderful _____ on him.

4. Amount / Number

Use the word *number* when you're writing about something that can be counted; use *amount* when you're writing about something that can't be counted. Examples: an *amount of peanut butter,* a *number of peanuts.* Use *number* if something is "countable," even if you don't know the exact count.

Complete:

(a) the _____ of secrecy

(b) the _____ of secrets

(c) the _____ of help

(d) the _____ of helpers

(e) the _____ of lemon drops

(f) the _____ of lemon flavoring

Most people don't make errors with *number;* they make errors by overusing *amount.* Here's a typical mistake: "I had a large amount of friends when I lived in Houston." Friends can be counted, even if you don't actually recall how many you had; therefore, it should be "I had a large *number* of friends."

The words *fewer* and *less* operate in the same way. *Fewer* is used as *number* is—with things that can be counted. *Less* is used as *amount* is—with things that can't be counted. Is the TV commercial that tells us one type of beer has "less calories" than another type grammatically correct? Yes _____ No _____

The words *many* and *much* also operate similarly. *Many* is used with things that can be counted; *much* modifies things that can't be counted. Study these correct examples:

CAN BE COUNTED	CANNOT BE COUNTED
the number of jokes	the amount of humor
fewer jokes	less humor
many jokes	much humor

5. Bare / Bear

The word *bare* is an adjective that means naked, plain, unadorned. It is also a verb that means to reveal. *Bear* has two basic meanings: it's a noun that refers to a certain animal; it's also a verb that means to carry a burden or to tolerate something. Examples: The room is too *bare;* it needs a few warm touches. He wants to *bare* his soul to you. You may encounter a grizzly *bear* in Glacier National Park. I can't *bear* to think about final exam week.

Complete:

(a) They _____ their pain in silence.

(b) Her face was _____ ; she had never liked wearing makeup.

(c) A polar _____ can be a dangerous animal.

(d) This description is a little _____ . Can you add a few good details?

(e) His heart can't _____ even the slightest stress.

(f) Let's _____ the facts so that the whole world can know the truth.

6. Coarse / Course

The word *course* means an academic subject, such as a mathematics course. It also means a path or route, such as the course of a river or a golf course. *Course* means a duration, as in the expression "throughout the course of history." Its most frequent use is probably in the phrase *of course.*

Coarse, on the other hand, is an adjective that means rough; it can describe such things as the texture of fabric or the sound of language.

Complete:

(a) His language was too _____ to be appropriate in the classroom.

(b) Throughout the _____ of her stay, she became more and more adjusted to life in Norway.

(c) Of _____ , I'd like a cup of coffee.

(d) Everybody should have a basic _____ in physics.

(e) Something went wrong with the cream pie, and it ended up tasting _____ and gritty.

7. Conscience / Conscious

Conscience is a noun; it's what is supposed to bother you when you do something wrong; roughly we could say it's your sense of right and wrong. The word *conscious* is an adjective that means aware. It's related to the noun *consciousness.* Examples: He had a guilty *conscience* after betraying his friend's trust. She was *conscious* of someone watching her.

Complete:

(a) If you're the one who took my wallet, I hope your _____ keeps you awake tonight.

(b) The judge asked the psychiatrist if the mass murderer who was on trial perhaps lacked a _____ .

(c) Please make a _____ attempt to use effective transitions in your next

paper.

(d) He was not _____ of the fact that he had inspired others to greatness.

(e) The problem of abused children disturbs the nation's _____ .

8. Finally / Finely

Finally means at last or eventually. *Finely* means delicately or in small pieces.

Complete:

(a) Sprinkle _____ diced tomatoes on the taco salad.

(b) We _____ got onto the freeway at noon.

(c) Your body is a _____ tuned machine, and it's sensitive to many things

that might surprise you.

(d) It's a big day in your life when you _____ move to your own place.

9. Have / Of

This problem is a little different. Sometimes students write the preposition *of* when they really mean the verb *have.* The only time this mistake occurs is after helping verbs such as *should, could, will, would, may, might,* and *must.* Use your S-V-C skill if this is a problem in your writing. In the middle of a verb phrase, you don't want a preposition. Here's a typical error: "I should *of* known better." Here's the correction: "I should *have* known better."

Label and underline the key parts of each clause and then complete:

(a) You must _____ been a beautiful baby.

(b) I would _____ given you a ride if I had known you needed one.

(c) She should _____ called me by now.

(d) We could _____ done so much more for them.

10. Hear / Here

Hear is the verb that means listen. *Here* is an adverb that designates a place.

Complete:

(a) Can you _____ me?

(b) She'd like to eat _____ .

(c) I want to _____ the score; then I'll turn off the radio.

(d) _____ is where he wants to stay.

11. It's / Its

It's is the contraction of *it is.* The word *its* is a possessive pronoun. Examples: *It's* a new day. The snake shed *its* skin.

Complete:

(a) Some people say that virtue is _____ own reward.

(b) I think _____ a shame that you won't stay.

(c) _____ amazing how much work you've done.

(d) The airplane lost 50 percent of the power in _____ left engine within

60 seconds of takeoff.

12. Passed / Past

Passed is a form of the verb *pass. Past* can be a noun or an adjective. Examples: They all *passed* the exam. You *passed* me on the street without saying a word. Who ever really forgets the *past*? (noun) Your *past* mistakes are forgiven. (adjective)

Complete:

(a) He's very nostalgic about the _____ .

(b) Leo _____ me during the last leg of the race.

(c) Your _____ accomplishments are impressive. What do you have

planned for the future?

13. Principal / Principle

We all remember that the *principal* is our pal. The noun also refers to a sum of money on which we can earn interest. But the problem most students have is that they don't realize the word *principal* is also an adjective that means main, central, most important. The word *principle* is a noun that means a basic truth, a law, a rule, a belief, a standard, or an ideal. Examples: Solving world hunger is the *principal* goal of the organization. Ozzie's *principal* problem is lack of confidence. This experiment demonstrates the *principle* of supply and demand. Charlie has no *principles*; he'll do anything for a price.

Complete:

(a) What's your _____ reason for choosing that major?

(b) For me, the _____ advantage of using a word processor is the speed

with which I can make revisions.

(c) Katharine Hepburn became famous portraying women of great

_____ .

(d) He objects to capital punishment on _____ .

(e) Your _____ asset is your zest for life.

(f) The _____ of self-determination for the physically disabled was the

topic of his speech.

14. Than / Then

Than is used to make comparisons. For example, a person can be *stronger than* someone else, and one climate can be *warmer than* another. *Then* is an adverb of time; it describes when an action occurred. For example, we say, *"Then* I woke up" and "If you decide you want to talk it over, *then* call me."

Complete:

(a) The skirt is shorter _____ it's supposed to be.

(b) His mouth was working faster _____ his brain.

(c) I got more _____ I bargained for.

(d) If you don't want to see him, _____ you'd better not answer the door-

bell.

(e) She used to say she hated all westerns; _____ she saw *High Noon.*

(f) My paper is less _____ perfect, but I need to let it sit for a few days;

_____ maybe I'll have some fresh ideas for rewriting.

15. Their / There / They're

Their is a possessive pronoun. It modifies a noun by showing that the noun belongs to someone. We speak of *their pencils, their cars, their future. There* is an indicator of location, as in "Let's go *there* now." It is also a sort of meaningless sentence starter, as in *"There* are a few problems we need to discuss." *They're* is the contraction of *they are,* as in *"They're* going to be here for an hour."

Complete:

(a) _____ willing to share _____ popcorn.

(b) _____ is nothing you can do about it.

(c) I'm afraid to go _____ for fear I might be recognized by one of

_____ agents.

(d) _____ willingness to cooperate is great.

(e) _____ likely to make mistakes once in a while, but

_____ hearts are always in the right place.

(f) _____ is definitely enough food to go around.

16. Threw / Through

Threw is the past tense of the verb *throw. Through* is a preposition.

Complete:

(a) They went _____ a great deal of hardship to get here.

(b) We'll stick together _____ thick and thin.

(c) She _____ $10 into the pot.

(d) He _____ a great fast ball earlier in his career.

17. To / Too / Two

To can be part of an infinitive verb phrase, as in "She wants *to* ride." *To* is also a preposition, as in "The poem *to* his daughter was never completed." *Two,* of course, is the number between one and three. It's *too* that gives writers the most trouble. *Too* is an "intensifier"; it makes the adjective that follows it more intense. Roughly, it means "excessively." For example, you can say, "You are *too* impatient," which means you are excessively impatient. *Too* has another meaning, which is "also." For example, you can write, "Please clean up this mess, and do the dishes, *too.*"

Complete:

(a) The ending of that movie is _____ sad; I can't stand

_____ watch it.

(b) Take the key _____ my heart.

(c) Your letter _____ your nephew apparently never arrived.

(d) The doctor gave the instructions _____ quickly.

(e) Jay believes that he can play football and find time for his studies,

_____ .

(f) I have _____ friends who are known _____ say, "You

can't be _____ careful."

(g) He was wearing _____ much after-shave lotion.

18. Weather / Whether

Weather, of course, refers to the climate. *Whether* is a conjunction used in sentences such as "I don't know *whether* I should sign up now or wait until tomorrow."

Complete:

(a) _____ you say yes or no, I'll always stand by you.

(b) The _____ might have had an effect on their performance.

(c) You have to decide _____ you'll go to Fargo or Bismarck.

19. Who's / Whose

Who's is the contraction of *who is*. *Whose* is a possessive pronoun, and you've worked with it as an embedding word.

Complete:

(a) I don't know _____ boots these are.

(b) A boy _____ reaching for the stars needs to keep his feet on the

ground.

(c) A person _____ voice sounded vaguely familiar called a few minutes

ago.

(d) The woman _____ going to be in charge is very well qualified.

20. You're / Your

You're is the contraction of *you are. Your* is a possessive pronoun.

Complete:

(a) It's _____ turn.

(b) If _____ ready, let's go.

(c) Do you know what _____ looking for?

(d) You need to take _____ umbrella today.

Please check your answers before continuing.

Answer Key for Troublesome Pairs

1.
an opportunity to serve	a record label
an educated guess	an hour-long show
a layperson's opinion	a satisfied smile
an apple a day	a union meeting
an idiotic suggestion	a January snowstorm
a Haitian custom	an upper-middle-class neighborhood
a heavy load	a terrific smile
a quirky light switch	an honest day's work
a nectarine	an April shower
an unfriendly gesture	a hot potato
an edible plant	an obstetrician's schedule
an album cover	an Italian import

2. (a) accept (c) except
   (b) except (d) accept, accept
3. (a) affect (c) affect
   (b) effect (d) effect
4. (a) amount (d) number
   (b) number (e) number
   (c) amount (f) amount

No, the beer commercial is incorrect; it should be "fewer calories" because calories can be counted.

5. (a) bear (d) bare
   (b) bare (e) bear
   (c) bear (f) bare
6. (a) coarse (d) course
   (b) course (e) coarse
   (c) course
7. (a) conscience (d) conscious
   (b) conscience (e) conscience
   (c) conscious

8. (a) finely   (c) finely
   (b) finally   (d) finally

9.   All answers are *have*.

10. (a) hear   (c) hear
   (b) here   (d) Here

11. (a) its   (c) It's
   (b) it's   (d) its

12. (a) past
   (b) passed   (c) past

13. (a) principal   (d) principle
   (b) principal   (e) principal
   (c) principle   (f) principle

14. (a) than   (d) then
   (b) than   (e) then
   (c) than   (f) than, then

15. (a) They're, their   (d) Their
   (b) There   (e) They're, their
   (c) there, their   (f) There

16. (a) through   (c) threw
   (b) through   (d) threw

17. (a) too, to   (e) too
   (b) to   (f) two, to, too
   (c) to   (g) too
   (d) too

18. (a) Whether   (c) whether
   (b) weather

19. (a) whose   (c) whose
   (b) who's   (d) who's

20. (a) your   (c) you're
   (b) you're   (d) your

Exercise One

Directions: Fill in the blanks with the correct choices.

1. Reindeer's milk has three times more protein _____ *(than/then)* cow's

   milk, and some people prefer the taste, _____ *(to/too/two)*.

2. The _____ *(principal/principle)* center of diamond trading in the

   United States is New York City's 47th Street; in fact, more _____

   (than/then) 75 percent of the action in the American diamond trade goes on

   _____ *(their/there/they're)*.

3. Richard Nixon was the first person _____ *(to/too/two)* put a tele-

   phone call _____ *(threw/through)* to the moon.

4. The _____ (principal/principle) of self-service, which of _____ (coarse/course) had a negative _____ (affect/ effect) on the employment of a great _____ (amount/number) of waiters and waitresses, goes all the way back _____ (to/too/two) 1885 when the first self-service restaurant, the Exchange Buffet, opened _____ (it's/its) doors near the New York Stock Exchange.

5. Joe Louis, _____ (who's/whose) considered by many to be the greatest fighter who ever lived, held the heavyweight title longer _____ (than/then) anyone else; if _____ (you're/your) up on _____ (you're/your) boxing trivia, you know that he was the champion from 1937 _____ (to/too/two) 1949.

6. Each of the precisely etched, _____ (finally/finely) carved faces of the presidents at Mt. Rushmore is _____ (to/too/two) times higher _____ (than/then) the Great Sphinx of Egypt.

7. The Eighteenth Amendment, which prohibited the sale of liquor in the United States, was the only one ever to be repealed. The American people _____ (finally/finely) _____ (threw/through) the amendment out on December 5, 1933, after almost 14 "dry years" had _____ (passed/past). Apparently, they came to the conclusion that, for adults, drinking alcohol should be considered less a matter of legislation _____ (than/then) a matter of individual _____ (conscience/conscious).

8. The first American husband and wife team to _____ (accept/except) the Nobel Prize was Dr. Carl F. Cori and Dr. Gerty T. Cori. _____ (Their/There/They're) work in medicine won them a joint prize in 1947.

9. The United States publishes a greater _____ (amount/number) of

 newspapers _____ (than/then) any other country.

10. _____ (It's/Its) a fact that _____ (their/there/they're) are

 exactly 20 possible first moves in chess.

11. If _____ (you're/your) ever watching a television sit-com and the

 laughter seems just a bit _____ (to/too/two) mechanical, it might

 _____ (have/of) been produced by a machine called a "Mackenzie."

 _____ (It's/Its) job is to cough up canned laughter for a considerable

 _____ (amount/number) of television shows.

12. Throughout the entire _____ (coarse/course) of American history,

 _____ (their/there/they're) was probably only one president who

 didn't let his spouse's views _____ (affect/effect) his political deci-

 sions in even the slightest way. That was James Buchanan, who served from 1857

 to 1861 and who was the only American president never _____

 (to/too/two) marry.

13. By the standards of centuries ago, it didn't really take _____ (to/

 too/two) long for the *Mayflower* to cross the Atlantic; in fact, the ship left Europe

 and arrived _____ (hear/here) in only _____ (to/

 too/two) months.

14. The presidential candidate who received the greatest _____ (amount/

 number) of votes in one election in American history was Richard M. Nixon. But

 he must _____ (bare/bear) the stigma of being the only president to

 resign, _____ (to/too/two).

15. During the time of the Civil War, _____ (their/there/they're) was no

 doubt that money could _____ (affect/effect) a young man's chances of serving in the military; to put it plainly, _____ *(a/an)* inductee could

pay someone else _____ *(to/too/two)* take his place if, of

_____ *(coarse/course)*, he could do so without disturbing his own

_____ *(conscience/conscious)* _____ *(to/too/two)*

much.

Exercise Two

PART A

Directions: Fill in each blank with the correct choice.

1. *The Heart of Hollywood* by Bob Thomas is _____ *(a/an)* interest-

    ing book that offers up a great deal of fascinating information on Hollywood's

    colorful _____ *(passed/past)*.   But _____ *(it's/its)*

    _____ *(principal/principle)* subject is the story of the Motion Picture

    and Television Relief Fund.

2. Leaders in the emerging movie industry first became _____ *(con-*

    science/conscious) of the need _____ *(to/too/two)* create such a

    fund shortly after the end of World War I. The war had had a very negative

    _____ *(affect/effect)* on the entertainment industry.

3. For one thing, it appears that the movie moguls might _____ *(have/of)*

    been counting on the war going on longer _____ *(than/then)* it actu-

    ally did, because when the armistice was signed, they were stuck with a consider-

    able _____ *(amount/number)* of suddenly passé war films that no one

    wanted to see. They _____ *(finally/finely)* had to write off

    _____ *(their/there/they're)* backlog of military movies as a financial

    loss because the entertainment-hungry public apparently couldn't

    _____ *(bare/bear)* living in the _____ *(passed/past)* one

more minute _____ (than/then) was necessary. _____ (It's/Its) not _____ (to/too/two) surprising that people wanted to move on to happier days—both on and off the silver screen.

4. _____ (Their/There/They're) was also _____ (a/an) epidemic of influenza that swept _____ (threw/through) the United States not _____ (to/too/two) long after the end of the war, and the movie industry suffered a great deal when medical authorities advised people _____ (to/too/two) decrease _____ (their/there/they're) risk of contagion by staying away from _____ (a/an) _____ (amount/number) of public places, including movie theaters.

5. Both factors had _____ (a/an) _____ (affect/effect), and the movie industry found itself facing _____ (it's/its) first major economic crisis. Of the hundreds of workers _____ (who's/whose) jobs simply disappeared, a lucky few were able _____ (to/too/two) return _____ (to/too/two) theater work or the vaudeville circuit, but the majority could find no other source of income, and for them, the proverbial cupboard was _____ (bare/bear).

PART B

Directions: Fill in each blank with the correct choice.

1. Earlier fund-raising efforts had been launched on behalf of entertainers who had left the Hollywood community to serve in the war; in peacetime, those efforts were _____ (than/then) turned toward the unemployed. Those who could afford to contribute simply _____ (passed/past) the hat, and for a time, simple, unorganized goodwill was sufficient, but just barely.

2. Time _____ (passed/past), and in the _____ (coarse/course) of the next decade, the 1920s, everything changed; the movie industry

became caught up in the postwar boom. People generally had money to spend, and

_____ *(weather/whether)* they had a little or a lot, they wanted to

spend a considerable _____ *(amount/number)* of it on entertainment.

So the young movie industry expanded rapidly, with enormous, lavish theaters,

many of them _____ *(baring/bearing)* a strange resemblance to tem-

ples or mosques, popping up all over the country. _____ *(Accept/Ex-*

cept) for the fact that most movie companies still maintained headquarters in New

York City, Hollywood was quickly becoming the _____ *(principal/*

principle) center for entertainment and escape in America. It became the place

where _____ *(you're/your)* dreams were supposed to turn into reality,

a place where _____ *(you're/your)* chances of being discovered, of

becoming _____ *(a/an)* overnight success, were just as good as any-

body else's. It became more _____ *(than/then)* a place; it became a

myth.

3. Some succeeded and succeeded beyond any of _____ *(their/there/*

they're) wildest expectations. One _____ *(principal/principle)* exam-

ple was Mary Pickford, _____ *(who's/whose)* annual salary of $ 1 mil-

lion made her perhaps the biggest salaried breadwinner in the nation in 1920.

4. But others did not share in the success manufactured by America's dream factory.

_____ *(Weather/Whether)* because of _____ *(to/too/*

two) little talent or _____ *(to/too/two)* few breaks, many of those

_____ *(who's/whose)* destiny had brought them to the West Coast

ended up with less _____ *(than/then)* _____ *(their/*

there/they're) share of the pie.

5. Leaders of the Hollywood community felt that it was a matter of

_____ *(conscience/conscious)*: they could not ignore the plight of the actors and actresses who had come to Hollywood expecting big bucks and sunny

_____ (weather/whether), only to find infrequent bit parts and storm

clouds.

PART C

Directions: **Fill in the blanks with the correct choices.**

1. The Motion Picture Branch of the Actor's Fund, which later was to evolve into the

    Motion Picture and Television Relief Fund, held _____ (it's/its) first

    meeting in the summer of 1921. Soon the fund was looking for

    _____ (a/an) administrator, and backers of the project urged the Rev-

    erend Neal Dodd to _____ (accept/except) the position. The Rever-

    end Dodd was _____ (a/an) unconventional and much-loved man, a

    man of great _____ (principal/principle) who defended Hollywood

    and _____ (it's/its) residents at a time when many of the nation's

    clergymen could hardly _____ (bare/bear) to _____

    (hear/here) the name of that "den of iniquity" spoken. Reverend Dodd, who was

    _____ (a/an) Episcopal priest, set up his first Hollywood church in

    _____ (a/an) vacant storefront and later turned fact into fiction by

    playing the role of a clergyman in more _____ (than/then) 300 mov-

    ies throughout the _____ (coarse/course) of his career.

2. At the end of September, the first assistance was given, and it went to

    _____ (to/too/two) people, a married couple who needed $40 to pay

    _____ (their/there/they're) hotel bill and rent _____

    (a/an) apartment. The husband, _____ (who's/whose) career as a

    character actor spanned 37 years, had acted in films for eight years; the wife had

    danced in the chorus.

3. The second person to _____ (accept/except) aid was a widow

   _____ (who's/whose) four children were living with her in a tent.

   When people were made _____ (conscience/conscious) of her situa-

   tion, one studio dispatched carpenters and lumber to help make the tent livable,

   and it was not _____ (to/too/two) long before casting offices were

   trying to help the woman secure acting jobs.

4. Throughout the years _____ (a/an) impressive _____

   (amount/number) of benefits were held on behalf of the fund, and the first was

   conducted in 1923. _____ (Accept/Except) for a very few, most of

   the important entertainers of the day, including Charlie Chaplin, Douglas Fairbanks,

   Mary Pickford, and Will Rogers, were _____ (their/there/they're).

5. _____ (Than/Then) in 1927 talkies were introduced with *The Jazz*

   Singer, and soon people were going to twice the number of movies they had seen

   in the silent era. Even in 1929, the year of the great stock market crash, people

   were buying _____ (a/an) unprecedented 110 million movie tickets a

   week. The lean years of the Great Depression might _____ (have/of)

   been devastating for the young film industry _____ (accept/except)

   for the fact that Americans seemed more willing _____ (than/then)

   ever to part with _____ (their/there/they're) few discretionary pen-

   nies in order to have an afternoon or evening of escape.

PART D

Directions: **Fill in each blank with the correct choice.**

1. But once again, a boom for the industry as a whole did not necessarily mean

   prosperity for each and every actor, actress, writer, or director. No one could

   _____ (have/of) foreseen how the sudden change in film technology would _____ *(affect/effect)* hundreds of careers. The addition of

sound _____ *(to/too/two)* the screen launched some careers and

sank others. Performers _____ *(who's/whose)* voices were

_____ *(to/too/two)* high-pitched were a classic example. Many of

those who had made a good living during the era of silent movies were suddenly

little more _____ *(than/then)* relics of the _____ *(passed/*

past). The future of films had suddenly and almost without warning

_____ *(passed/past)* them by. And in _____ *(a/an)* unset-

tling _____ *(amount/number)* of cases, those who were suddenly

unemployed had little to show for _____ *(their/there/they're)* earlier

successes.

2. Again, the Motion Picture Relief Fund helped out, functioning as the

_____ *(principal/principle)* source of aid for hundreds of people. One

interesting example of a person supported by the fund during this period was

Joseph H. Hazelton, who had been a "program boy" at Ford's Theater the night

that President Abraham Lincoln was shot. After he had been supported by the fund

during a period in which he was _____ *(to/too/two)* sick to work, he

wrote a story about the tragedy of Lincoln's assassination and sold it to a magazine

for $50. According to *The Heart of Hollywood*, he _____ *(than/then)*

sent his entire check to the fund along with a note that said, "I want to be a life

member."

3. The fund quickly developed a reputation for assisting the down-and-out among the

Hollywood community and doing so without _____ *(to/too/two)*

much fussing with red tape. Rather _____ *(than/then)* make people

who needed help wait and wait, the administrators of the program decided to

operate on the _____ *(principal/principle)* of help first, questions later. Bob Thomas, the author of *The Heart of Hollywood,* tells about funds being used to "dry out" an alcoholic writer, to cap the teeth of _____ *(a/an)* young actress who couldn't afford much-needed dental work, and to buy a toupee for _____ *(a/an)* actor who couldn't get work and who thought it had something to do with the fact that he was getting a little _____ *(bare/bear)* on top.

4. _____ *(Threw/Through)* the years, the fund continued to grow and evolve, eventually expanding _____ *(to/too/two)* meet the needs of those who would later work in another medium—television. Finding that it could not rely exclusively upon charitable contributions, the Motion Picture and Television Relief Fund began a payroll deduction plan in 1932, asking all studio workers to contribute one half of one percent of _____ *(their/there/they're)* salaries, _____ *(accept/except)* for those actors and actresses _____ *(who's/whose)* earnings totaled less _____ *(than/then)* $200 a week. A weekly radio show and occasional star-studded benefits also helped fill the fund's coffers.

5. In the early 1940s the fund realized one of _____ *(it's/its)* dreams by building the Motion Picture Country House, and by the late 1940s, the Motion Picture Country Hospital had been completed. Both projects and all building projects since _____ *(than/then)* have been financed without the use of any borrowed money. The fund spends no more _____ *(than/then)* it raises, but the commitment and talent of many in the entertainment community ensure that what is needed can be raised. Even the royalties from the sale of *The Heart of Hollywood,* the book that _____ *(bares/bears)* witness to this unusual story, were donated in _____ *(their/there/they're)* entirety to the fund.

Exercise Three

Directions: Fill in the blanks with the correct choices.

You've heard the expression "Put on a happy face"? Well, as corny and trite as it   1

sounds, _____ *(their/there/they're)* might be something to that little nug-   2

get of down-home advice. According _____ *(to/too/two)* a recent report   3

from the University of California at San Francisco, _____ *(it's/its)* often   4

true that by the simple act of smiling a person can generate happy feelings, and by   5

frowning, a person can generate sad feelings. In other words, facial expressions do   6

frequently _____ *(affect/effect)* emotions. Of _____ *(coarse/*   7

course), the converse—that emotions usually have an _____ *(affect/*   8

effect) upon facial expressions—is a truth that we all generally _____   9

(accept/except). But now _____ *(it's/its)* believed that, in the words of Dr.   10

Paul Ekman, a professor of psychiatry at the University of California, "You become what   11

you put on _____ *(you're/your)* face."   12

_____ *(Threw/Through)* tests that measure heart rate, skin tempera-   13

ture, respiration, and muscle tension, scientists have long been able   14

_____ *(to/too/two)* determine the _____ *(affect/effect)* of   15

emotions on the body. But one of the _____ *(principal/principle)* assump-   16

tions of the scientists' work was that it is basically a one-way street: they thought that   17

certain emotions normally triggered certain corresponding physical states. But the   18

California study is interesting because one of _____ *(it's/its)* conclusions   19

is that the opposite is also true: certain physical states, specifically facial expressions,   20

were found to trigger particular emotional states, or at least the physical sensations that   21

we normally associate with those emotional states.   22

PART B

Directions: Fill in each blank with the correct choice.

Dr. Ekman began his research using actors because of _____ *(their/there/* 1

they're) relatively high degree of skill in making certain kinds of faces on demand, or 2

in other words, in artificial situations when _____ *(their/there/they're)* is 3

no natural reason to feel anger, disgust, joy, or relief. In his tests with professional 4

actors, Ekman found that by making a _____ *(conscience/conscious)* at- 5

tempt to move _____ *(their/there/they're)* facial muscles into certain pat- 6

terns the actors were able to produce corresponding physical states in 7

_____ *(their/there/they're)* bodies. For instance, _____ 8

(a/an) actor _____ *(who's/whose)* face showed disgust could be expected 9

_____ *(to/too/two)* exhibit a large _____ *(amount/number)* 10

of physical symptoms that scientists associate with the emotion of disgust. These might 11

include very specific changes in heart rate, breathing, muscle contractions, and skin 12

temperature. To put it very simply, actors could make themselves feel disgusted just 13

by looking disgusted. 14

   Dr. Ekman was pleased with the results of the study, and most of his colleagues 15

were, _____ *(to/too/two)*, _____ *(accept/except)* for a few 16

critics who said, in essence, "Well, the study might _____ *(have/of)* shown 17

something about actors, but _____ *(their/there/they're)* a special breed. If 18

something is true of actors, is it _____ *(than/then)* necessarily true of 19

anyone else?" So the researchers assembled a group of college freshmen, who appar- 20

ently were thought to be more typical of the general public _____ *(than/* 21

then) actors were, and the study was repeated. In the end, _____ 22

(weather/whether) the study involved actors or college students, _____ 23

(it's/ its) results were the same: it did show that putting on a certain kind of face did ₂₄

produce corresponding physical changes in the body. ₂₅

Part of the task of the study was _____ *(to/too/two)* figure out what ₂₆

facial configurations were recognized by most people as being characteristic of certain ₂₇

emotions. The researchers paired facial features and body reactions for seven emo- ₂₈

tions: amusement, anger, contempt, disgust, fear, sadness, and surprise. ₂₉

_____ *(Than/Then)* they taught _____ *(their/there/they're)* ₃₀

research subjects to make the appropriate faces. For instance, to show fear ₃₁

_____ *(a/an)* individual was asked to raise the eyebrows and pull them ₃₂

together, tighten the area under the brows, and _____ *(finally/finely),* pull ₃₃

the jaw back. According to the researchers, this took a typical subject a few minutes, ₃₄

and _____ *(than/then)* before _____ *(to/too/two)* long, he or ₃₅

she actually began to feel afraid. ₃₆

PART C

Directions: **Fill in each blank with the correct choice.**

"Of what possible use is this type of information?" _____ *(you're/your)* ₁

probably asking. Well, the most obvious guess might be that if you just make yourself ₂

look happy, _____ *(you're/your)* going to find yourself feeling happy. But ₃

unfortunately, that's *not* among Dr. Ekman's conclusions. In fact, he says that the ₄

evidence of the link between facial expressions and corresponding changes in the body ₅

is the weakest for the smile, and that is probably because a person ₆

_____ *(who's/whose)* smiling may be experiencing any one of ₇

_____ *(a/an)* whole range of emotions. In fact, according to Dr. Ekman, ₈

_____ *(their/there/they're)* are 18 kinds of smiles. There's the smile that ₉

you smile when you meet _____ *(a/an)* old boyfriend or girlfriend, a person ₁₀ that you can't _____ *(bare/bear)* the thought of any longer. And there's the 11

smile you smile when you've just become _____ *(conscience/conscious)* 12

that _____ *(you're/your)* zipper is down or _____ *(you're/* 13

your) blouse is partially unbuttoned, and _____ *(you're/your)* less 14

_____ *(than/then)* halfway _____ *(threw/through)* 15

_____ *(you're/your)* presentation to the entire class. Obviously, a smile is 16

a very complicated and subtle thing. 17

So what does the study have to offer us? Basically, it has _____ 18

(to/too/two) things that may be of some value. The _____ *(principal/prin-* 19

ciple) use could be in the medical field where someday doctors might learn how to assist 20

patients so that _____ *(their/there/they're)* able to learn to use happy and 21

peaceful facial expressions to create happier and more peaceful conditions inside 22

_____ *(their/there/they're)* bodies. _____ *(It's/Its)* not 23

_____ *(to/too/two)* likely that this is going to happen any time soon, but 24

stranger things have happened in the _____ *(passed/past),* and some re- 25

searchers think _____ *(it's/its)* a real possibility for the future. 26

PART D

Directions: **Fill in each blank with the correct choice.**

The other use might appeal to someone _____ *(who's/whose)* not exactly 1

a man or woman of _____ *(principal/principle).* That use involves figuring 2

out how to beat a lie detector test. Lie detectors, of _____ *(coarse/* 3

course), measure physical reactions that are triggered by certain states of mind. If 4

_____ *(a/an)* person _____ *(who's/whose)* being evaluated 5

lies, the tester can supposedly pick up on small physiological changes that are, to put 6

it very simply, triggered by a guilty _____ *(conscience/conscious)* or by 7 the test-taker's knowledge that the truth is not being told. But what if the person 8

_____ *(who's/whose)* veracity is being tested could just put on 9

_____ *(a/an)* innocent face, which, in turn, could create the correspond- 10

ingly "innocent" physiological state within the body? Dr. Ekman says that lie detectors 11

are already being beaten this way and that people involved in espionage have for years 12

_____ *(passed/past)* lie detector tests using the _____ *(prin-* 13

cipal/principle) of what we might call "facial feature control." _____ 14

(Their/There/They're) often experts at achieving a desired _____ *(affect/* 15

effect) when in the position of trying to gain security clearance _____ 16

(threw/through) successful performances on lie detector tests and other forms of evalu- 17

ation. "If they weren't," he asks, "how did we get so many spies in security jobs in the 18

government?" 19

UNIT 7: Capitalization

There are many fine points of capitalization, but these basic guidelines will meet most of the needs of college writers.

1. Titles of poems, short stories, plays, books, newspapers, magazines, television shows, radio programs, and movies. Capitalize each word with the exception of conjunctions, prepositions, and articles *(a, an,* and *the).* The first and last words of a title are always capitalized, no matter what part of speech they are. (Titles of poems and short stories are also enclosed within double quotation marks; titles of books, newspapers, and the other things listed above are normally underlined.)
    Correct examples: "The Love Song of J. Alfred Prufrock," "Air and Angels," "Delight in Disorder," "On the Death of Dr. Robert Levet," *The Valley of Horses, The Milwaukee Journal, Pro Football Digest, St. Elsewhere, The Cosby Show, One Flew over the Cuckoo's Nest, Butch Cassidy and the Sundance Kid, On the Waterfront.*

2. Brand names. Brand names are always capitalized.
    Correct examples: Bisquick buttermilk baking mix, Nike running shoes, Clinique cosmetics, Arrow shirts, Sylvania light bulbs, Head & Shoulders shampoo.

3. Breeds of animals. Capitalize the name of a breed of animal if it is derived from another proper (capitalized) noun. The names that are capitalized below are derived from the names of nationalities, which are always capitalized. Use your dictionary if you are in doubt.
    Correct examples: alley cat, Persian cat, Old English sheepdog, beagle, French poodle, quarter horse, Arabian horse.

4. Buildings and institutions. The names of buildings and institutions are always capitalized.

Correct examples: the White House, the Taj Mahal, the Superdome, St. Joseph's Hospital, the University of Iowa, the Berkeley Psychic Institute.

5. Companies and corporations. The names of companies and corporations are always capitalized.

Correct examples: Colgate-Palmolive Company; Harper & Row, Publishers, Inc.; Mobil Oil Corporation, Lockheed Aircraft Corporation.

6. Days of the week. The days of the week are always capitalized.

Correct examples: Monday, Tuesday.

7. Directions. The names of directions are normally *not* capitalized. Capitalize them only when they name or modify an entire region—a whole section of a country or a continent.

Correct examples: I live four miles west of the lake. Her study covered the era when the South was at war with the North.

8. Geographical locations and words derived from them. All of these are capitalized: the names of cities, counties, states, nations, lakes, rivers, oceans, mountain ranges, parks, continents, and planets.

Correct examples: Seattle, Washington, Blue Lake, the Atlantic Ocean, the Allegheny Mountains, France, Jupiter, Mars.

TWO SPECIAL NOTES: Most words that are derived from these location words are also capitalized; for example, *Switzerland* is capitalized, and so is *Swiss* cheese. The word *Mexico* is capitalized, and so is *Mexican* art.

Normally, the word *earth* is not capitalized, but when it refers to the entire planet, it is. *These are correct examples*: The earth in some parts of the country has a reddish color. The Earth is not the largest planet that revolves around the sun.

9. Historical periods. Names of historical periods are usually capitalized. If you are in doubt, consult your dictionary.

Correct examples: the Renaissance, the Pleistocene Age, the Middles Ages.

10. Holidays. The names of holidays and holy days are always capitalized.

Correct examples: Christmas, Yom Kippur, Thanksgiving.

11. I. The word *I* is always capitalized.

12. Months of the year. The months of the year are always capitalized.

Correct examples: January, February, March.

A SPECIAL NOTE: Although the months are capitalized, the seasons are usually not. Capitalize the name of a season only if it is part of the formal name of something else, such as a dance or a celebration of some sort. *These are correct examples*: I won't see you again until next winter. Our school's famous Fall Festival was only a modest financial success this year, but the Spring Fling will probably be a bigger money-maker.

13. Mother and father. Mistakes are often made in capitalizing or not capitalizing person nouns such as *mother, father, mom,* and *dad.* But the rule is really very simple: Do not capitalize these words when they are preceded by a possessive noun or pronoun. *Study these correct examples*:

1. (a) I have always considered *Dad* a perfectionist.
   (b) I have always considered *my dad* a perfectionist.

2. (a) I met *Father* at the restaurant.
   (b) I met *my neighbor's father* at the restaurant.

Fill in the blanks with *Mother* or *mother*:

3. I have known your _____ for 24 years.

4. I told _____ that I'd be back in an hour.

5. What movie do you want to see tonight, _____ ?

6. Dianna's _____ is known for her great sense of humor.

7. The twins loved to confuse their _____ .

8. I asked my brother, "When did _____ say she'd call?"

9. She had known her friend's _____ for seven years.

10. My _____ is a very busy woman.

[*Answers.* (3) mother; (4) Mother; (5) Mother; (6) mother; (7) mother; (8) Mother; (9) mother; and (10) mother.]

14. Names of people and pets. Names of people and pets are always capitalized.
   Correct examples: Mary Richards, Sarah Zellman, John Brown, Snoopy, Fluffy, Killer.

15. One-of-a-kind events. Large one-of-a-kind events are normally capitalized.
   Correct examples: the Orange Bowl, the World Series, the War of 1812.

16. Organizations and associations. The names of organizations and associations are capitalized. Once again, articles, conjunctions, and prepositions are not capitalized.
   Correct examples: American Civil Liberties Union, Children's Literature Association, National Aeronautics and Space Administration, National Council of Teachers of English.

17. Political parties. The names of political parties and words derived from them are capitalized. (Note, however, that the word *party* is not.)
   Correct examples: the Republican party, the Democratic candidate, the Socialist platform, the Communists.

18. Religions. The names of religions and words derived from them are capitalized.
   Correct examples: the Jewish people, the Protestants' representative, the Mormons, the Baptist minister.

19. The first word in a sentence. The first word of a new sentence is capitalized, and this is also true of quoted sentences that are a part of larger sentences.
   Correct example: The note said, "Your books have been overdue for a month. Please return them and pay your fine."

20. Personal titles. Personal titles are capitalized only when they directly precede a person's name or when they are used as a form of direct address. This is true for words such as president, general, mayor, doctor, king, queen, professor, dean, and pope.

Correct examples: Do you realize that President Reagan's press conference is on television right now? Do you realize that the president's press conference is on television right now? The reporter asked, "When did you first know of this situation, Mr. President?"

Exercise One

Directions: Make changes below, applying what you've learned about capitalization.

1. Experts at the new york museum of modern art, after studying french artist henri matisse's *le bateau* for more than six weeks, discovered that the painting had been hung upside down.

2. Geoffrey chaucer once wrote, "love is blind," and william shakespeare used that line, too.

3. The lincoln memorial in washington, d.c., has 36 columns.

4. Ernest hemingway, the great american novelist who gave us *the sun also rises, a farewell to arms, for whom the bell tolls, the old man and the sea,* and other important works, was supposedly very reluctant to travel on fridays.

5. It was in a movie called *sudden impact* that clint eastwood first said, "make my day."

6. The best-selling car in history was the volkswagen beetle.

7. Three of every four russian doctors are women.

8. It was once suggested by president jimmy carter that each president be elected for a single six-year term of office.

9. In the frontier days of the west, cheyenne, wyoming, was nicknamed "hell on wheels."

10. John lindsay, a former mayor of new york city, made his acting debut in the movie *rosebud* in 1975.

Correct each exercise and discuss any questions you have before continuing.

Exercise Two

Directions: Make changes below, applying what you've learned about capitalization.

1. The president who dedicated the statue of liberty in the fall of 1886 was grover cleveland.

2. According to the nursery rhyme, monday's child is fair of face, and tuesday's child is full of grace.

3. The empire state building, a principal tourist attraction for those who are considering a trip to the east coast, has 6500 windows.

4. In one of the most gruesome and bizarre episodes of world war II, almost a thousand retreating japanese soldiers were killed by crocodiles in waist-deep water off ramree island on february 19, 1945. The island is just west of burma in the bay of bengal, which is in the indian ocean.

5. William shakespeare's father once served as mayor of the city of stratford-on-avon in england.

6. According to statistics, more railroad crossing accidents occur on sunday than on any other day, and that's true no matter what the season—summer, winter, spring, or fall.

7. The famous sphinx of egypt faces east.

8. The best-selling brand of cigarette in the western world is marlboro.

9. The first city to host the annual major league all-star game was chicago, illinois.

10. A common misconception is that the catholic church's feast of the immaculate conception, which is observed every december 8, celebrates the virgin birth of jesus; actually, it honors the fact that mary, christ's mother, was free from original sin.

Exercise Three

Directions: Make changes below, applying what you've learned about capitalization.

1. The two presidents whose names are on the declaration of independence are thomas jefferson and john adams. The presidents who signed the constitution are george washington and james madison.

2. According to the encyclopaedia britannica, terriers were so named because they were used to attack vermin that lived in the earth *(terre)*. Most terriers originated in the british isles; however, one variety, the miniature schnauzer or rat terrier, was bred in germany. Some sources list as many as 20 breeds of this kind of dog, including irish terriers, border terriers, welsh terriers, scotch terriers, fox terriers, and boston terriers.

3. Most of the planets were known to the ancient astronomers; however, uranus was discovered in relatively recent times—1781.

4. The a. c. nielsen company, a famous market research firm, has cornered a great deal of the television rating business in america. According to the nielsen ratings, the sixth most popular television show in the season that began in october 1957 and ended in april 1958 was *the life and legend of wyatt earp*. The seventh most popular television show in the autumn of 1977 and the spring of 1978 was *little house on the prairie*.

5. According to the hindu religion, the individual soul never dies; it moves on a path of continual rebirth and evolution until it eliminates all desire and realizes its unity with brahman, which is thought to be the absolute, the force that created and still permeates the entire universe. The hindus believe that every soul will eventually achieve unity with brahman, and this state is believed to be one of perfect bliss.

6. When the austrian composer wolfgang amadeus mozart was only 13 years old, his father lost his position and his income because he was devoting so much of his time to accompanying his children on concert tours of europe. Until leopold mozart was once again making money, the young wolfgang supported the family.

7. *Webster's new collegiate dictionary* defines the pronoun *i* as "someone aware of possessing a personal individuality."

8. The three principal political parties in west germany are the christian democrats, the free democrats, and the social democrats.

9. Fanny bullock workman, an early feminist of the victorian era, was known for many achievements, including her successful and unprecedented climb of the karakoram mountains in india in 1912.

10. The people who make campbell's soup were once penalized by the federal trade commission for deceptive television advertising: the ftc discovered that in one ad marbles had been placed in the bottom of a bowl of soup in order to push the vegetables and noodles to the top and make the soup appear chunkier. In another incident, the federal trade commission required the makers of ocean spray cranberry juice cocktail to run a corrective ad after one commercial claimed that a glass of the cranberry cocktail provided more "food energy" than other breakfast drinks. *Food energy* is just another term for calories.

Exercise Four

Directions: **Make changes below, applying what you've learned about capitalization. This exercise is divided into three sections.**

(a) Most of the words, images, and customs that we associate with halloween were ₁ derived from other countries and other cultures. For instance, the word *pumpkin* comes ₂ from the old french word *pumpion,* and that word in turn was derived from *pepon,* the ₃ greek word for melon. The custom of carving pumpkins into jack-o'-lanterns hails from ₄ ireland where, for centuries, irish children hollowed out large potatoes, turnips, and ₅ rutabagas, carved evil-looking faces on them, and placed candles inside. The children ₆ then placed the lanterns in window sills to scare evil spirits away. When irish immigrants ₇ came to america in large numbers in the nineteenth century, they brought their tradi- ₈ tions with them, but the perfectly suited and widely available american pumpkin was 9

soon substituted for the other vegetables. 10

(b) The word *witch* comes from *wicca,* which is an old english word for sorcerer or 11

sorceress. Witches became associated with halloween in a number of ways that can 12

be traced back to both pagan and christian times. When november 1 was established 13

as all saints' day by the christian church, it was thought that witches and devils gathered 14

the night before—on october 31—to mock the religious festival with unholy doings of 15

their own. 16

(c) The black cat, one of the most common images of the annual fall ritual of hallow- 17

een, has a rich history as a magical and spooky animal. The cat was considered a god 18

by the ancient egyptians. In greek legend, a woman who had been transformed into a 19

feline was chosen to be the priestess of hecate. As the goddess of sorcery and ruler 20

of the night, hecate took all witches under her patronage. 21

Sources

The examples and exercises in *Easy Writer II* were drawn from the following sources. Books are arranged alphabetically by title; magazine and newspaper articles are arranged alphabetically by article title.

Books

The American Heritage Dictionary of the English Language, ed. William Morris, American Heritage Publishing Co., Inc., and Houghton Mifflin Company, New York, 1975.

The Best by Peter Passell and Leonard Ross, Farrar, Straus and Giroux, New York, 1974.

The Book of Firsts by Patrick Robertson, Bramhall House, Crown Publishers, Inc., New York, 1982.

The Book of Lists #3 by Amy Wallace, David Wallechinsky, and Irving Wallace, William Morrow and Company, Inc., New York, 1983.

Can Elephants Swim? by Robert M. Jones, Time-Life Books, New York, 1969.

Cross Your Fingers, Spit In Your Hat by Alvin Schwartz and Glen Rounds, J.B. Lippincott Company, Philadelphia and New York, 1974.

The Dance Encyclopedia by Anatole Chujoy and P.W. Manchester, Simon and Schuster, New York, 1967.

Deep Song: The Dance Story of Martha Graham by Ernestine Stodelle, Schirmer Books, New York, 1984.

Dick Clark's The First 25 Years of Rock & Roll by Michael Uslan and Bruce Solomon, Delacorte Press, New York, 1981.

Encyclopaedia Britannica, Volumes 7 and 22, Encyclopaedia Britannica, Inc., William Benton, Publisher, Chicago, 1963.

The Encyclopedia of Sports by Frank G. Menke, A.S. Barnes and Company, New York, 1960.

The Great American Sports Book by George Gipe, A Dolphin Book, Doubleday & Company, Inc., Garden City, New York, 1978.

The Healing Heart by Norman Cousins, W. W. Norton & Company, New York, 1983.

The Heart of Hollywood by Bob Thomas, Price/Stern/Sloan, Publishers, Inc., Los Angeles, California, 1971.

How to Raise a Street-Smart Child by Grace Hechinger, Facts On File Publications, New York, 1984.

Incredible Animals, A to Z, National Wildlife Federation, 1985.

Joan Embery's Collection of Amazing Animal Facts by Joan Embery with Ed Lucaire, Delacorte Press, New York, 1983.

Knock on Wood: An Encyclopedia of Talismans, Charms, Superstitions & Symbols, Carole Potter, Beaufort Books, Inc., New York, 1983.

Life-spans, Or, How Long Things Last by Frank Kendig and Richard Hutton, Holt, Rinehart and Winston, New York, 1979.

The Misunderstood Child by Larry B. Silver, McGraw-Hill Book Company, New York, 1984.

More FYI, For Your Information, ed. Nat Brandt, M. Evans and Company, Inc., New York, 1983.

The People's Almanac #2 by David Wallechinsky and Irving Wallace, Bantam Books, New York, 1978.

The People's Almanac #3 by David Wallechinsky and Irving Wallace, Bantam Books, New York, 1981.

Pictorial History of American Sports by John Durant and Otto Bettmann, A. S. Barnes and Company, New York, 1952.

The Presidents, Tidbits & Trivia by Sid Frank and Arden Davis Melick, Greenwich House, a division of Arlington House, Inc., distributed by Crown Publishers, Inc., New York, 1984.

The Quintessential Quiz Book by Norman G. Hickman, St. Martin's Press, New York, 1979.

The Rolling Stone Encyclopedia of Rock & Roll, eds. Jon Pareles and Patricia Romanowski, Rolling Stone Press/Summit Books, New York, 1983.

The Rule Book by Stephen M. Kirschner, Barry J. Pavelec, and Jeffrey Feinman, A Dolphin Book, Doubleday & Company, Inc., Garden City, New York, 1979.

Speaker's Treasury of Anecdotes About the Famous by James C. Humes, Harper & Row, Publishers, Inc., New York, 1978.

Stay Tuned, A Concise History of American Broadcasting by Christopher H. Sterling and John M. Kittros, Wadsworth Publishing Co., Belmont, California, 1978.

This Day in Sports by John G. Fetros, Newton K. Gregg, Publisher, Novato, California, 1974.

Van Gogh by Gerald E. Finley, Tudor Publishing Company, New York, 1966.

The Westerners by Dee Brown, Holt, Rinehart and Winston, New York, 1974.

Your Five-Year-Old, Sunny and Serene by Louise Bates Ames and Frances L. Ilg, A Delta Book, Dell Publishing Co., Inc., 1979.

Magazine and Newspaper Articles

"A Cutthroat Business," by Philip Jacobson, *Connoisseur,* December 1984.

"A Sense of Control," by Elizabeth Hall, *Psychology Today,* December 1984.

"A very special crystal: Mystique of diamonds still endures," by Dennis R. Getto, *The Milwaukee Journal,* April 24, 1985.

"An aching America," UPI, *The Milwaukee Journal,* October 22, 1985.

"An Ancient 'Nuclear Winter,'" by Sharon Begley, *Newsweek,* October 14, 1985.

"After 73 years, a Titanic Find," *Time,* September 16, 1985.

"Bakelite Envy, Depression-Era Plastic Costume Jewelry Has Become a Hot Item," by Andrea DiNoto, *Connoisseur,* July 1985.

"Coffee trivia," *The Milwaukee Journal,* April 24, 1985.

"Death of an American Icon," by Jack Kroll, *Newsweek,* August 23, 1982.

"Facing up to feelings: Your expressions may trigger physical reactions," Los Angeles Times service, *The Milwaukee Journal,* June 18, 1985.

"Ferrets fancied by city dwellers," by Caroline Nichols, *Milwaukee Sentinel,* October 7, 1985.

"Fish—For Health," *Vogue,* July 1985.

"Following in the footsteps of Rachel Carson," by Robert W. Smith, *USA Today,* April 5, 1985.

"For every region, a special food," by Dan Sperling, *USA Today,* October 8, 1985.

"Getting there without motion sickness," by Cynthia Dennis, *The Milwaukee Journal,* April 29, 1985.

"Houses from Sears," by Nelson Groffman, *Country Living,* June 1984.

"Little swamis," by Claire Warga, *Psychology Today,* January 1985.

"Looking for Mr. Good Bear," *Newsweek,* December 24, 1984.

"Mabel K. Staupers and the Integration of Black Nurses into the Armed Forces," by Darlene Clark Hine, in *Black Leaders of the Twentieth Century,* eds. John Hope Franklin and August Meier, University of Illinois Press, Urbana, Illinois, 1982.

"Manhattan Serenade," by David Ansen, *Newsweek,* February 3, 1986.

"Name Calling," by Harris Dienstfrev, *Psychology Today,* January 1983.

"New Bodies For Sale," *Newsweek,* May 27, 1985.

"Nuclear winter and carbon dioxide," by John Maddox, *Nature,* December 13, 1984.

"Nutty pets often the owner's fault," UPI, *The Milwaukee Sentinel,* April 26, 1985.

"Overachievers—when toil gets them in trouble," *Vogue,* May 1985.

"Pets can pose problems," UPI, *The Milwaukee Journal,* June 9, 1985.

"Rah, rah, rah: As spirit grows, so do souvenir sales," UPI, *The Milwaukee Journal,* April 11, 1985.

"Remember Them?" Jacquelyn Mitchard, *The Milwaukee Journal,* March 17, 1985.

"Ruth Gordon: her life and work had 'this zing,'" by Michael Gordon, Washington Post Service, *The Milwaukee Journal,* August 31, 1985.

"The Secret Payoff of Hypochondria," *Vogue*, August 1983.

"So THAT'S what it was!" by Michael Bauman, *The Milwaukee Journal*, October 2, 1985.

"Strong, special bond sustains sisters through life," by Barbara Bisantz Raymond, *USA Today*, August 8, 1983.

"They're still making 501 jeans the old-fashioned way," *The Milwaukee Journal*, April 17, 1985.

"Thieves like popular cars, too," *The Milwaukee Journal*, May 4, 1985.

"Titanic: The questions remain," Duane Valentry, copyright 1985 Duane Valentry, News America Syndicate, *The Milwaukee Journal*, April 15, 1985.

"To sleep, perchance to dream," by Elizabeth Stark, *Psychology Today*, October 1984.

"The US trivia team has a quiz for you," by Gary C. Rummler, *The Milwaukee Journal*, June 12, 1985.

"Washington married into money," AP, *The Milwaukee Journal*, April 29, 1985.

"What Makes a Top Executive?" by Morgan W. McCall, Jr., and Michael M. Lombardo, *Psychology Today*, February 1983.

"What's black and orange and scary?" by Tony Staffieri, *The Milwaukee Journal*, October 17, 1985.

"Will the real impostor please stand up?" by Jeff Meer, *Psychology Today*, April 1985.

Index

For the convenience of the teacher who wants to locate an item quickly, this index includes a few traditional terms that are not actually used in *Easy Writer II*. For example, the index contains a reference to the "conjunctive adverb," but the book teaches the concept of the conjunctive adverb without using a label for it.